On Core Mathematics

Grade 3

HOUGHTON MIFFLIN HARCOURT

Cover photo credit: Garry Gay/Alamy

Printed in the U.S.A.

ISBN 978-0-547-57523-0

21 1026 20 19 18 17 16

4500596685 ^ B C D E F G

Table of Contents

Operations and Algebraic Thinking

▶ **Represent and solve problems involving multiplication and division.**

▶ **Understand properties of multiplication and the relationship between multiplication and division.**

▶ **Multiply and divide within 100.**

▶ **Solve problems involving the four operations, and identify and explain patterns in arithmetic.**

Number and Operations in Base Ten

▶ **Use place value understanding and properties of operations to perform multi-digit arithmetic.**

Number and Operations – Fractions

▶ **Develop understanding of fractions as numbers.**

Measurement and Data

▶ **Solve problems involving measurement and estimation of intervals of time, liquid volumes, and masses of objects.**

▶ **Represent and interpret data.**

▶ **Geometric measurement: understand concepts of area and relate area to multiplication and to addition.**

▶ **Geometric measurement: recognize perimeter as an attribute of plane figures and distinguish between linear and area measures.**

Geometry

▶ **Reason with shapes and their attributes.**

Name ______________________________

COMMON CORE STANDARD CC.3.OA.1

Lesson Objective: Model and skip count objects in equal groups to find how many there are.

Count Equal Groups

Equal groups have the same number in each group.

There are 3 tulips in each of 4 vases. How many tulips are there in all?

Step 1 Think: there are 4 vases, so draw **4** circles to show **4** equal groups.

Step 2 Think: there are 3 tulips in each vase, so draw **3** dots in each group.

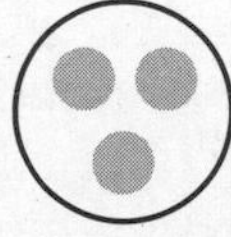   

Step 3 Skip count by 3s to find how many in all: 3, **6**, **9**, **12**

There are **4** equal groups with **3** tulips in each group.

So, there are **12** tulips in all.

1. Draw 3 groups of 5. Skip count to find how many.

_____ in all

Count equal groups to find how many.

2.

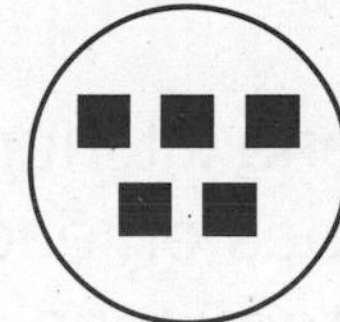 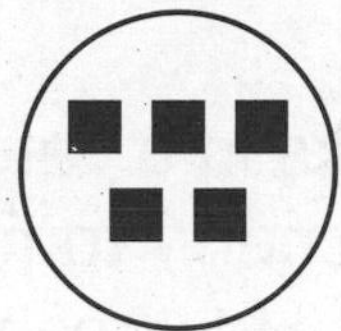

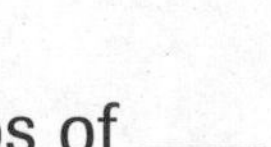

____ groups of ____

____ in all

3.

____ groups of ____

____ in all

Name ______________________

Lesson 1
CC.3.OA.1

Count Equal Groups

Draw equal groups. Skip count to find how many.

1. 2 groups of 2 ___4___

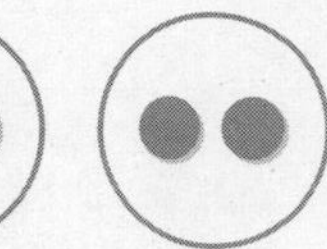

2. 3 groups of 6 ______

3. 5 groups of 3 ______

4. 4 groups of 5 ______

Count equal groups to find how many.

5.

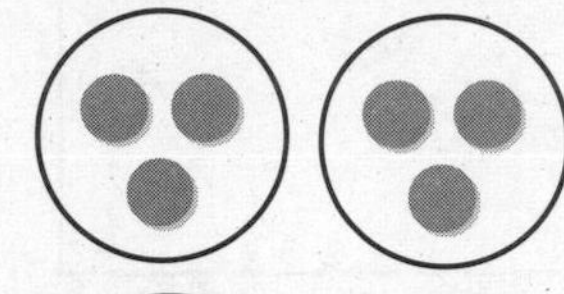
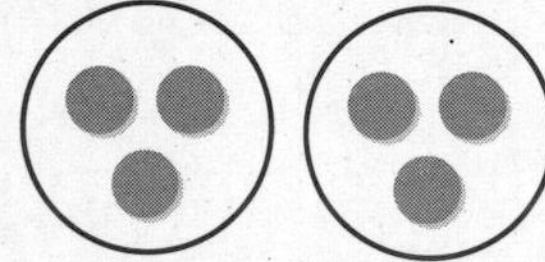

______ groups of ______

______ in all

6.

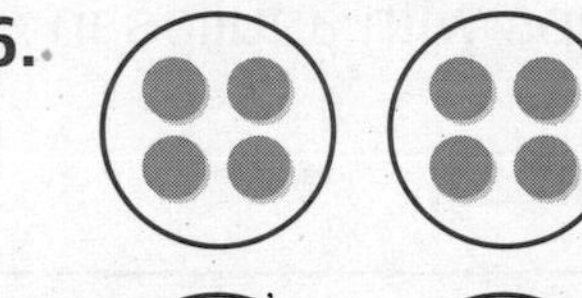
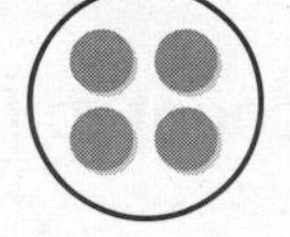
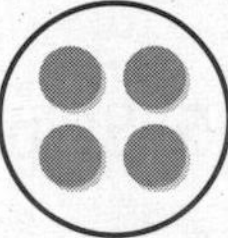

______ groups of ______

______ in all

Problem Solving REAL WORLD

7. Marcia puts 2 slices of cheese on each sandwich. She makes 4 cheese sandwiches. How many slices of cheese does Marcia use in all?

____

8. Tomas works in a cafeteria kitchen. He puts 3 cherry tomatoes on each of 5 salads. How many tomatoes does he use?

____

Name ______________________________

Lesson 2

COMMON CORE STANDARD CC.3.OA.1

Lesson Objective: Write an addition sentence and a multiplication sentence for a model.

Algebra • Relate Addition and Multiplication

You can add to find how many in all.

You can also multiply to find how many in all when you have equal groups.

2 + 2 + 2

$3 \times 2 = 6$

The **factors** are 3 and 2.
The **product** is 6.

So, $2 + 2 + 2 = 6$ and $3 \times 2 = 6$.

Write related addition and multiplication sentences for the model.

1.

___ + ___ + ___ + ___ = ___

___ × ___ = ___

2.

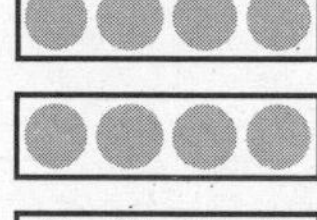

___ + ___ + ___ = ___

___ × ___ = ___

Draw a quick picture to show the equal groups. Then write related addition and multiplication sentences.

3. 4 groups of 3

___ + ___ + ___ + ___ = ___

___ × ___ = ___

4. 2 groups of 3

___ + ___ = ___

___ × ___ = ___

Name ______________________________

Lesson 2
CC.3.OA.1

Relate Addition and Multiplication

Draw a quick picture to show the equal groups. Then write related addition and multiplication sentences.

1. 3 groups of 5

5 + **5** + **5** = **15**

3 × **5** = **15**

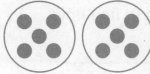

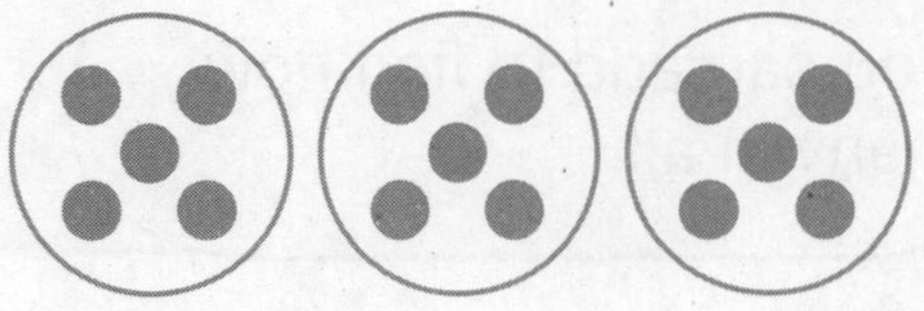

2. 3 groups of 4

___ + ___ + ___ = ___

___ × ___ = ___

3. 4 groups of 3

___ + ___ + ___ + ___ = ___

___ × ___ = ___

4. 5 groups of 2

___ + ___ + ___ + ___ + ___ = ___

___ × ___ = ___

Complete. Write a multiplication sentence.

5. 7 + 7 + 7 = ___

___ × ___ = ___

6. 3 + 3 + 3 = ___

___ × ___ = ___

Problem Solving REAL WORLD

7. There are 6 jars of pickles in a box. Ed has 3 boxes of pickles. How many jars of pickles does he have in all? Write a multiplication sentence to find the answer.

___ × ___ = ___ jars

8. Each day, Jani rides her bike 5 miles. How many miles does Jani ride in all in 4 days? Write a multiplication sentence to find the answer.

___ × ___ = ___ miles

Name ______________________________

Lesson 3

COMMON CORE STANDARD CC.3.OA.2

Lesson Objective: Use models to explore the meaning of partitive (sharing) division.

Size of Equal Groups

When you **divide**, you separate into equal groups.

Use counters or draw a quick picture. Make equal groups. Complete the table.

Counters	Number of Equal Groups	Number in Each Group
24	6	■

The number in each group is unknown, so divide.

Place 1 counter at a time in each group until all 24 counters are used.

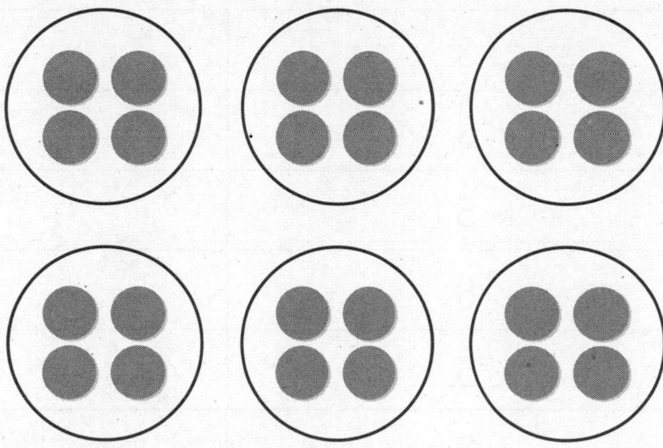

There are 4 counters in each of 6 groups.

Use counters or draw a quick picture. Make equal groups. Complete the table.

	Counters	Number of Equal Groups	Number in Each Group
1.	12	2	
2.	10	5	
3.	16	4	
4.	24	3	
5.	15	5	

Name ______________________________

Lesson 3

CC.3.OA.2

Size of Equal Groups

Use counters or draw a quick picture. Make equal groups. Complete the table.

	Counters	Number of Equal Groups	Number in Each Group
1.	15	3	5
2.	21	7	
3.	28	7	
4.	32	4	
5.	9	3	
6.	18	3	
7.	20	5	
8.	16	8	
9.	35	5	
10.	24	3	

Problem Solving REAL WORLD

11. Alicia has 12 eggs that she will use to make 4 different cookie recipes. If each recipe calls for the same number of eggs, how many eggs will she use in each recipe?

____

12. Brett picked 27 flowers from the garden. He plans to give an equal number of flowers to each of 3 people. How many flowers will each person get?

____

Name ______________________________

COMMON CORE STANDARD CC.3.OA.2

Lesson Objective: Use models to explore the meaning of quotative (measurement) division.

Number of Equal Groups

Complete the table. Use counters to help find the number of equal groups.

Counters	Number of Equal Groups	Number in Each Group
18	■	3

The number of equal groups is unknown, so divide.
Circle groups of 3 counters until all 18 counters are in a group.

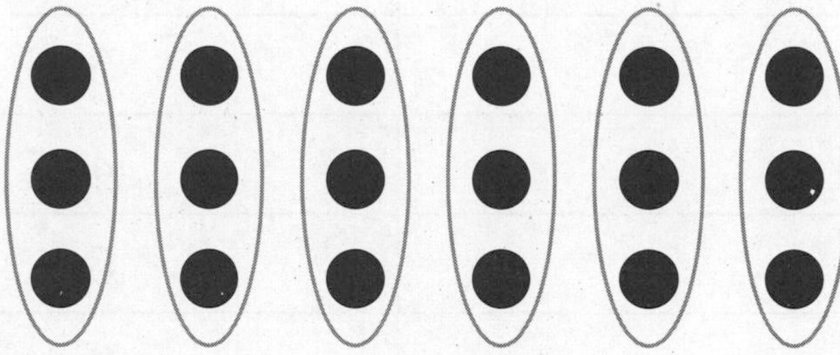

There are 6 groups of 3 counters each.

Draw counters. Then circle equal groups. Complete the table.

	Counters	Number of Equal Groups	Number in Each Group
1.	24		4
2.	20		5
3.	21		7
4.	36		4

Name ______________________________

Lesson 4

CC.3.OA.2

Number of Equal Groups

Draw counters. Then circle equal groups. Complete the table.

	Counters	Number of Equal Groups	Number in Each Group
1.	24	3	8
2.	35		7
3.	30		5
4.	16		4
5.	12		6
6.	36		9
7.	18		3
8.	15		5
9.	28		4
10.	27		3

Problem Solving REAL WORLD

11. In his bookstore, Toby places 21 books on shelves, with 7 books on each shelf. How many shelves does Toby need?

____

12. Mr. Holden has 32 quarters in stacks of 4 on his desk. How many stacks of quarters are on his desk?

____

Name ______________________________

COMMON CORE STANDARD CC.3.OA.2

Lesson Objective: Model division by using equal groups and bar models.

Model with Bar Models

Use counters to find 15 ÷ 5.

Step 1 Use 15 counters. Draw 5 circles to show the number of equal groups.

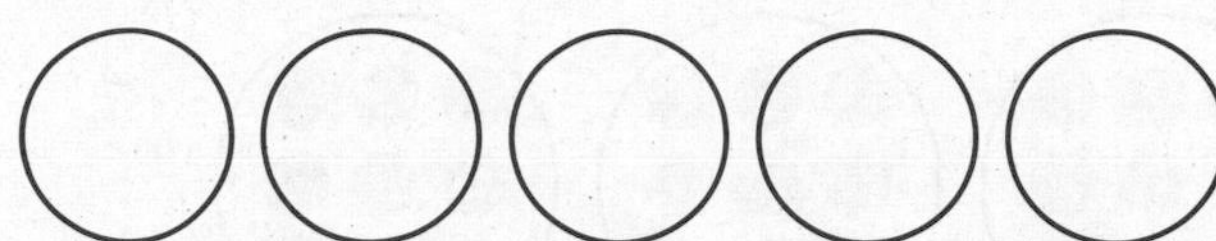

Step 2 Place 1 counter at a time in each circle.

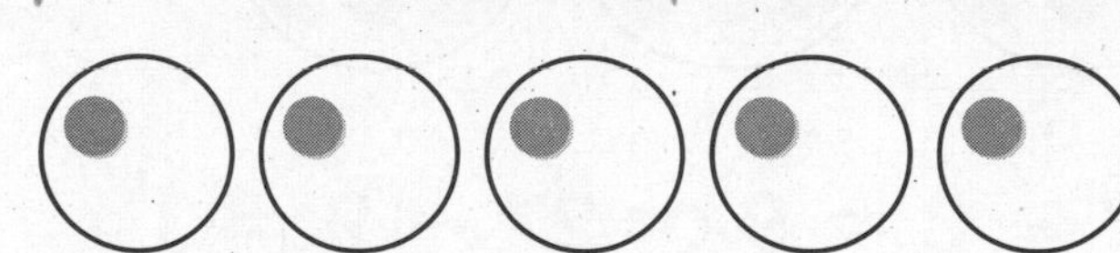

Step 3 Continue until you have placed all 15 counters.

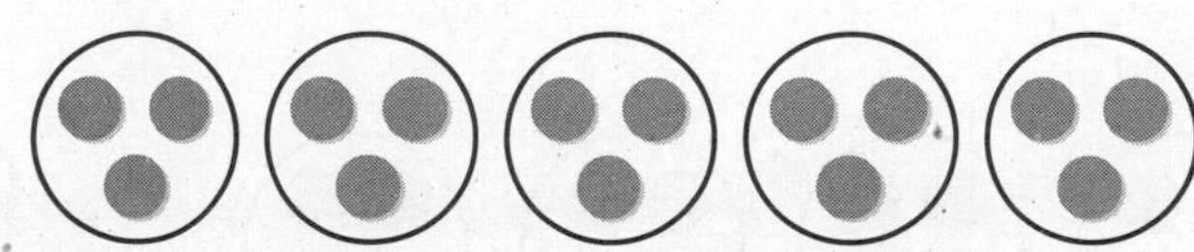

Step 4 Count the number of counters in each circle.

There are **3** counters in each of the 5 groups.

You can use a bar model to show how the parts of a problem are related.

- There are 15 counters.
- There are 5 equal groups.
- There are 3 counters in each group.

Write a division equation for the model.

15 ÷ 5 = **3**

Write a division equation for the picture.

1\.

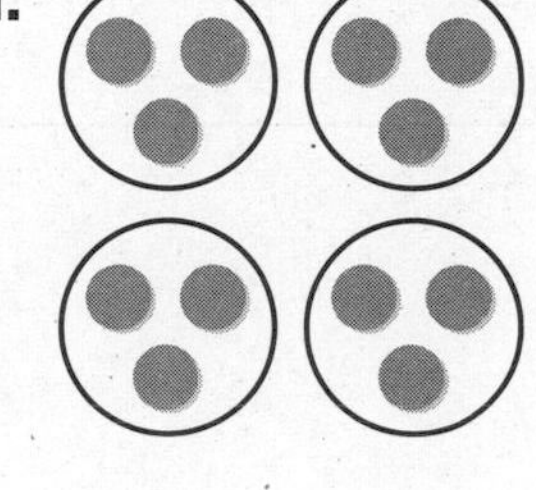

____

____

2\.

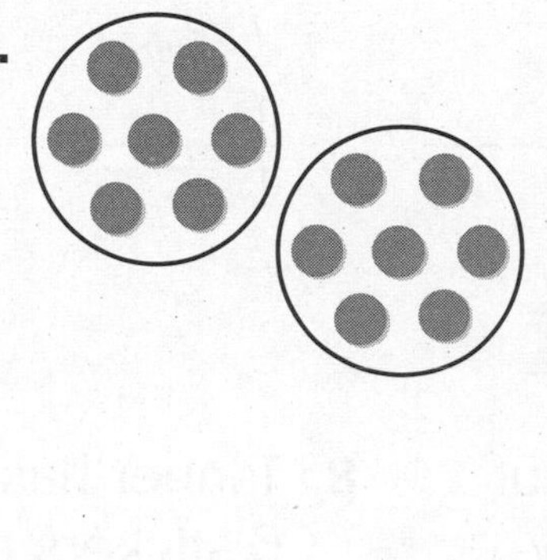

____

____

3\.

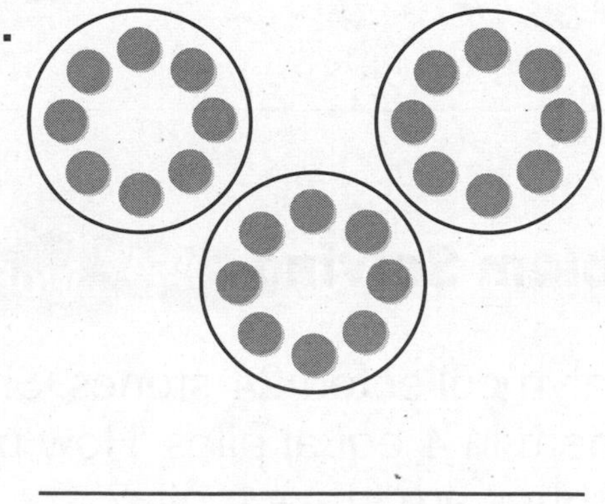

____

____

Name ______________________

Lesson 5

CC.3.OA.2

Model with Bar Models

Write a division equation for the picture.

1. 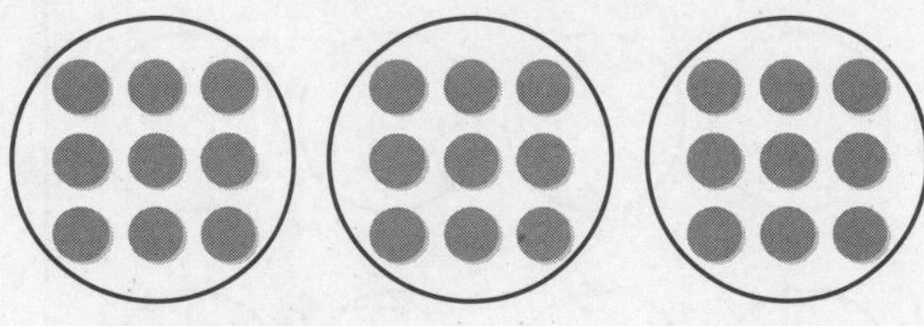

27 ÷ 3 = 9 or 27 ÷ 9 = 3

2. 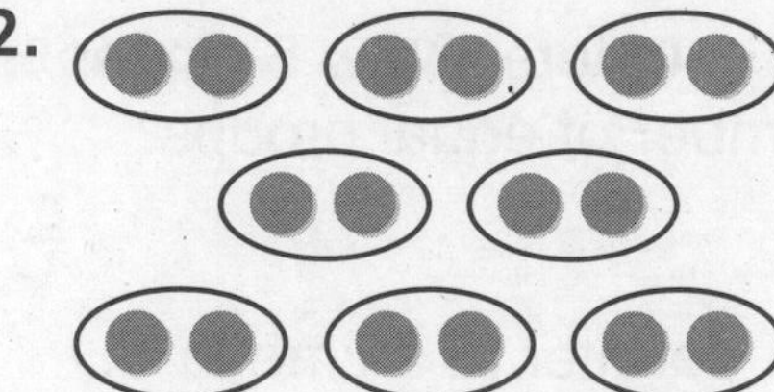

____

3. 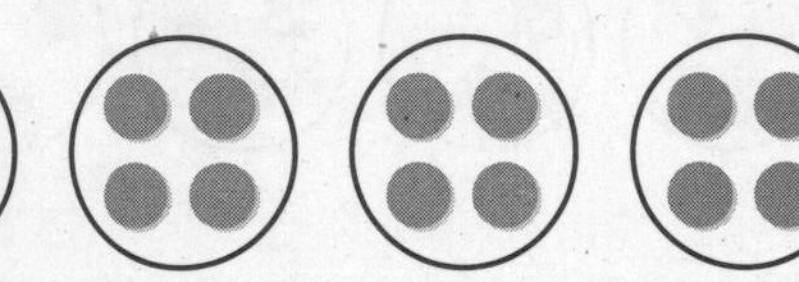

____

4. 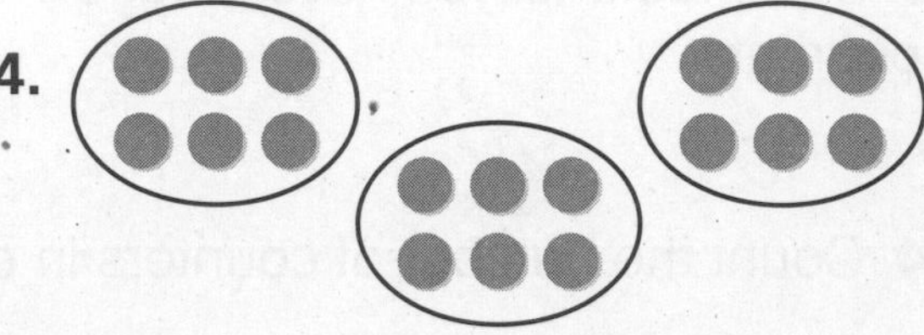

____

Complete the bar model to solve. Then write a division equation for the bar model.

5. There are 15 postcards in 3 equal stacks. How many postcards are in each stack?

___	___	___

15 postcards

____

6. There are 21 key rings. How many groups of 3 key rings can you make?

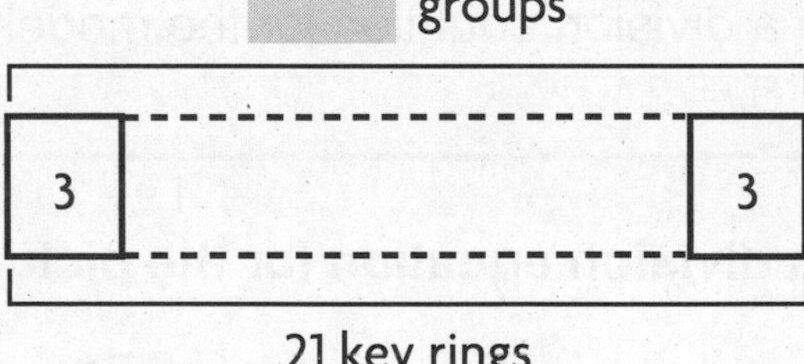

____

Problem Solving

7. Jalyn collected 24 stones. She put them in 4 equal piles. How many stones are in each pile?

____

8. Tanner has 30 stickers. He puts 6 stickers on each page. On how many pages does he put stickers?

____

Name ______________________________

Lesson 6

COMMON CORE STANDARD CC.3.OA.3

Lesson Objective: Model and skip count on a number line to find how many there are.

Skip Count on a Number Line

When you have **equal groups**, you can skip count on a number line to find how many in all.

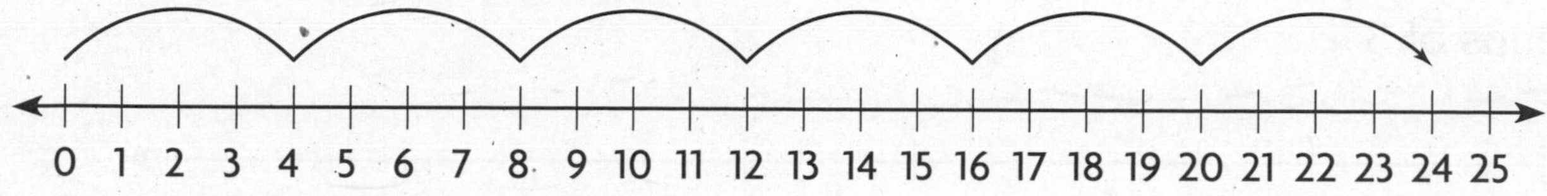

How many jumps are there? **6**

How long is each jump? **4 spaces**

Think: 6 jumps of 4 shows 6 groups of 4.

Multiply. **6 × 4**

6 × 4 = **24**

1. Skip count by drawing jumps on the number line. Find how many in 4 jumps of 4. Then write the product.

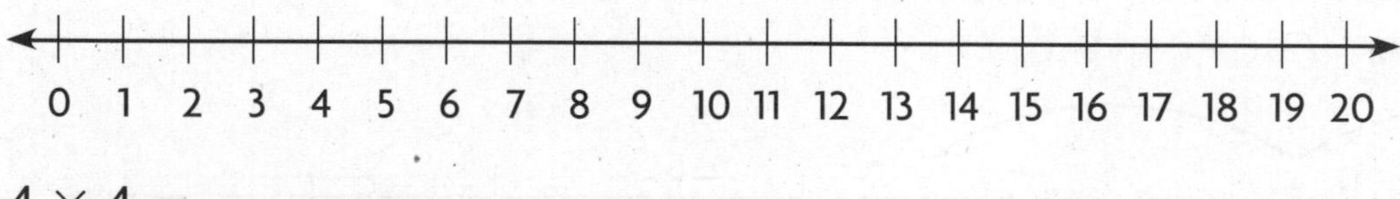

4 × 4 = ____

2. Draw jumps on the number line to show 6 groups of 3. Then find the product.

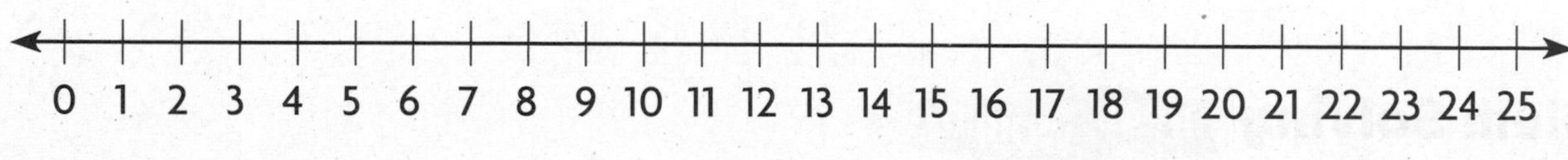

6 × 3 = ____

3. Write the multiplication sentence the number line shows.

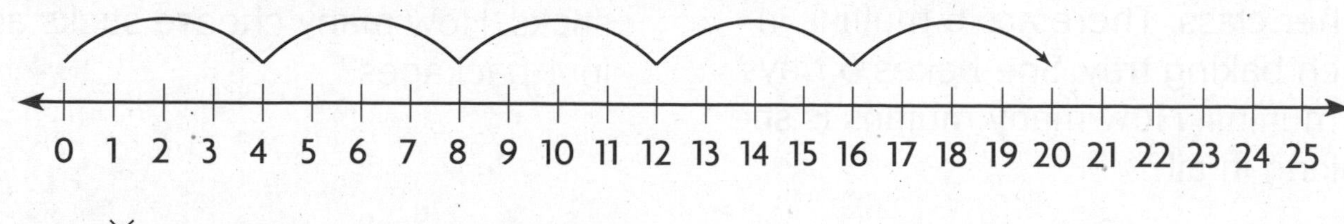

____ × ____ = ____

Name ______________________________

Lesson 6
CC.3.OA.3

Skip Count on a Number Line

Draw jumps on the number line to show equal groups. Find the product.

1. 6 groups of 3

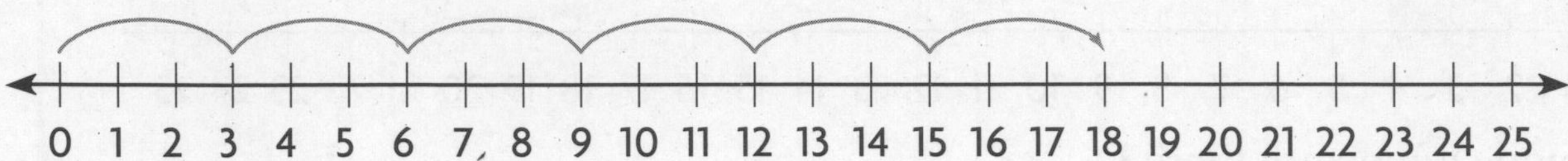

$6 \times 3 =$ **18**

2. 3 groups of 5

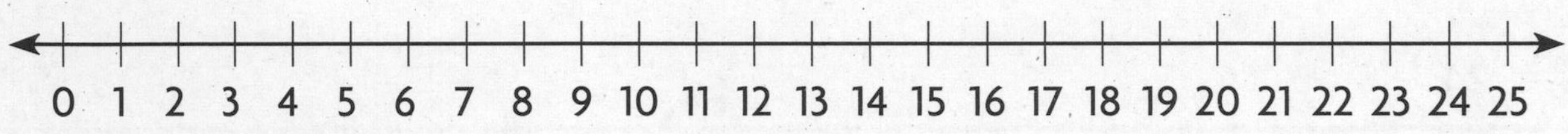

$3 \times 5 =$ ______

Write the multiplication sentence the number line shows.

3. 2 groups of 6

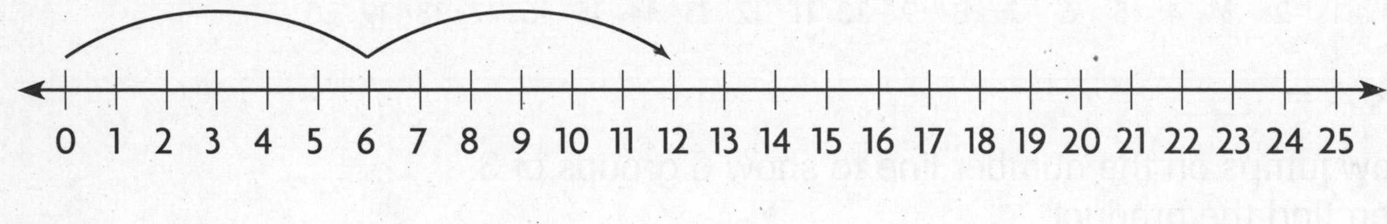

______ $\times$ ______ $=$ ______

Problem Solving REAL WORLD

4. Allie is baking muffins for students in her class. There are 6 muffins in each baking tray. She bakes 5 trays of muffins. How many muffins is she baking in all?

____

5. A snack package has 4 cheese sticks. How many cheese sticks are in 4 packages?

____

Name ______________________

Lesson 3

COMMON CORE STANDA[illegible] CC.3.OA.3

Lesson Objective: Draw a [illegible]re, count by 2s, or use doubles to multip[illegible] [illegible]ith the factors 2 and 4.

Multiply with 2 and 4

You can skip count to help you find a product.

Find the product. 4 × 3

Step 1 Use cubes to model 4 groups of 3.

Step 2 Skip count by 3s four times to find how many in all.

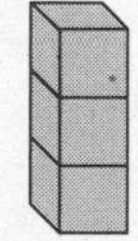
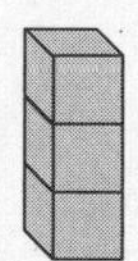
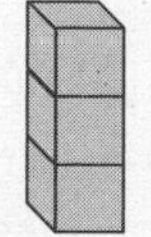
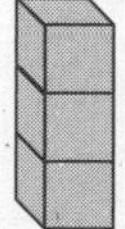

3, 6, 9, 12

4 groups of 3 is equal to **12**.

So, 4 × 3 = 12.

Write a multiplication sentence for the model.

1.

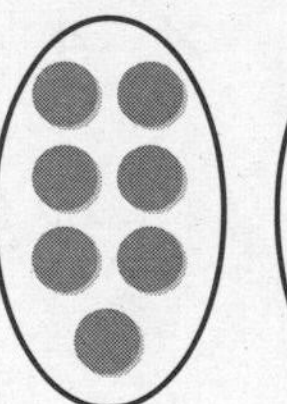
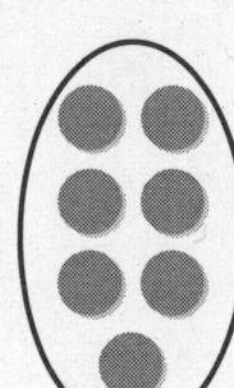

_____ × _____ = _____

2.

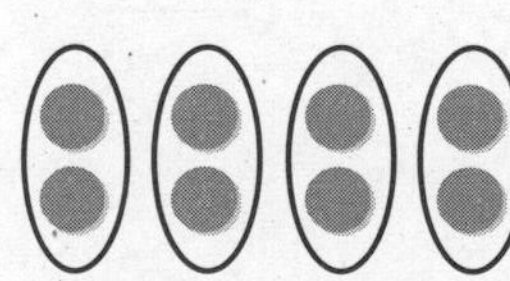

_____ × _____ = _____

Find the product.

3. 2 × 3	**4.** 4 × 8	**5.** 2 × 6	**6.** 4 × 1	**7.** 2 × 9
8. 2 × 2	**9.** 4 × 9	**10.** 2 × 5	**11.** 4 × 5	**12.** 4 × 7

Name ______________________________

Lesson 8
CC.3.OA.3

Multiply with 2 and 4

Write a multiplication sentence for the model.

1. 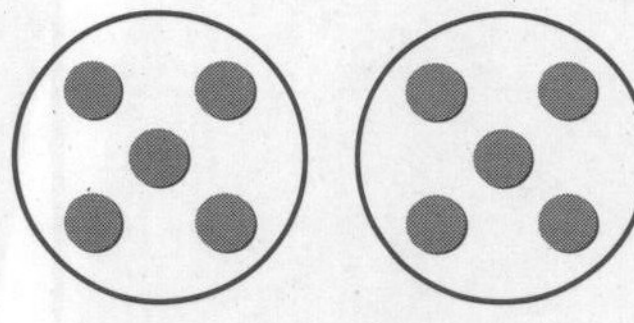

Think: There are 2 groups of 5 counters.

$\underline{2} \times \underline{5} = \underline{10}$

2. 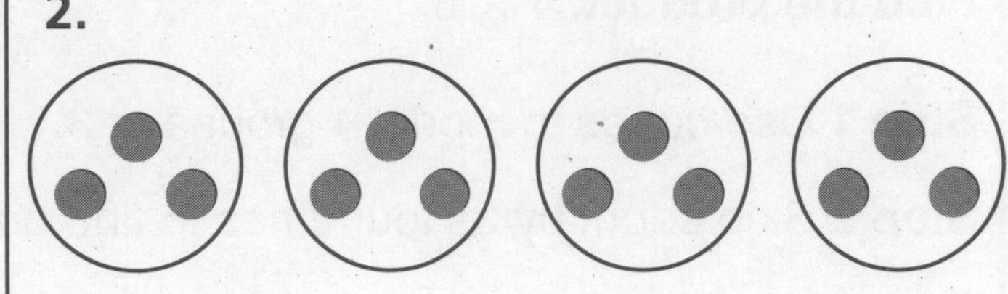

____ × ____ = ____

Find the product.

3. 2×6

4. 4×8

5. 2×3

6. 4×6

7. 4×4

8. 2×7

9. 4×5

10. 2×4

Problem Solving 

11. On Monday, Steven read 9 pages of his new book. To finish the first chapter on Tuesday, he needs to read double the number of pages he read on Monday. How many pages does he need to read on Tuesday?

____

12. Courtney's school is having a family game night. Each table has 4 players. There are 7 tables in all. How many players are at the game night?

____

Name ______________________________

COMMON CORE STANDARD CC.3.OA.3

Lesson Objective: Use skip counting, a number line, or a bar model to multiply with the factors 5 and 10.

Multiply with 5 and 10

You can use an array to multiply with 5.

Find the product. 5×4

Step 1 Make an array to show 5×4.
Show 5 rows of 4 tiles.

Step 2 Count the tiles.
5 rows of 4 tiles = 20 tiles

So, $5 \times 4 =$ **20**.

You can use doubles to multiply with 10.

Find the product. 6×10

Think: $5 + 5 = 10$

Multiply with 5. $6 \times 5 =$ **30**

Then double the product. **30** + 30 = **60**

So, $6 \times 10 =$ **60**.

Find the product.

1. $2 \times 5 =$ ______ 2. $10 \times 2 =$ ______ 3. $5 \times 5 =$ ______ 4. $5 \times 1 =$ ______

5. $10 \times 1 =$ ______ 6. $10 \times 5 =$ ______ 7. $3 \times 5 =$ ______ 8. $10 \times 7 =$ ______

9. 10×4 10. 6×5 11. 9×5 12. 10×3

13. 5×2 14. 10×6 15. 8×5 16. 10×8

Name ______________________

Lesson 9

CC.3.OA.3

Multiply with 5 and 10

Find the product.

1. $5 \times 7 =$ 35
2. $5 \times 1 =$ ______
3. $2 \times 10 =$ ______
4. ______ $= 8 \times 5$
5. $1 \times 10 =$ ______
6. ______ $= 4 \times 5$
7. $5 \times 10 =$ ______
8. $7 \times 5 =$ ______
9. ______ $= 5 \times 5$
10. $5 \times 8 =$ ______
11. ______ $= 5 \times 9$
12. $10 \times 0 =$ ______
13. 5×6
14. 10×7
15. 5×3
16. 10×4
17. 5×0
18. 10×8
19. 5×2
20. 10×6

Problem Solving REAL WORLD

21. Ginger takes 10 nickels to buy some pencils at the school store. How many cents does Ginger have to spend?

____

22. The gym at Evergreen School has three basketball courts. There are 5 players on each of the courts. How many players are there in all?

____

Name ______________________________

Lesson 10

COMMON CORE STANDARD CC.3.OA.3

Lesson Objective: Draw a picture, use 5s facts and addition, doubles, or a multiplication table to multiply with the factors 3 and 6.

Multiply with 3 and 6

You can use a number line to multiply with 3 or 6.

Find the product. 6 × 3

The factor 6 tells you to make **6 jumps**.

The factor 3 tells you each jump should be **3 spaces**.

Step 1 Start at 0.
Make 6 jumps of 3 spaces.

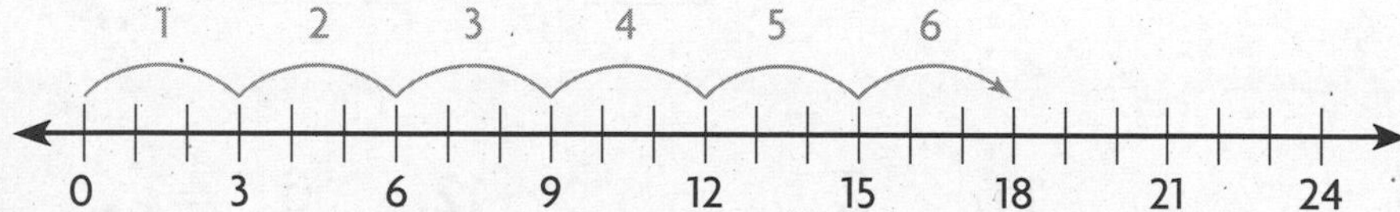

Step 2 The number you land on is the product.

So, 6 × 3 = 18.

Find the product.

1. 3 × 1 = _____ **2.** _____ = 2 × 6 **3.** 8 × 3 = _____ **4.** 6 × 6 = _____

5. 3 × 0 = _____ **6.** 5 × 6 = _____ **7.** _____ = 3 × 5 **8.** 9 × 6 = _____

9. $\begin{array}{r} 3 \\ \times\ 9 \\ \hline \end{array}$ **10.** $\begin{array}{r} 6 \\ \times\ 4 \\ \hline \end{array}$ **11.** $\begin{array}{r} 7 \\ \times\ 3 \\ \hline \end{array}$ **12.** $\begin{array}{r} 1 \\ \times\ 6 \\ \hline \end{array}$

13. $\begin{array}{r} 10 \\ \times\ 6 \\ \hline \end{array}$ **14.** $\begin{array}{r} 3 \\ \times\ 6 \\ \hline \end{array}$ **15.** $\begin{array}{r} 6 \\ \times\ 7 \\ \hline \end{array}$ **16.** $\begin{array}{r} 4 \\ \times\ 3 \\ \hline \end{array}$

Name ____________________

Multiply with 3 and 6

Find the product.

1. $6 \times 4 =$ 24
   Think: You can use doubles.
   $3 \times 4 = 12$
   $12 + 12 = 24$

2. $3 \times 7 =$ ____

3. ____ $= 2 \times 6$

4. ____ $= 3 \times 5$

5. $1 \times 3 =$ ____

6. ____ $= 6 \times 8$

7. $3 \times 9 =$ ____

8. ____ $= 6 \times 6$

9. 4×3

10. 6×5

11. 2×3

12. 6×3

13. 10×6

14. 3×6

15. 7×6

16. 3×0

17. 9×6

18. 3×3

19. 10×3

20. 1×6

Problem Solving REAL WORLD

21. James got 3 hits in each of his baseball games. He has played 4 baseball games. How many hits has he had in all?

____

22. Mrs. Burns is buying muffins. There are 6 muffins in each box. If she buys 5 boxes, how many muffins will she buy?

____

Name ______________________________

COMMON CORE STANDARD CC.3.OA.3

Lesson Objective: Model division by using arrays.

Model with Arrays

You can use arrays to model division.

How many rows of 6 tiles each can you make with 24 tiles?

Use square tiles to make an array. Solve.

Step 1 Use 24 tiles.

Step 2 Make as many rows of 6 as you can.

You can make **4** rows of 6.

So, there are **4** rows of 6 tiles in 24.

Use square tiles to make an array. Solve.

1. How many rows of 7 are in 28? ______________

2. How many rows of 5 are in 15? ______________

Make an array. Then write a division equation.

3. 18 tiles in 3 rows ______________

4. 20 tiles in 4 rows ______________

5. 14 tiles in 2 rows ______________

6. 36 tiles in 4 rows ______________

Name ______________________

Model with Arrays

Use square tiles to make an array. Solve.

1. How many rows of 4 are in 12?

   3 rows

2. How many rows of 3 are in 21?

   ______

3. How many rows of 6 are in 30?

   ______

4. How many rows of 9 are in 18?

   ______

Make an array. Then write a division equation.

5. 20 tiles in 5 rows

   ______

6. 28 tiles in 7 rows

   ______

7. 18 tiles in 9 rows

   ______

8. 36 tiles in 6 rows

   ______

Problem Solving REAL WORLD

9. A dressmaker has 24 buttons. He needs 3 buttons to make one dress. How many dresses can he make with 24 buttons?

   ______

10. Liana buys 36 party favors for her 9 guests. She gives an equal number of favors to each guest. How many party favors does each guest get?

   ______

Name ______________________

Divide by 2

Lesson 14

COMMON CORE STANDARD CC.3.OA.3

Lesson Objective: Use models to represent division by 2.

You can draw a picture to show how to divide.

Find the quotient. 16 ÷ 2

Step 1 Draw 16 counters.

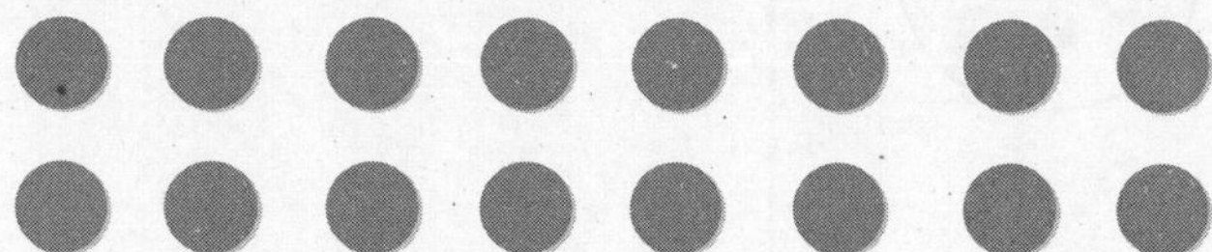

Step 2 Circle groups of 2. Continue circling groups of 2 until all 16 counters are in groups.

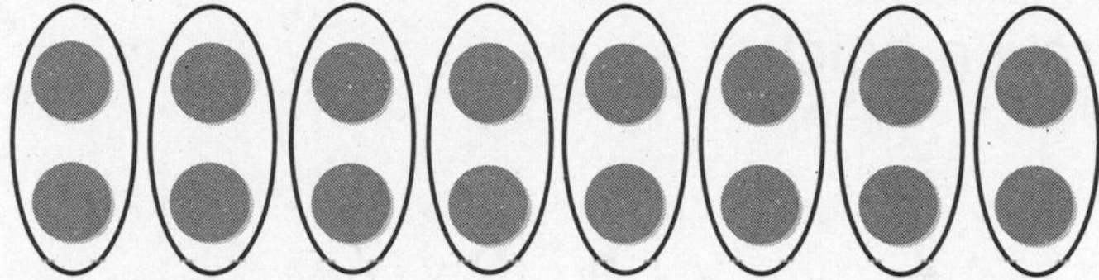

There are **8** groups of **2**.
So, 16 ÷ 2 = **8**.

Write a division equation for the picture.

1.

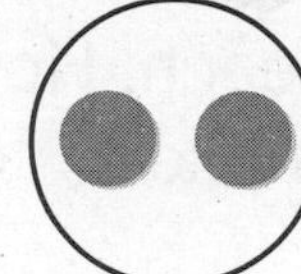

____

2.

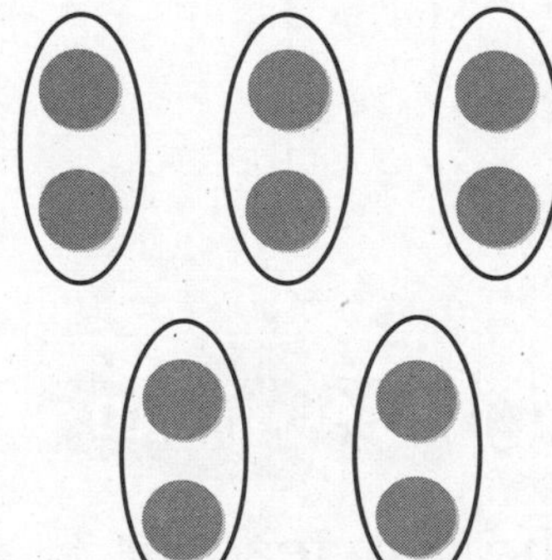

____

Name ______________________________

Divide by 2

Write a division equation for the picture.

1. 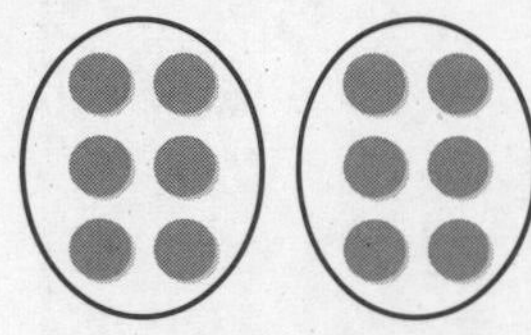

$12 \div 2 = 6$ or
$12 \div 6 = 2$

2. 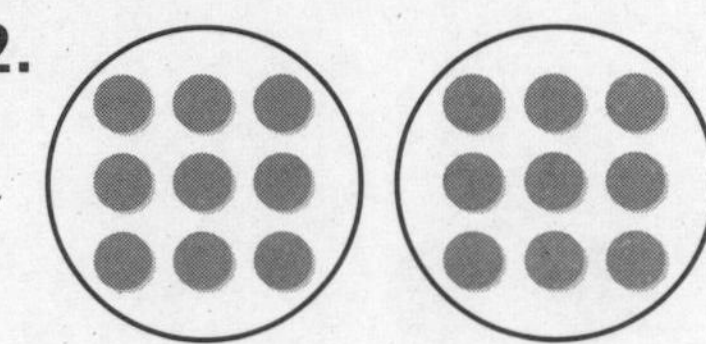

____
____

3. 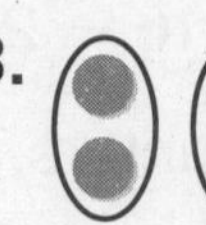   

____
____

Find the quotient. You may want to draw a quick picture to help.

4. ____ $= 14 \div 2$

5. ____ $= 4 \div 2$

6. $16 \div 2 =$ ____

7. $2\overline{)18}$

8. $2\overline{)12}$

9. $2\overline{)14}$

Problem Solving 

10. Mr. Reynolds, the gym teacher, divided a class of 16 students into 2 equal teams. How many students were on each team?

____

11. Sandra has 10 books. She divides them into groups of 2 each. How many groups can she make?

____

Name ______________________________

Lesson 15

COMMON CORE STANDARD CC.3.OA.3

Lesson Objective: Count up by 5s, count back on a number line, or use 10s facts and doubles to divide by 5.

Divide by 5

You can use a hundred chart and count up to help you divide.

Find the quotient. 30 ÷ 5

Step 1 Count up by 5s until you reach 30. Circle the numbers you say in the count.

Step 2 Count the number of times you count up.

5, 10, 15, ____, ____, ____

1 2, ____, ____, ____, ____

Step 3 Use the number of times you count up to complete the equation.

You counted up by 5 ____ times.

So, 30 ÷ 5 = ____.

1	2	3	4	(5)	6	7	8	9	(10)
11	12	13	14	15	16	17	18	19	20
21	22	23	24	25	26	27	28	29	30
31	32	33	34	35	36	37	38	39	40
41	42	43	44	45	46	47	48	49	50
51	52	53	54	55	56	57	58	59	60
61	62	63	64	65	66	67	68	69	70
71	72	73	74	75	76	77	78	79	80
81	82	83	84	85	86	87	88	89	90
91	92	93	94	95	96	97	98	99	100

Use the hundred chart and count up to solve.

1. 20 ÷ 5 = ____

2. 35 ÷ 5 = ____

3. 40 ÷ 5 = ____

Find the quotient.

4. 25 ÷ 5 = ____

5. ____ = 45 ÷ 5

6. 10 ÷ 5 = ____

7. ____ = 15 ÷ 5

8. 50 ÷ 5 = ____

9. ____ = 5 ÷ 5

Name ____________________

Lesson 15
CC.3.OA.3

Divide by 5

Use count up or count back on a number line to solve.

1. 40 ÷ 5 = 8

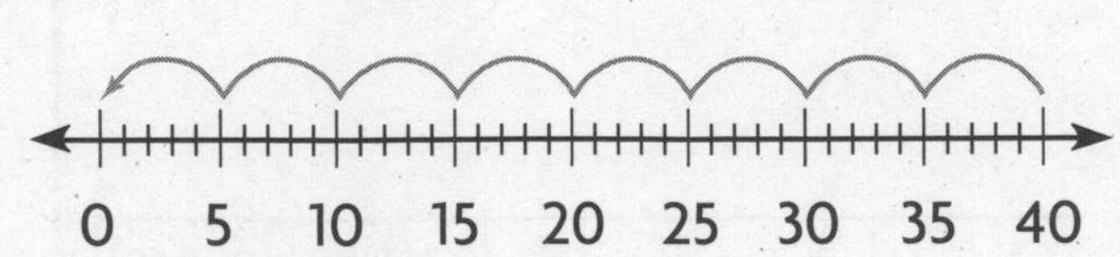

2. 25 ÷ 5 = ____

Find the quotient.

3. ____ = 10 ÷ 5

4. ____ = 30 ÷ 5

5. 14 ÷ 2 = ____

6. 5 ÷ 5 = ____

7. 45 ÷ 5 = ____

8. ____ = 60 ÷ 10

9. ____ = 15 ÷ 5

10. 18 ÷ 2 = ____

11. ____ = 0 ÷ 5

12. 20 ÷ 5 = ____

13. 25 ÷ 5 = ____

14. ____ = 35 ÷ 5

15. $5\overline{)20}$

16. $10\overline{)70}$

17. $5\overline{)15}$

18. $5\overline{)40}$

Problem Solving REAL WORLD

19. A model car maker puts 5 wheels in each kit. A machine makes 30 wheels at a time. How many packages of 5 wheels can be made from the 30 wheels?

____

20. A doll maker puts a small bag with 5 hair ribbons inside each box with a doll. How many bags of 5 hair ribbons can be made from 45 hair ribbons?

____

Name ____________________

COMMON CORE STANDARD CC.3.OA.4

Lesson Objective: Use repeated subtraction, a related multiplication fact, or a multiplication table to divide by 8.

Divide by 8

You can use a number line to divide by 8.

Find the quotient. 24 ÷ 8

Step 1 Start at 24. Count back by 8s as many times as you can until you reach 0. Draw the jumps on the number line.

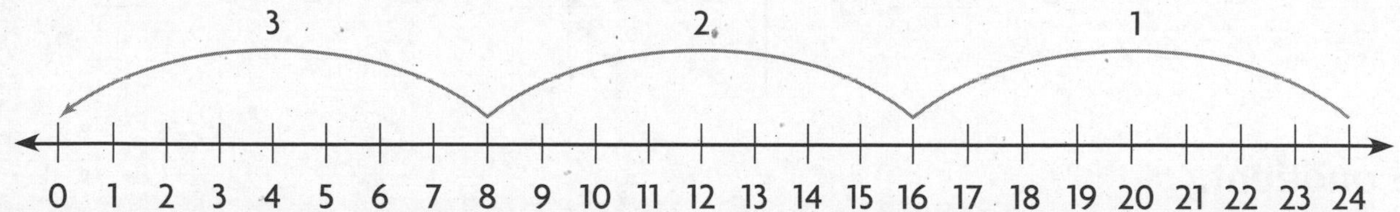

Step 2 Count the number of times you jumped back 8.

You jumped back by 8 **three** times.

So, 24 ÷ 8 = **3**.

Find the unknown factor and quotient.

1. ____ × 8 = 72 72 ÷ 8 = ____

2. 8 × ____ = 48 48 ÷ 8 = ____

3. 8 × ____ = 40 40 ÷ 8 = ____

4. ____ × 8 = 16 16 ÷ 8 = ____

Find the quotient.

5. 32 ÷ 8 = ____

6. ____ = 8 ÷ 8

7. 64 ÷ 8 = ____

8. 56 ÷ 8 = ____

9. ____ = 16 ÷ 8

10. 40 ÷ 8 = ____

11. 24 ÷ 8 = ____

12. ____ = 72 ÷ 8

13. 48 ÷ 8 = ____

Name ______________________________

Lesson 17
CC.3.OA.4

Divide by 8

Find the unknown factor and quotient.

1. $8 \times$ <u>4</u> $= 32$ $32 \div 8 =$ ____

2. $3 \times$ ____ $= 27$ $27 \div 3 =$ ____

3. $8 \times$ ____ $= 8$ $8 \div 8 =$ ____

4. $8 \times$ ____ $= 72$ $72 \div 8 =$ ____

Find the quotient.

5. ____ $= 24 \div 8$

6. $40 \div 8 =$ ____

7. ____ $= 56 \div 8$

8. $14 \div 2 =$ ____

9. $8\overline{)64}$

10. $7\overline{)28}$

11. $8\overline{)16}$

12. $8\overline{)48}$

Find the unknown number.

13. $16 \div p = 8$

$p =$ ____

14. $25 \div$ ■ $= 5$

■ $=$ ____

15. $24 \div a = 3$

$a =$ ____

16. $k \div 10 = 8$

$k =$ ____

Problem Solving REAL WORLD

17. Sixty-four students are going on a field trip. There is 1 adult for every 8 students. How many adults are there?

____

18. Mr. Chen spends $32 for tickets to a play. If the tickets cost $8 each, how many tickets does Mr. Chen buy?

____

Name ______________________ 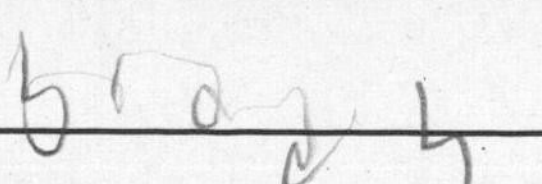

Lesson 19

COMMON CORE STANDARD CC.3.OA.5

Lesson Objective: Model multiplication with the factors 1 and 0.

Algebra • Multiply with 1 and 0

Find the product.

4 × 0 = ■

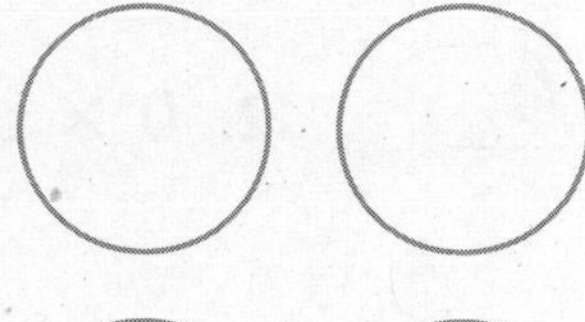

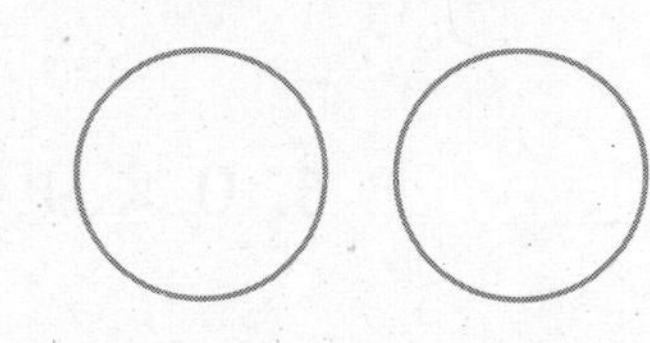

Model 4 × 0.
Each circle contains 0 counters.

4 circles × 0 counters = 0 counters

Zero Property of Multiplication
The product of zero and any number is zero.

So, 4 × 0 = 0 and 0 × 4 = 0.

Find the product.

6 × 1 = ■

Model 6 × 1.
Each circle contains 1 star.

6 circles × 1 star = 6 stars

Identity Property of Multiplication
The product of any number and 1 is that number.

So, 6 × 1 = 6 and 1 × 6 = 6.

Find the product.

1. 9 × 0 = ______ **2.** 1 × 5 = ______ **3.** 0 × 10 = ______ **4.** 8 × 1 = ______

5. 0 × 3 = ______ **6.** 7 × 1 = ______ **7.** 5 × 0 = ______ **8.** 1 × 2 = ______

Name ______________________

Multiply w h 1

Find the produ

1. $1 \times$ = 4
2. $0 \times 8 =$ 0
3. $0 \times 4 =$ 0
4. $1 \times 6 =$ 6

5. 3) = ___
6. $0 \times 9 =$ 0
7. $8 \times 1 =$ 8
8. $1 \times 2 =$ 2

9. $\times 6 =$ ___
10. $4 \times 0 =$ 0
11. $7 \times 1 =$ 7
12. $1 \times 5 =$ 5

13. $3 \times 1 =$ 3
14. $0 \times 7 =$ 0
15. $1 \times 9 =$ 9
16. $5 \times 0 =$ 0

17. 10×1 = 10
18. $2 \times 0 =$ 0
19. $5 \times 1 =$ 5
20. $1 \times 0 =$ 0

21. 0×0 0
22. $1 \times 3 =$ 3
23. $9 \times 0 =$ 0
24. $1 \times 1 =$ 1

Proble Solving REAL WORLD

25. Pete in the school play. His teac r gave 1 copy of the play to e h of 6 students. How many cop of the play did the teacher har out?

6 copivs

26. There are 4 egg cartons on the table. There are 0 eggs in each carton. How many eggs are there in all?

0 eggs

Name ______________________________

COMMON CORE STANDARD CC.3.OA

Lesson Objective: Divide using the rules for 1 and 0.

Algebra • Division Rules for 1 and 0

Division rules can help you understand how to divide with 1 and 0.

Rule A: Any number divided by 1 equals that number.

$5 \div 1 = \mathbf{5}$ or $1\overline{)5}$ with quotient **5**

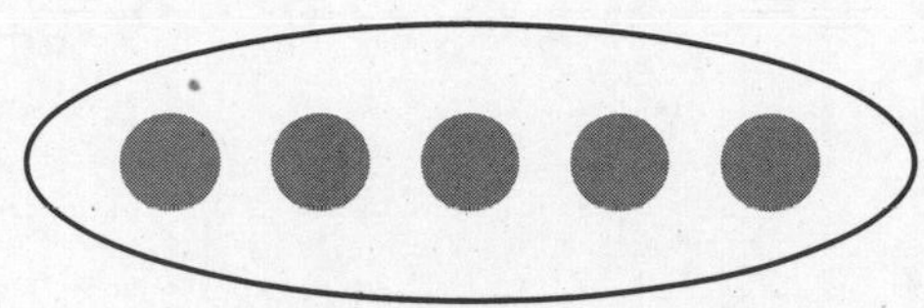

One group of 5

Rule B: Any number (except 0) divided by itself equals 1.

$5 \div 5 = \mathbf{1}$ or $5\overline{)5}$ with quotient **1**

Five groups of 1

Rule C: Zero divided by any number (except 0) equals 0.

$0 \div 5 = \mathbf{0}$ or $5\overline{)0}$ with quotient **0**

Five groups of 0

Rule D: You cannot divide by 0.

Find the quotient.

1. $4 \div 1 =$ ____ **2.** $2 \div 2 =$ ____ **3.** $8 \div 1 =$ ____ **4.** $7 \div 7 =$ ____

5. $0 \div 8 =$ ____ **6.** $0 \div 9 =$ ____ **7.** $4 \div 4 =$ ____ **8.** $6 \div 1 =$ ____

9. $6 \div 6 =$ ____ **10.** $0 \div 4 =$ ____ **11.** $0 \div 2 =$ ____ **12.** $3 \div 1 =$ ____

Name ______________________________

Lesson 22
CC.3.OA.5

Division Rules for 1 and 0

Find the quotient.

1. $3 \div 1 =$ 3
2. $8 \div 8 =$ ____
3. ____ $= 0 \div 6$
4. $2 \div 2 =$ ____

5. ____ $= 9 \div 1$
6. $0 \div 2 =$ ____
7. $0 \div 3 =$ ____
8. ____ $= 0 \div 4$

9. $7\overline{)7}$
10. $1\overline{)6}$
11. $9\overline{)0}$
12. $1\overline{)5}$

13. $1\overline{)0}$
14. $4\overline{)4}$
15. $1\overline{)10}$
16. $2\overline{)2}$

Problem Solving REAL WORLD

17. There are no horses in the stables. There are 3 stables in all. How many horses are in each stable?

____

18. Jon has 6 kites. He and his friends will each fly 1 kite. How many people in all will fly a kite?

____

Name ______________________________

Lesson 23

COMMON CORE STANDARD CC.3.OA.6

Lesson Objective: Use bar models and arrays to relate multiplication and division as inverse operations.

Algebra • Relate Multiplication and Division

You can use an array to complete 21 ÷ 3 = _____.

Use 21 counters.
Make 3 equal rows.

There are 7 counters in each row.

3 rows of 7 = 21

So, 21 ÷ 3 = 7

The 21 tells the total number of counters in the array.
The 3 stands for the number of equal rows.
The 7 stands for the number of counters in each row.

You can use a related multiplication fact to check your answer.

21 ÷ 3 = 7 **3 × 7 = 21**

So, 3 rows of 7 represents 21 ÷ 3 = 7 or 3 × 7 = 21.

Complete.

1. 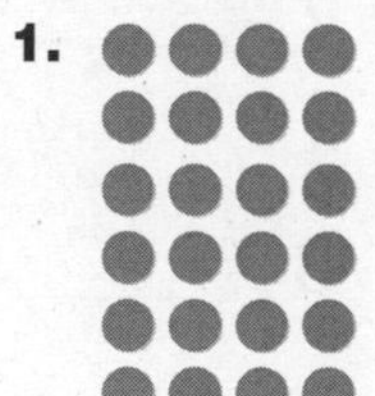

6 rows of _____ = 24

6 × _____ = 24

24 ÷ 6 = _____

2. 

3 rows of _____ = 27

3 × _____ = 27

27 ÷ 3 = _____

3. 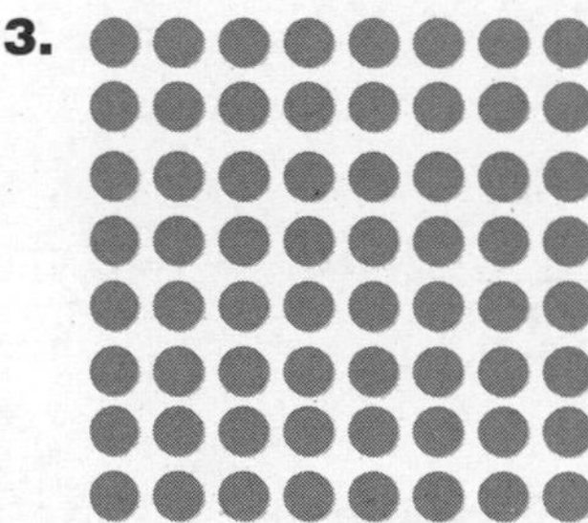

8 rows of _____ = 64

8 × _____ = 64

64 ÷ 8 = _____

Complete the equations.

4. 6 × _____ = 42 42 ÷ _____ = 6

5. 9 × _____ = 54 54 ÷ _____ = 9

Name ____________________

Relate Multiplication and Division

Complete the equations.

1. 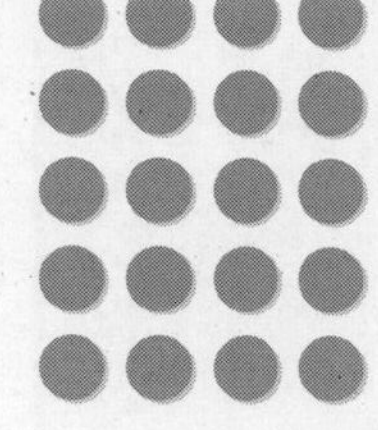

5 rows of 4 = 20

5 × 4 = 20

20 ÷ 5 = 4

2. 

4 rows of _____ = 24

4 × _____ = 24

24 ÷ 4 = _____

3. 

3 rows of _____ = 24

3 × _____ = 24

24 ÷ 3 = _____

Complete the equations.

4. 4 × _____ = 28   28 ÷ 4 = _____

5. 6 × _____ = 36   36 ÷ 6 = _____

6. 7 × _____ = 35   35 ÷ 7 = _____

7. 7 × _____ = 21   21 ÷ 7 = _____

8. 9 × _____ = 27   27 ÷ 9 = _____

9. 2 × _____ = 16   16 ÷ 2 = _____

10. 4 × _____ = 36   36 ÷ 4 = _____

11. 8 × _____ = 40   40 ÷ 8 = _____

Problem Solving REAL WORLD

12. Mr. Martin buys 36 muffins for a class breakfast. He places them on plates for his students. If he places 9 muffins on each plate, how many plates does Mr. Martin use?

____

13. Ralph read 18 books during his summer vacation. He read the same number of books each month for 3 months. How many books did he read each month?

____

Name ___________________________

Lesson 24

COMMON CORE STANDARD CC.3.OA.7

Lesson Objective: Use the Commutative or Distributive Property or known facts to multiply with the factor 7.

Multiply with 7

Pablo is making gift bags for his party. He puts 7 pencils in each bag. How many pencils will he need for 3 gift bags?

Find 3 × 7.

You can use a number line to find the product.

Step 1 Draw a number line.

Step 2 Start at 0. Draw 3 jumps of **7**.

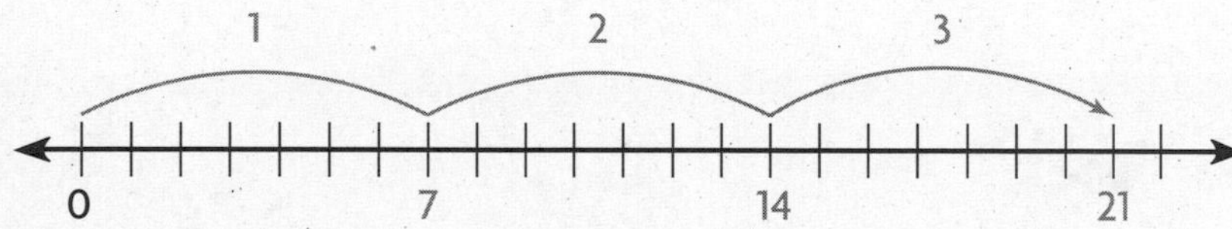

3 × 7 = **21**

So, Pablo will need __21__ pencils for 3 gift bags.

Find the product.

1. _____ = 0 × 7 **2.** 5 × 7 = _____ **3.** 4 × 7 = _____ **4.** _____ = 6 × 7

5. 7 × 7 = _____ **6.** _____ = 7 × 9 **7.** 1 × 7 = _____ **8.** _____ = 7 × 2

9. 10 × 7 **10.** 7 × 8 **11.** 7 × 0 **12.** 7 × 3 **13.** 9 × 7

14. 6 × 7 **15.** 7 × 5 **16.** 1 × 7 **17.** 7 × 7 **18.** 4 × 7

Name ______________________

Multiply with 7

Find the product.

1. $6 \times 7 =$ 42

2. ____ $= 7 \times 9$

3. ____ $= 1 \times 7$

4. $3 \times 7 =$ ____

5. $7 \times 7 =$ ____

6. ____ $= 2 \times 7$

7. $7 \times 8 =$ ____

8. ____ $= 4 \times 7$

9. 7×5

10. 7×1

11. 6×7

12. 7×4

13. 2×7

14. 10×7

15. 3×7

16. 7×9

17. 8×7

18. 7×0

Problem Solving REAL WORLD

19. Julie buys a pair of earrings for \$7. Now she would like to buy the same earrings for 2 of her friends. How much will she spend for all 3 pairs of earrings?

____

20. Owen and his family will go camping in 8 weeks. There are 7 days in 1 week. How many days are in 8 weeks?

____

Name ______________________________

Lesson 25

COMMON CORE STANDARD CC.3.OA.7

Lesson Objective: Use doubles, a number line, or the Associative Property of Multiplication to multiply with the factor 8.

Multiply with 8

You can break apart arrays to multiply with 8.

Candace works at a candle shop.
She places candles in a box for display.
The box has 7 rows of 8 candles.
How many candles are in the box in all?

You can break apart an array to find 7×8.

Step 1 Draw 7 rows of 8 squares.

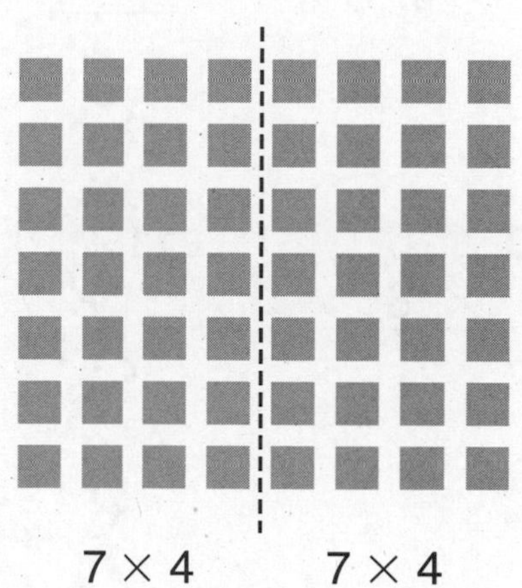

Step 2 Draw a dashed line to break apart the array into two smaller arrays to show facts you know.

$7 \times 8 = (7 \times 4) + (7 \times 4)$

$7 \times 8 = 28 + 28$

$7 \times 8 = 56$

So, there are 56 candles in the box.

Find the product.

1. $3 \times 8 =$ ______
2. ______ $= 0 \times 8$
3. $2 \times 8 =$ ______
4. $4 \times 8 =$ ______
5. ______ $= 9 \times 8$
6. $5 \times 8 =$ ______
7. $8 \times 10 =$ ______
8. ______ $= 8 \times 8$
9. 7×8
10. 10×8
11. 8×4
12. 8×3
13. 1×8

Name ______________________________

Lesson 25

CC.3.OA.7

Multiply with 8

Find the product.

1. $8 \times 10 =$ 80
2. $8 \times 8 =$ ____
3. $8 \times 5 =$ ____
4. $3 \times 8 =$ ____
5. ____ $= 4 \times 8$
6. $8 \times 7 =$ ____
7. $6 \times 8 =$ ____
8. ____ $= 9 \times 8$
9. 8×2
10. 6×8
11. 8×7
12. 0×8
13. 8×5
14. 8×8
15. 9×8
16. 8×3
17. 8×1
18. 4×8

Problem Solving REAL WORLD

19. There are 6 teams in the basketball league. Each team has 8 players. How many players are there in all?

    ____

20. Lynn has 4 stacks of quarters. There are 8 quarters in each stack. How many quarters does Lynn have in all?

    ____

21. Tomas is packing 7 baskets for a fair. He is placing 8 apples in each basket. How many apples are there in all?

    ____

22. There are 10 pencils in each box. If Jenna buys 8 boxes, how many pencils will she buy?

    ____

Name ______________________________

COMMON CORE STANDARD CC.3.OA.7

Lesson Objective: Use the Distributive Property with addition or subtraction or patterns to multiply with the factor 9.

Multiply with 9

Ana goes to the pet store to buy a fish. The store has 3 fish tanks. Each tank has 9 fish. How many fish in all are in the tanks?

You can use counters to find the product.

Find 3 × 9.

Step 1 Make 3 groups of 9 counters.

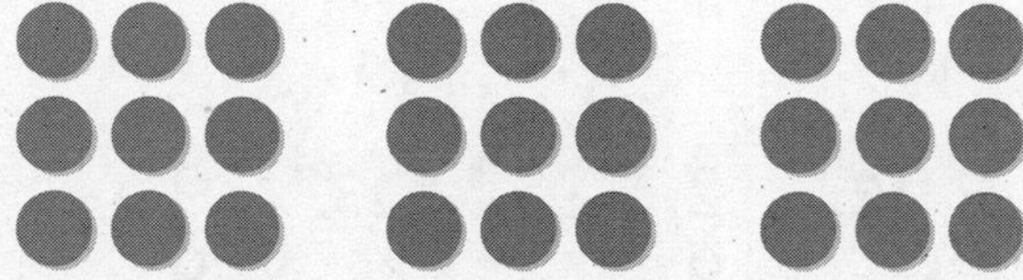

Step 2 Skip count by 9s to find the total number of counters.

9, 18, 27 counters

3 × 9 = 27

So, there are 27 fish in all in the tanks.

Find the product.

1. 4 × 9 = _____ **2.** 6 × 9 = _____ **3.** 3 × 9 = _____ **4.** 7 × 9 = _____

5. 1 × 9 = _____ **6.** _____ = 8 × 9 **7.** 9 × 5 = _____ **8.** _____ = 0 × 9

9. $\begin{array}{r} 2 \\ \times\ 9 \\ \hline \end{array}$ **10.** $\begin{array}{r} 9 \\ \times\ 9 \\ \hline \end{array}$ **11.** $\begin{array}{r} 9 \\ \times\ 3 \\ \hline \end{array}$ **12.** $\begin{array}{r} 9 \\ \times\ 4 \\ \hline \end{array}$ **13.** $\begin{array}{r} 10 \\ \times\ 9 \\ \hline \end{array}$

Name ________________________

Lesson 26
CC.3.OA.7

Multiply with 9

Find the product.

1. $10 \times 9 =$ 90 **2.** $2 \times 9 =$ ____ **3.** $9 \times 4 =$ ____ **4.** $0 \times 9 =$ ____

5. $1 \times 9 =$ ____ **6.** $8 \times 9 =$ ____ **7.** $9 \times 5 =$ ____ **8.** $6 \times 9 =$ ____

9. 9×4 **10.** 5×9 **11.** 9×7 **12.** 2×9 **13.** 9×9

14. 10×9 **15.** 3×9 **16.** 9×8 **17.** 6×9 **18.** 9×1

Problem Solving REAL WORLD

19. There are 9 positions on the softball team. Three people are trying out for each position. How many people in all are trying out?

____

20. Carlos bought a book for $9. Now he would like to buy 4 other books for the same price. How much will he have to pay in all for the other 4 books?

____

Name ______________________

COMMON CORE STANDARD CC.3.OA.7

Lesson Objective: Write related multiplication and division facts.

Algebra • Write Related Facts

Related facts are a set of related multiplication and division equations.

Write the related facts for the array.

There are **4** equal rows of tiles.
There are **6** tiles in each row.
There are **24** tiles.
Write 2 multiplication equations and 2 division equations for the array.

factor × factor = product

4 × 6 = **24**

6 × 4 = **24**

dividend ÷ divisor = quotient

24 ÷ 4 = 6

24 ÷ 6 = 4

The equations show how the numbers 4, 6, and 24 are related.

So, the related facts are **4 × 6 = 24**, **6 × 4 = 24**, **24 ÷ 4 = 6**, and **24 ÷ 6 = 4**.

Write the related facts for the array.

1. 

______________ ______________

______________ ______________

2.  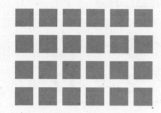

______________ ______________

______________ ______________

3. 

______________ ______________

______________ ______________

4.  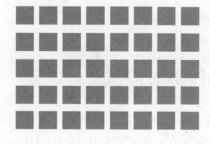

______________ ______________

______________ ______________

Name ______________________

Lesson 27
CC.3.OA.7

Write Related Facts

Write the related facts for the array.

1.

$2 \times 6 = 12$

$6 \times 2 = 12$

$12 \div 2 = 6$

$12 \div 6 = 2$

2. 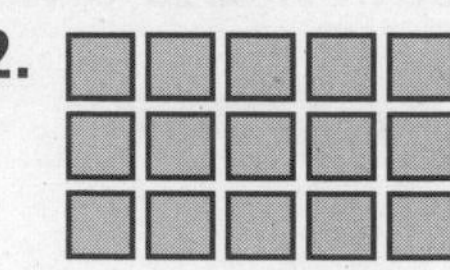

____

____

____

____

3.

____

____

____

____

Write the related facts for the set of numbers.

4. 3, 7, 21

____

____

____

____

5. 2, 9, 18

____

____

____

____

6. 4, 8, 32

____

____

____

____

Complete the related facts.

7. $4 \times 9 =$ _____

$9 \times$ _____ $= 36$

$36 \div$ _____ $= 4$

_____ $\div 4 = 9$

8. _____ $\times 7 = 35$

_____ $\times 5 = 35$

_____ $\div 7 = 5$

$35 \div 5 =$ _____

9. $6 \times$ _____ $= 18$

$3 \times 6 =$ _____

$18 \div$ _____ $= 3$

_____ $\div 3 = 6$

Problem Solving REAL WORLD

10. CDs are on sale for $5 each. Jennifer has $45 and wants to buy as many as she can. How many CDs can Jennifer buy?

____

11. Mr. Moore has 21 feet of wallpaper. He cuts it into sections that are each 3 feet long. How many sections does Mr. Moore have?

____

Name ______________________________

COMMON CORE STANDARD CC.3.OA.7

Lesson Objective: Use repeated subtraction, a number line, or a multiplication table to divide by 10.

Divide by 10

You can use a multiplication table to divide by 10.

×	0	1	2	3	4	5	6	7	8	9	10
0	0	0	0	0	0	0	0	0	0	0	0
1	0	1	2	3	4	5	6	7	8	9	10
2	0	2	4	6	8	10	12	14	16	18	20
3	0	3	6	9	12	15	18	21	24	27	30
4	0	4	8	12	16	20	24	28	32	36	40
5	0	5	10	15	20	25	30	35	40	45	50
6	0	6	12	18	24	30	36	42	48	54	60
7	0	7	14	21	28	35	42	49	56	63	70
8	0	8	16	24	32	40	48	56	64	72	80
9	0	9	18	27	36	45	54	63	72	81	90
10	0	10	20	30	40	50	60	70	80	90	100

Find the quotient. $30 \div 10$

Think of a related multiplication fact.

$10 \times ■ = 30$

Step 1 Find the row for the factor, 10. This number is the divisor.

Step 2 Look across the row to find the product, 30. This number is the dividend.

Step 3 Look up to the top row to find the unknown factor, 3. This is the quotient.

Since $10 \times 3 = 30$, then $30 \div 10 = 3$.

So, $30 \div 10 = 3$.

Find the unknown factor and quotient.

1. $10 \times$ _____ $= 70$ _____ $= 70 \div 10$

2. $10 \times$ _____ $= 20$ $20 \div 10 =$ _____

Find the quotient.

3. $60 \div 10 =$ _____   **4.** $80 \div 10 =$ _____   **5.** $100 \div 10 =$ _____

6. $10\overline{)50}$ **7.** $10\overline{)90}$ **8.** $10\overline{)30}$

Name ______________________

Divide by 10

Find the unknown factor and quotient.

1. $10 \times$ <u>2</u> $= 20$ $20 \div 10 =$ <u>2</u>

2. $10 \times$ ____ $= 70$ $70 \div 10 =$ ____

3. $10 \times$ ____ $= 80$ $80 \div 10 =$ ____

4. $10 \times$ ____ $= 30$ $30 \div 10 =$ ____

Find the quotient.

5. $60 \div 10 =$ ____

6. ____ $= 40 \div 4$

7. $20 \div 2 =$ ____

8. $50 \div 10 =$ ____

9. $90 \div 10 =$ ____

10. $10 \div 10 =$ ____

11. ____ $= 30 \div 10$

12. $40 \div 10 =$ ____

13. $10\overline{)40}$

14. $10\overline{)70}$

15. $10\overline{)100}$

16. $10\overline{)20}$

Problem Solving

17. Pencils cost 10¢ each. How many pencils can Brent buy with 90¢?

____

18. Mrs. Marks wants to buy 80 pens. If the pens come in packs of 10, how many packs does she need to buy?

____

Name ______________________

Lesson 29

COMMON CORE STANDARD CC.3.OA.7

Lesson Objective: Use equal groups, a number line, or a related multiplication fact to divide by 3.

Divide by 3

You can draw a picture to show how to divide.

Find the quotient.

21 ÷ 3

Step 1 Draw 21 counters to show the dividend.

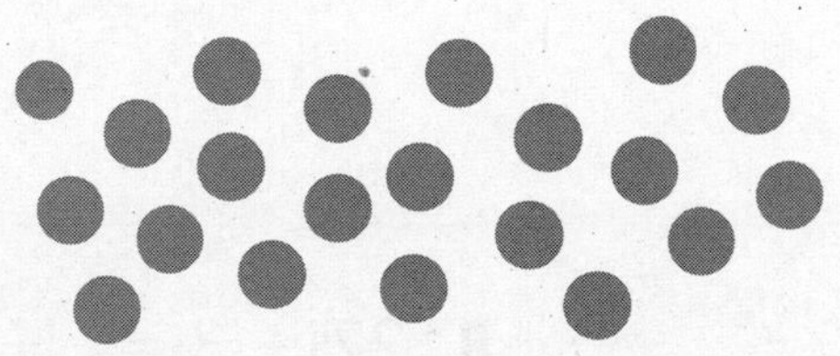

Step 2 Circle groups of 3 to show the divisor.

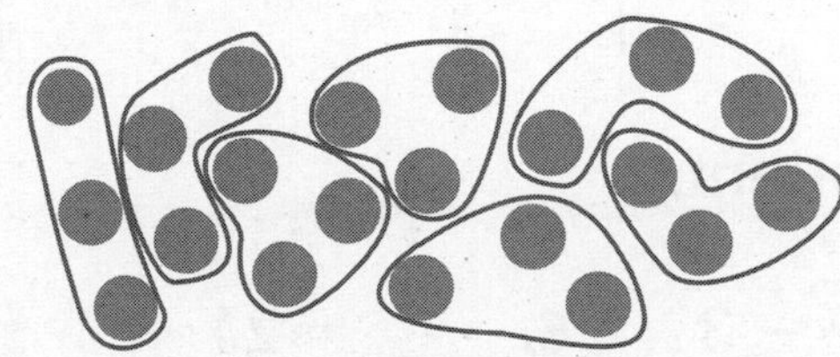

Step 3 Count the groups.

There are 7 groups of 3. So, the quotient is 7.

You can use a related multiplication fact to check your answer.

Think: 7 × 3 = 21

So, 21 ÷ 3 = 7.

Circle groups of 3 to find the quotient.

1. 9 ÷ 3 = ____

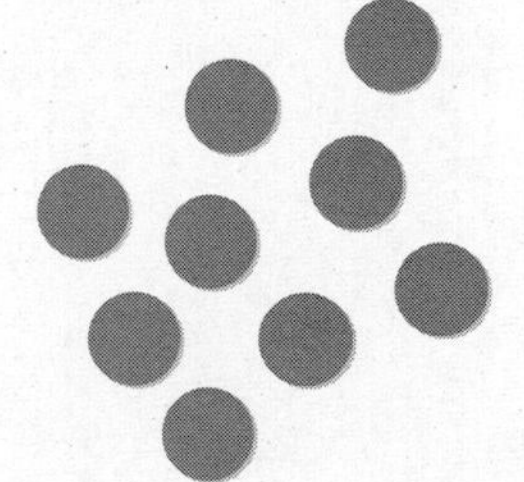

2. 15 ÷ 3 = ____

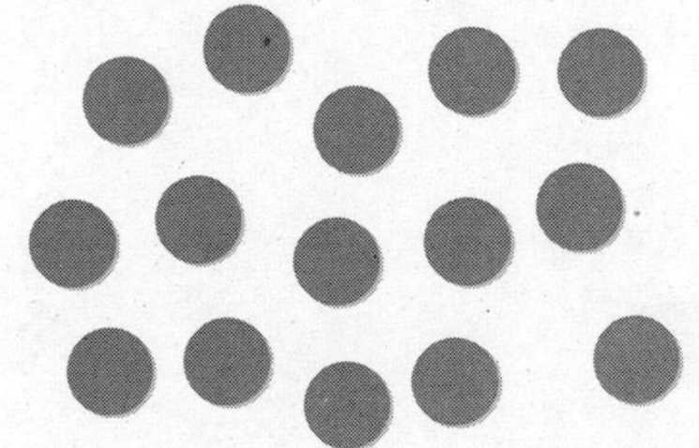

3. ____ = 6 ÷ 3

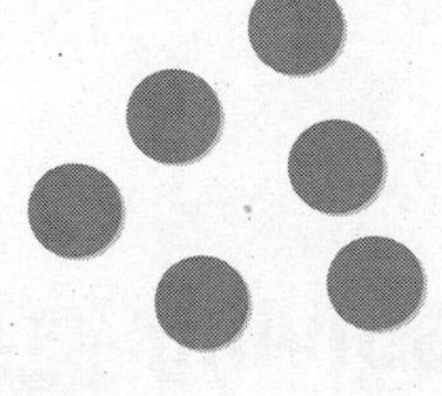

Find the quotient.

4. 12 ÷ 3 = ____ **5.** 18 ÷ 3 = ____ **6.** 24 ÷ 3 = ____ **7.** 27 ÷ 3 = ____

Name ______________________________

Divide by 3

Find the quotient. Draw a quick picture to help.

1. $12 \div 3 =$ 4

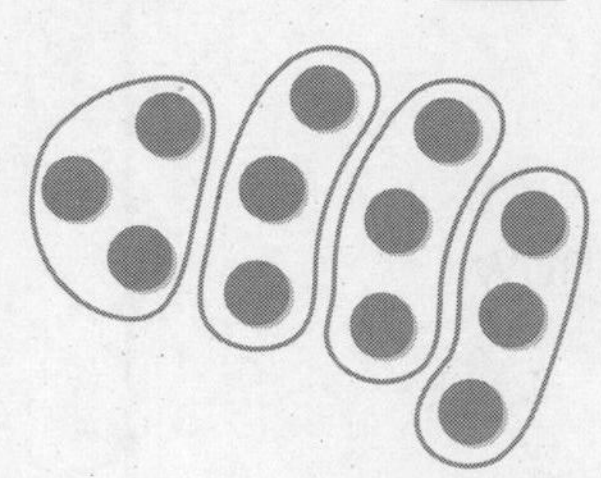

2. $24 \div 3 =$ ____

3. ____ $= 6 \div 3$

4. $40 \div 5 =$ ____

Find the quotient.

5. ____ $= 15 \div 3$

6. ____ $= 21 \div 3$

7. $16 \div 2 =$ ____

8. $27 \div 3 =$ ____

9. $0 \div 3 =$ ____

10. $9 \div 3 =$ ____

11. ____ $= 30 \div 3$

12. ____ $= 12 \div 4$

13. $3\overline{)12}$

14. $3\overline{)15}$

15. $3\overline{)24}$

16. $3\overline{)9}$

Problem Solving

17. The principal at Miller Street School has 12 packs of new pencils. She will give 3 packs to each third-grade class. How many third-grade classes are there?

____

18. Mike has \$21 to spend at the mall. He spends all of his money on bracelets for his sisters. Bracelets cost \$3 each. How many bracelets does he buy?

____

Name ______________________________

Lesson 30

COMMON CORE STANDARD CC.3.OA.7

Lesson Objective: Use an array, equal groups, factors, or a related multiplication fact to divide by 4.

Divide by 4

One way to divide is to count back on a number line.

Find the quotient.
12 ÷ 4

Start at 12.

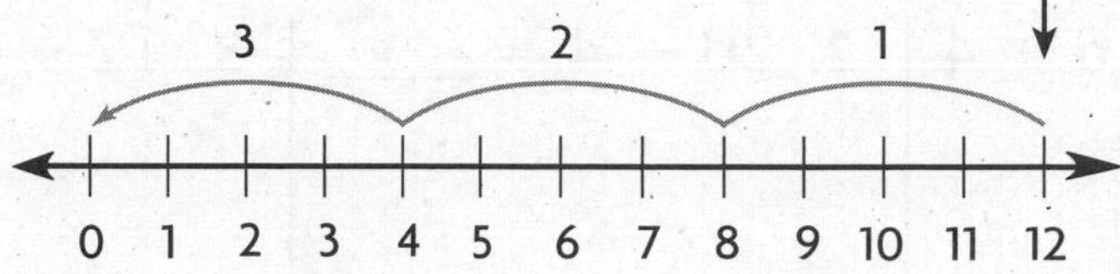

Count back by 4s as many times as you can until you reach 0.

Count the number of times you jumped back 4. **3 times**

So, 12 ÷ 4 = 3.

Find the quotient.
32 ÷ 4

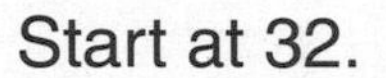
Start at 32.

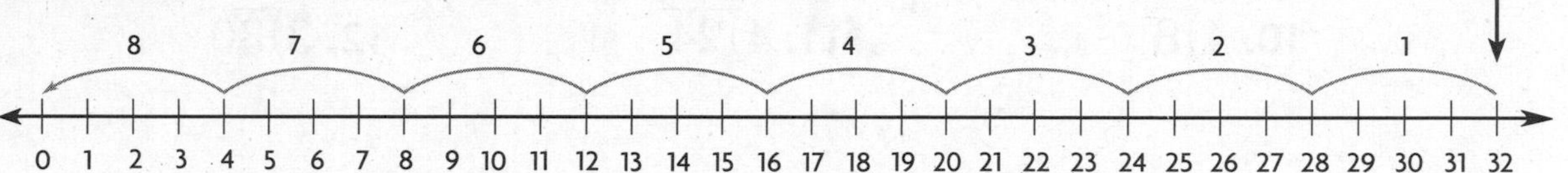

Count back by 4s as many times as you can until you reach 0.

Count the number of times you jumped back 4. **8 times**

So, 32 ÷ 4 = 8.

Find the quotient.

1. 24 ÷ 4 = ____ **2.** ____ = 12 ÷ 3 **3.** 16 ÷ 4 = ____ **4.** ____ = 8 ÷ 4

5. 4 ÷ 2 = ____ **6.** ____ = 28 ÷ 4 **7.** 36 ÷ 4 = ____ **8.** 20 ÷ 4 = ____

Find the unknown number.

9. 4 ÷ 4 = ▲ **10.** 40 ÷ 10 = t **11.** 8 ÷ 2 = g **12.** 21 ÷ 7 = m

▲ = ____ t = ____ g = ____ m = ____

Name ____________________

Divide by 4

Draw tiles to make an array. Find the quotient.

1. 4 = 16 ÷ 4

2. 20 ÷ 4 = ____

3. 12 ÷ 4 = ____

4. 10 ÷ 2 = ____

Find the quotient.

5. 24 ÷ 3 = ____

6. ____ = 8 ÷ 2

7. 32 ÷ 4 = ____

8. ____ = 28 ÷ 4

9. $4\overline{)36}$

10. $4\overline{)8}$

11. $4\overline{)24}$

12. $3\overline{)30}$

Find the unknown number.

13. 20 ÷ 5 = a

a = ____

14. 32 ÷ 4 = p

p = ____

15. 40 ÷ 10 = ■

■ = ____

16. 18 ÷ 3 = x

x = ____

Problem Solving REAL WORLD

17. Ms. Higgins has 28 students in her gym class. She puts them in 4 equal groups. How many students are in each group?

____

18. Andy has 36 CDs. He buys a case that holds 4 CDs in each section. How many sections can he fill?

____

Name ___________________________

Lesson 31

COMMON CORE STANDARD CC.3.OA.7

Lesson Objective: Use equal groups, a related multiplication fact, or factors to divide by 6.

Divide by 6

You can use a multiplication table to divide by 6.

Find the quotient. 42 ÷ 6

Think of a related multiplication fact.
6 × ■ = 42

Find the row for the factor, 6.

Look right to find the product, **42**.

Look up to find the unknown factor, 7.

7 is the factor you multiply by 6 to get the product, 42.

So, 6 × **7** = 42.

Use this related multiplication fact to find the quotient.

Since 6 × **7** = 42, then 42 ÷ 6 = **7**.

So, 42 ÷ 6 = **7**.

×	0	1	2	3	4	5	6	7	8	9	10
0	0	0	0	0	0	0	0	0	0	0	0
1	0	1	2	3	4	5	6	7	8	9	10
2	0	2	4	6	8	10	12	14	16	18	20
3	0	3	6	9	12	15	18	21	24	27	30
4	0	4	8	12	16	20	24	28	32	36	40
5	0	5	10	15	20	25	30	35	40	45	50
6	0	6	12	18	24	30	36	42	48	54	60
7	0	7	14	21	28	35	42	49	56	63	70
8	0	8	16	24	32	40	48	56	64	72	80
9	0	9	18	27	36	45	54	63	72	81	90
10	0	10	20	30	40	50	60	70	80	90	100

Find the unknown factor and quotient.

1. 6 × ____ = 30 30 ÷ 6 = ____

2. 6 × ____ = 48 48 ÷ 6 = ____

3. 6 × ____ = 18 18 ÷ 6 = ____

4. 6 × ____ = 24 24 ÷ 6 = ____

Find the quotient.

5. 6 ÷ 6 = ____

6. 48 ÷ 6 = ____

7. 54 ÷ 6 = ____

8. 12 ÷ 6 = ____

9. 0 ÷ 6 = ____

10. 36 ÷ 6 = ____

11. 6 ÷ 1 = ____

12. 18 ÷ 6 = ____

Name ____________________

Lesson 31
CC.3.OA.7

Divide by 6

Find the unknown factor and quotient.

1. $6 \times$ 7 $= 42$ $42 \div 6 =$ 7
2. $6 \times$ ____ $= 18$ $18 \div 6 =$ ____
3. $4 \times$ ____ $= 24$ $24 \div 4 =$ ____
4. $6 \times$ ____ $= 54$ $54 \div 6 =$ ____

Find the quotient.

5. ____ $= 24 \div 6$
6. $48 \div 6 =$ ____
7. ____ $= 6 \div 6$
8. $12 \div 6 =$ ____

9. $6\overline{)36}$
10. $6\overline{)54}$
11. $6\overline{)30}$
12. $1\overline{)6}$

Find the unknown number.

13. $p = 42 \div 6$

    $p =$ ____
14. $18 \div 3 = q$

    $q =$ ____
15. $r = 30 \div 6$

    $r =$ ____
16. $60 \div 6 = s$

    $s =$ ____

Problem Solving REAL WORLD

17. Lucas has 36 pages of a book left to read. If he reads 6 pages a day, how many days will it take Lucas to finish the book?

    ____

18. Juan has $24 to spend at the bookstore. If books cost $6 each, how many books can he buy?

    ____

Name ______________________________

COMMON CORE STANDARD CC.3.OA.7

Lesson Objective: Use an array, a related multiplication fact, or equal groups to divide by 7.

Divide by 7

You can use counters to divide by 7.

Find the quotient. 35 ÷ 7

Step 1 Draw 7 circles to show 7 groups. Place 1 counter in each group.

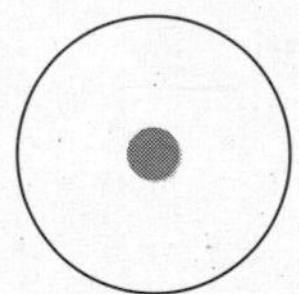 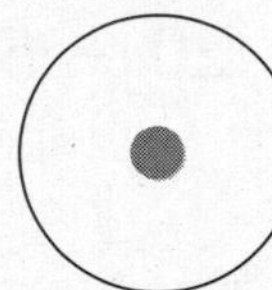 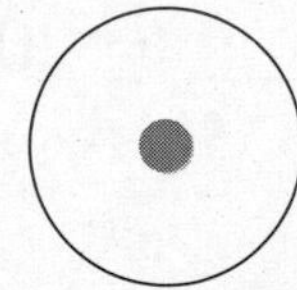 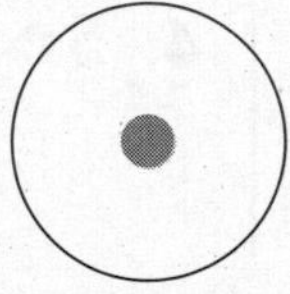 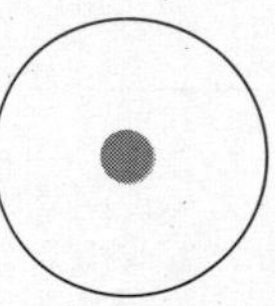 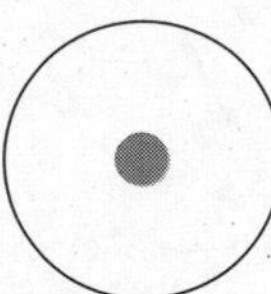 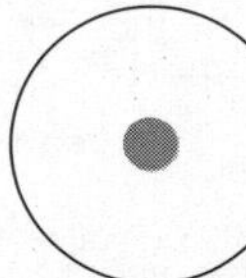

Step 2 Continue placing 1 counter at a time in each group until all 35 counters are placed.

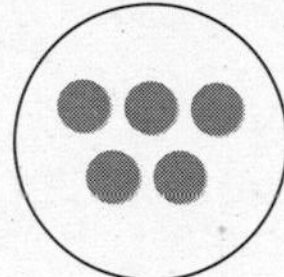 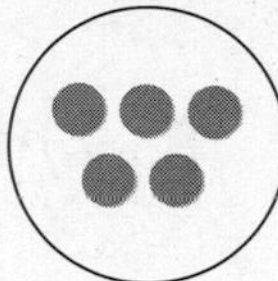 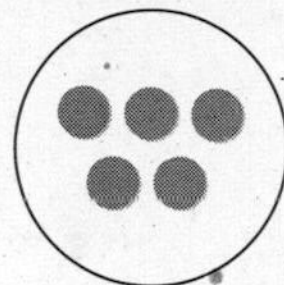 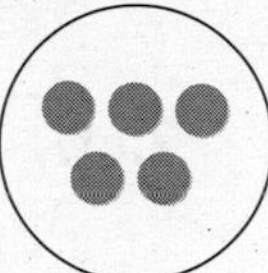 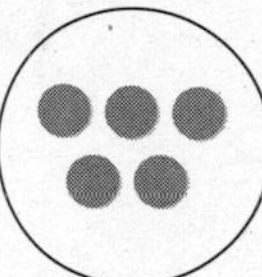 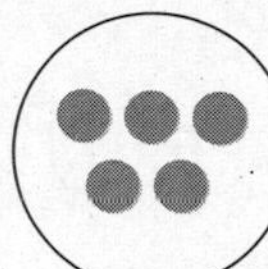 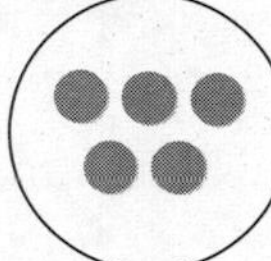

There are 5 counters in each group.

So, 35 ÷ 7 = 5.

Find the unknown factor and quotient.

1. 7 × ____ = 63 63 ÷ 7 = ____ | **2.** 7 × ____ = 7 7 ÷ 7 = ____

3. 7 × ____ = 14 14 ÷ 7 = ____ | **4.** 7 × ____ = 28 28 ÷ 7 = ____

Find the quotient.

5. ____ = 56 ÷ 7 **6.** 21 ÷ 7 = ____ **7.** 42 ÷ 7 = ____ **8.** 28 ÷ 7 = ____

9. ____ = 35 ÷ 7 **10.** 63 ÷ 7 = ____ **11.** 49 ÷ 7 = ____ **12.** 70 ÷ 7 = ____

Name ______________________

Divide by 7

Find the unknown factor and quotient.

1. $7 \times$ 6 $= 42$ $42 \div 7 =$ 6

2. $7 \times$ ____ $= 35$ $35 \div 7 =$ ____

3. $7 \times$ ____ $= 7$ $7 \div 7 =$ ____

4. $5 \times$ ____ $= 20$ $20 \div 5 =$ ____

Find the quotient.

5. $7\overline{)21}$

6. $7\overline{)14}$

7. $6\overline{)48}$

8. $7\overline{)63}$

9. ____ $= 35 \div 7$

10. $0 \div 7 =$ ____

11. ____ $= 56 \div 7$

12. $32 \div 8 =$ ____

Find the unknown number.

13. $56 \div 7 = e$

$e =$ ______

14. $k = 32 \div 4$

$k =$ ______

15. $g = 49 \div 7$

$g =$ ______

16. $28 \div 7 = s$

$s =$ ______

Problem Solving REAL WORLD

17. Twenty-eight players sign up for basketball. The coach puts 7 players on each team. How many teams are there?

____

18. Roberto read 42 books over 7 months. He read the same number of books each month. How many books did Roberto read each month?

____

Name ______________________________

Lesson 33

COMMON CORE STANDARD CC.3.OA.7

Lesson Objective: Use equal groups, factors, or a related multiplication fact to divide by 9.

Divide by 9

You can use repeated subtraction to divide by 9.

Find the quotient.
36 ÷ 9

Step 1 Start with 36. Subtract 9 as many times as you can until you reach 0. Write the answers.

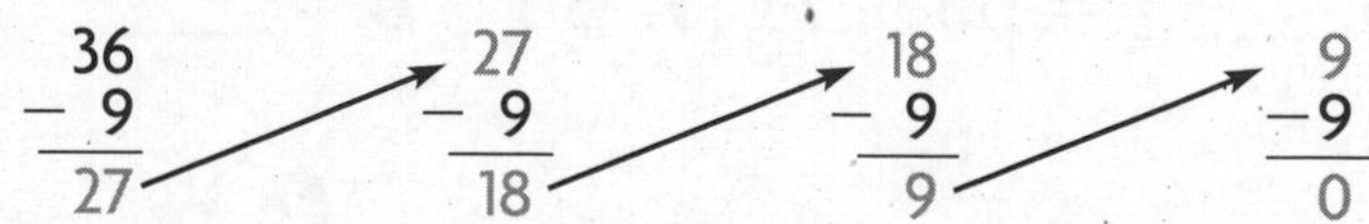

Step 2 Count the number of times you subtract 9.

You subtracted 9 **four** times.

So, 36 ÷ 9 = **4**.

Find the quotient.

1. 9 ÷ 9 = ____
2. 27 ÷ 9 = ____
3. 18 ÷ 9 = ____
4. 36 ÷ 9 = ____
5. ____ = 72 ÷ 9
6. ____ = 63 ÷ 9
7. 45 ÷ 9 = ____
8. ____ = 18 ÷ 9
9. ____ = 54 ÷ 9
10. $9\overline{)63}$
11. $9\overline{)81}$
12. $9\overline{)36}$
13. $8\overline{)48}$
14. $4\overline{)36}$
15. $7\overline{)28}$

Name ______________________

Lesson 33
CC.3.OA.7

Divide by 9

Find the quotient.

1. 4 = 36 ÷ 9
2. 30 ÷ 6 = _____
3. _____ = 81 ÷ 9
4. 27 ÷ 9 = _____
5. 9 ÷ 9 = _____
6. _____ = 63 ÷ 7
7. 36 ÷ 6 = _____
8. _____ = 90 ÷ 9
9. $9\overline{)63}$
10. $9\overline{)18}$
11. $7\overline{)49}$
12. $9\overline{)45}$

Find the unknown number.

13. $48 \div 8 = g$

    $g =$ _____

14. $s = 72 \div 9$

    $s =$ _____

15. $m = 0 \div 9$

    $m =$ _____

16. $54 \div 9 = n$

    $n =$ _____

Problem Solving REAL WORLD

17. A crate of oranges has trays inside that hold 9 oranges each. There are 72 oranges in the crate. If all trays are filled, how many trays are there?

    ____

18. Van has 45 new baseball cards. He puts them in a binder that holds 9 cards on each page. How many pages does he fill?

    ____

Name ______________________

COMMON CORE STANDARD CC.3.OA.8

Lesson Objective: Solve addition and subtraction problems by using the strategy *draw a diagram.*

Problem Solving • Model Addition and Subtraction

Kim sold 127 tickets to the school play. Jon sold 89 tickets. How many more tickets did Kim sell than Jon?

Read the Problem	Solve the Problem
What do I need to find? I need to find how many more tickets Kim sold than Jon ______.	Complete the bar model. Kim [127 tickets] Jon [89 tickets] ■ tickets
What information do I need to use? I know that Kim sold 127 tickets and Jon sold 89 tickets.	Subtract to find the unknown part. 127 – 89 = 38 ■ = 38 tickets
How will I use the information? I will draw a bar model to help me see what operation to use to solve the problem.	So, Kim sold 38 more tickets than Jon.

1. Kasha collected 76 fall leaves. She collects 58 more leaves. How many leaves does she have now?

____

2. Max has 96 stamps. Pat has 79 stamps. How many more stamps does Max have than Pat?

____

Name ______________________________

Lesson 34

CC.3.OA.8

Problem Solving • Model Addition and Subtraction

Use the bar model to solve the problem.

1. Elena went bowling. Elena's score in the first game was 127. She scored 16 more points in the second game than in the first game. What was her total score?

127	16

▲ points

127 + 16 = ▲

143 = ▲

127	143

■ points

127 + 143 = ■

270 = ■

270 points

2. Mike's Music sold 287 CDs on the first day of a 2-day sale. The store sold 96 more CDs on the second day than on the first day. How many CDs in all were sold during the 2-day sale?

____ CDs	____ CDs

★ CDs

★ =

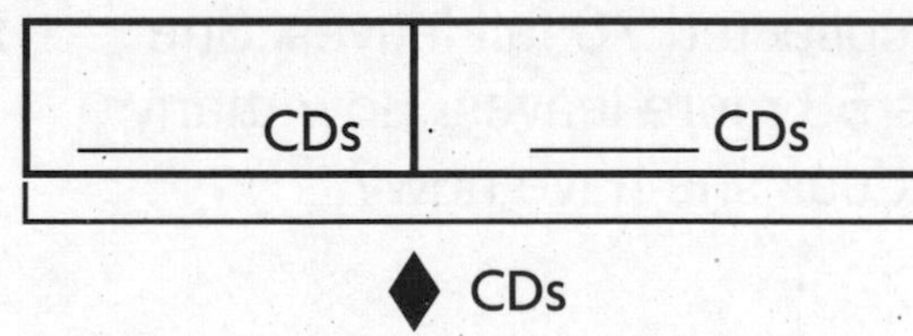

♦ CDs

♦ =

____

Name ____________________

Lesson 35

COMMON CORE STANDARD CC.3.OA.8

Lesson Objective: Solve one- and two-step problems by using the strategy *draw a diagram.*

Problem Solving • Model Multiplication

There are 2 rows of flute players in a marching band. Each row has 7 students. How many flute players are there in all?

Read the Problem	Solve the Problem
What do I need to find? I need to find how many __flute players__ are in the marching band.	Complete the bar model to show the flute players. Write 7 in each box to show the 7 students in each of the 2 groups. | __7__ | __7__ | __14__ students
What information do I need to use? I know there are __2__ rows. There are __7__ students in each row.	
How will I use the information? I will draw a __bar model__ to help me see what __operation__ I need to use to solve the problem.	Since there are equal groups, I can multiply to find the number of flute players in the band. __2__ × __7__ = __14__ So, there are __14__ flute players in all.

1. The Coopers put a new floor in the bathroom. There are 5 rows of 6 red tiles. How many tiles did they use?

____

2. Tommy has a jar of coins. He makes 8 piles of 4 quarters. How many quarters does Tommy have in all?

____

Name ______________________

Problem Solving • Model Multiplication

Draw a diagram to solve each problem.

1. Robert put some toy blocks into 3 rows. There are 5 blocks in each row. How many blocks are there in all?

   15 blocks

2. Mr. Fernandez is putting tiles on his kitchen floor. There are 2 rows with 9 tiles in each row. How many tiles are there in all?

   ____

3. In Jillian's garden, there are 3 rows of carrots, 2 rows of string beans, and 1 row of peas. There are 8 plants in each row. How many plants are there in all?

   ____

4. In Sorhab's classroom, there are 3 rows with 7 desks in each row. How many desks are there in all?

   ____

5. Maya visits the movie rental store. On one wall, there are 6 DVDs on each of 5 shelves. On another wall, there are 4 DVDs on each of 4 shelves. How many DVDs are there in all?

   ____

6. The media center at Josh's school has a computer area. The first 4 rows have 6 computers each. The fifth row has 4 computers. How many computers are there in all?

   ____

Name ______________________________

Lesson 36

COMMON CORE STANDARD CC.3.OA.8

Lesson Objective: Solve multiplication problems by using the strategy *make a table*.

Problem Solving • Multiplication

Lucy's mother is making punch for the students. For each pitcher, she uses 1 can of fruit juice, 1 bottle of ginger ale, and 6 scoops of sherbet. How much of each ingredient will she need to make 5 pitchers of punch?

Read the Problem

What do I need to find?

I need to find how much of each ingredient Lucy's mother needs to make 5 pitchers of punch.

What information do I need to use?

Lucy's mother uses __1__ can of fruit juice, __1__ bottle of ginger ale, and __6__ scoops of sherbet for each pitcher.

How will I use the information?

I will make a __table__ to show the total amounts of each ingredient Lucy's mother needs.

Solve the Problem

First, make a table with the information.

Number of Pitchers	1	2	3	4	5
Cans of Fruit Juice	1	2	3	4	5
Bottles of Ginger Ale	1	2	3	4	5
Scoops of Sherbet	6	12	18	24	30

Next, look for information in the table that will help you solve the problem.

Look for a pattern. The cans of fruit juice and the bottles of ginger ale increase by 1. The scoops of sherbet increase by 6. Complete the table.

So, Lucy's mother will need 5 cans of fruit juice, 5 bottles of ginger ale, and 30 scoops of sherbet.

1. Suppose Lucy's mother decides to make 2 more pitchers of punch. How many scoops of sherbet would she need for 7 pitchers of punch? **Explain** your answer.

____

____

2. Jake gives his dog 4 chew bones and 1 dog toy each month. How many chew bones and how many toys will Jake give his dog in 5 months?

____

Name ______________________

Problem Solving • Multiplication

Solve.

1. Henry has a new album for his baseball cards. He uses pages that hold 6 cards and pages that hold 3 cards. If Henry has 36 cards, how many different ways can he put them in his album?

Pages with 6 Cards	1	2	3	4	5
Pages with 3 Cards	10	8	6	4	2
Total Cards	36	36	36	36	36

Henry can put the cards in his album **5** ways.

2. Ms. Hernandez has 17 tomato plants that she wants to plant in rows. She will put 2 plants in some rows and 1 plant in the others. How many different ways can she plant the tomato plants? Make a table to solve.

Rows with 2 Plants	
Rows with 1 Plant	
Total Plants	

Ms. Hernandez can plant the tomato plants ______ ways.

3. Bianca has a total of 25¢. She has some nickels and pennies. How many different combinations of nickels and pennies could Bianca have? Make a table to solve.

Number of Nickels	
Number of Pennies	
Total Value	

Bianca could have ______ combinations of 25¢.

Name ________________________

Lesson 37

COMMON CORE STANDARD CC.3.OA.8

Lesson Objective: Solve two-step problems by using the strategy *act it out.*

Problem Solving • Two-Step Problems

Chloe bought 5 sets of books. Each set had the same number of books. She donated 9 books to her school. Now she has 26 books left. How many books were in each set that Chloe bought?

Read the Problem	Solve the Problem
What do I need to find? I need to find how many __books__ were in each __set__.	First, begin with the number of books left. Add the number of books donated. books left → 26 + books donated → 9 = *t*, total number of books → *t* $26 + 9 = t$ __35__ = *t*
What information do I need to use? I need to use the information given: Chloe bought __5__ sets of books. She donated __9__ books. She has __26__ books left.	Then divide to find the number of books in each set. *t*, total number of books → 35 ÷ sets of books → 5 = *s*, books in each set → *s* $35 \div 5 = s$ __7__ = *s*
How will I use the information? I will use the information to __act out__ the problem.	So, __7__ books were in each set.

Solve the problem.

1. Jackie had 6 equal packs of pencils. Her friend gave her 4 more pencils. Now she has 52 pencils. How many pencils were in each pack?

____

2. Tony had 4 equal sets of sports cards. He gave his friends 5 cards. Now he has 31 cards. How many cards were in each set?

____

Name ______________________

Lesson 37

CC.3.OA.8

Problem Solving • Two-Step Problems

Solve the problem.

1. Jack has 3 boxes of pencils with the same number of pencils in each box. His mother gives him 4 more pencils. Now Jack has 28 pencils. How many pencils are in each box?

   Think: I can start with 28 counters and act out the problem.

   8 pencils

2. The art teacher has 48 paintbrushes. She puts 8 paintbrushes on each table in her classroom. How many tables are in her classroom?

   ____

3. Ricardo has 2 cases of video games with the same number of games in each case. He gives 4 games to his brother. Ricardo has 10 games left. How many video games were in each case?

   ____

4. Patty has $20 to spend on gifts for her friends. Her mother gives her $5 more. If each gift costs $5, how many gifts can she buy?

   ____

5. Joe has a collection of 35 DVD movies. He received 8 of them as gifts. Joe bought the rest of his movies over 3 years. If he bought the same number of movies each year, how many movies did Joe buy last year?

   ____

6. Liz has a 24-inch-long ribbon. She cuts nine 2-inch pieces from her original ribbon. How much of the original ribbon is left?

   ____

Name ______________________________

Lesson 38

COMMON CORE STANDARD CC.3.OA.8

Lesson Objective: Perform operations in order when there are no parentheses.

Order of Operations

Danny buys a marker for $4. He also buys 5 pens for $2 each. How much money does he spend?

You can write $4 + 5 \times 2 = c$ to describe and solve the problem.

Find $4 + 5 \times 2 = c$.

When there is more than one type of operation in an equation, use the **order of operations**, or the set of rules for the order in which to do operations.

Order of Operations

First: Multiply and divide from left to right.

Then: Add and subtract from left to right.

Step 1 Multiply from left to right.

$4 + 5 × $2 = c

↑ multiply

$4 + **$10** = c

So, Danny spends **$14** .

Step 2 Next, add from left to right.

$4 + $10 = c

↑ add

$14 = c

Write *correct* if the operations are listed in the correct order. If not correct, write the correct order of operations.

1. $5 + 6 \times 3$ add, multiply

____

2. $20 \div 4 - 3$ divide, subtract

____

Follow the order of operations to find the unknown number.

3. $9 - 7 + 2 = k$

$k =$ ____

4. $8 + 2 \times 5 = m$

$m =$ ____

5. $7 \times 8 - 6 = g$

$g =$ ____

6. $16 + 4 \div 2 = s$

$s =$ ____

7. $12 - 6 \div 2 = y$

$y =$ ____

8. $36 \div 6 + 13 = f$

$f =$ ____

Name ______________________

Lesson 38
CC.3.OA.8

Order of Operations

Write *correct* if the operations are listed in the correct order. If not correct, write the correct order of operations.

1. $45 - 3 \times 5$ subtract, multiply

   multiply, subtract

2. $3 \times 4 \div 2$ divide, multiply

   ____

3. $5 + 12 \div 2$ divide, add

   ____

4. $7 \times 10 + 3$ add, multiply

   ____

Follow the order of operations to find the unknown number.

5. $6 + 4 \times 3 = n$

   $n =$ ______

6. $8 - 3 + 2 = k$

   $k =$ ______

7. $24 \div 3 + 5 = p$

   $p =$ ______

8. $12 - 2 \times 5 = r$

   $r =$ ______

9. $7 \times 8 - 6 = j$

   $j =$ ______

10. $4 + 3 \times 9 = w$

    $w =$ ______

Problem Solving REAL WORLD

11. Shelley bought 3 kites for $6 each. She gave the clerk $20. How much change should Shelley get?

    ____

12. Tim has 5 apples and 3 bags with 8 apples in each bag. How many apples does Tim have in all?

    ____

Name ______________________________

Lesson 39

COMMON CORE STANDARD CC.3.OA.9

Lesson Objective: Identify and describe whole-number patterns and solve problems.

Algebra • Number Patterns

A **pattern** is an ordered set of numbers or objects. The order helps you predict what will come next.

Use the addition table to find patterns.

+	0	1	2	3	4
0	0	1	2	3	4
1	1	2	3	4	5
2	2	3	4	5	6
3	3	4	5	6	7
4	4	5	6	7	8

- Color the row that starts with 1. What pattern do you see?

  The numbers increase by 1.

- Color the column that starts with 1. What pattern do you see?

  The numbers increase by 1. The numbers are the same as in the row starting with 1.

- Circle the sum of 4 in the column you colored. Circle the addends for that sum. What two addition sentences can you write for that sum of 4?

  3 + 1 = 4 and 1 + 3 = 4

  The addends are the same. The sum is the same.

The **Commutative Property of Addition** states that you can add two or more numbers in any order and get the same sum.

Use the addition table to find the sum.

1. 2 + 3 = ___ 3 + 2 = ___

2. 2 + 0 = ___ 0 + 2 = ___

Find the sum. Then use the Commutative Property of Addition to write the related addition sentence.

3. 3 + 0 = ___

___ + ___ = ___

4. 4 + 1 = ___

___ + ___ = ___

5. 2 + 3 = ___

___ + ___ = ___

Name ______________________

Lesson 39
CC.3.OA.9

Number Patterns

Find the sum. Then use the Commutative Property of Addition to write the related addition sentence.

1. 9 + 2 = 11
2 + 9 = 11

2. 4 + 7 = ____
____ + ____ = ____

3. 3 + 6 = ____
____ + ____ = ____

4. 3 + 10 = ____
____ + ____ = ____

5. 6 + 7 = ____
____ + ____ = ____

6. 7 + 5 = ____
____ + ____ = ____

7. 8 + 9 = ____
____ + ____ = ____

8. 0 + 4 = ____
____ + ____ = ____

9. 9 + 6 = ____
____ + ____ = ____

Is the sum even or odd? Write *even* or *odd*.

10. 5 + 2 ____________

11. 6 + 4 ____________

12. 1 + 0 ____________

13. 5 + 5 ____________

14. 3 + 8 ____________

15. 7 + 7 ____________

Problem Solving REAL WORLD

16. Ada writes 10 + 8 = 18 on the board. Maria wants to use the Commutative Property of Addition to rewrite Ada's addition sentence. What number sentence should Maria write?

____

17. Jackson says he has an odd number of model cars. He has 6 cars on one shelf and 8 cars on another shelf. Is Jackson correct? **Explain.**

____

____

____

Name ______________________

Lesson 42

COMMON CORE STANDARD CC.3.NBT.1

Lesson Objective: Round 2- and 3-digit numbers to the nearest ten or hundred.

Round to the Nearest Ten or Hundred

When you **round** a number, you find a number that tells you *about* how much or *about* how many.

Use place value to round 76 to the nearest ten.

Step 1 Look at the digit to the right of the tens place.

- If the ones digit is 5 or more, the tens digit increases by one.
- If the ones digit is less than 5, the tens digit stays the same.

Step 2 Write zero for the ones digit.

76
↑
ones place

The digit in the ones place is 6.

$6 > 5$

So, the digit 7 in the tens place increases to 8.

So, 76 rounded to the nearest ten is **80**.

Think: To round to the nearest hundred, look at the tens digit. So, 128 rounded to the nearest hundred is **100**.

128
↑
tens place

Round to the nearest ten.

1. 24 ________ **2.** 15 ________ **3.** 47 ________

4. 42 ________ **5.** 81 ________ **6.** 65 ________

Round to the nearest hundred.

7. 176 ________ **8.** 395 ________ **9.** 431 ________

10. 421 ________ **11.** 692 ________ **12.** 470 ________

Name ______________________

Round to the Nearest Ten or Hundred

Locate and label 739 on the number line. Round to the nearest hundred.

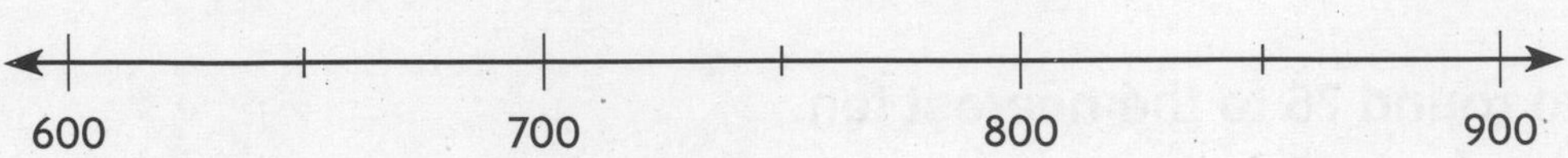

1. 739 is between 700 and 800.

2. 739 is closer to ______ than it is to ______.

3. 739 rounded to the nearest hundred is ______.

Round to the nearest ten and hundred.

4. 363 ______ ______

5. 829 ______ ______

6. 572 ______ ______

7. 209 ______ ______

8. 663 ______ ______

9. 949 ______ ______

10. 762 ______ ______

11. 399 ______ ______

12. 402 ______ ______

Problem Solving REAL WORLD

13. The baby elephant weighs 435 pounds. What is its weight rounded to the nearest hundred pounds?

____

14. Jayce sold 218 cups of lemonade at his lemonade stand. What is 218 rounded to the nearest ten?

____

Name ______________________

Lesson 43

COMMON CORE STANDARD CC.3.NBT.1

Lesson Objective: Use compatible numbers and rounding to estimate sums.

Estimate Sums

An **estimate** is a number close to an exact amount.

You can use **compatible numbers** to estimate. Compatible numbers are easy to compute mentally and are close to the real numbers.

Estimate. Use compatible numbers.

73 + 21 = ■

So, 73 + 21 is about 100.

$$\begin{array}{r} 73 \\ +21 \\ \hline \end{array} \longrightarrow \begin{array}{r} 75 \\ +25 \\ \hline 100 \end{array}$$

Another way to estimate is to round numbers to the same place value.

Estimate. Round each number to the nearest hundred. 214 + 678 = ■

Step 1 Look at the digit to the right of the hundreds place.

- 1 < 5, so the digit 2 stays the same.
- 7 > 5, so the digit 6 increases by 1 to become 7.

$$\begin{array}{r} 214 \\ +678 \\ \hline \end{array} \longrightarrow \begin{array}{r} 200 \\ +700 \\ \hline 900 \end{array}$$

Step 2 Write zeros for the tens and ones places.

So, 214 + 678 is about 900.

Use rounding or compatible numbers to estimate the sum.

1. $\begin{array}{r} 42 \\ +\ 36 \\ \hline \end{array}$ $\begin{array}{r} \_\_\_\_ \\ +\ \_\_\_\_ \\ \hline \end{array}$

2. $\begin{array}{r} 523 \\ +\ 117 \\ \hline \end{array}$ $\begin{array}{r} \_\_\_\_ \\ +\ \_\_\_\_ \\ \hline \end{array}$

3. $\begin{array}{r} 235 \\ +\ 374 \\ \hline \end{array}$ $\begin{array}{r} \_\_\_\_ \\ +\ \_\_\_\_ \\ \hline \end{array}$

4. $\begin{array}{r} 23 \\ +\ 99 \\ \hline \end{array}$ $\begin{array}{r} \_\_\_\_ \\ +\ \_\_\_\_ \\ \hline \end{array}$

5. $\begin{array}{r} 254 \\ +\ 167 \\ \hline \end{array}$ $\begin{array}{r} \_\_\_\_ \\ +\ \_\_\_\_ \\ \hline \end{array}$

6. $\begin{array}{r} 299 \\ +\ 199 \\ \hline \end{array}$ $\begin{array}{r} \_\_\_\_ \\ +\ \_\_\_\_ \\ \hline \end{array}$

Name ______________________

Lesson 43
CC.3.NBT.1

Estimate Sums

Use rounding or compatible numbers to estimate the sum.

1. 198 + 727 → 200 + 725 = 925

2. 87 + 34 → ____ + ____

3. 222 + 203 → ____ + ____

4. 52 + 39 → ____ + ____

5. 256 + 321 → ____ + ____

6. 302 + 412 → ____ + ____

7. 519 + 124 → ____ + ____

8. 790 + 112 → ____ + ____

9. 547 + 326 → ____ + ____

10. 325 + 458

____ + ____ = ____

11. 620 + 107

____ + ____ = ____

Problem Solving REAL WORLD

12. Stephanie read 72 pages on Sunday and 83 pages on Monday. About how many pages did Stephanie read during the two days?

____

13. Matt biked 345 miles last month. This month he has biked 107 miles. Altogether, about how many miles has Matt biked last month and this month?

____

Name ______________________

Lesson 44

COMMON CORE STANDARD CC.3.NBT.1

Lesson Objective: Use compatible numbers and rounding to estimate differences.

Estimate Differences

You can use what you know about estimating sums to estimate differences.

Estimate. Use compatible numbers.
78 − 47 = ■

Think: Compatible numbers are easy to subtract.

78	⟶	75
− 47	⟶	− 50
		25

So, 78 − 47 is about **25**.

Another way to estimate is to round to the same place value.

Estimate. Round each number to the nearest hundred. 687 − 516 = ■

Step 1 Look at the digit to the right of the hundreds place.

- 8 > 5, so the digit in the hundreds place increases by 1.
- 1 < 5, so the digit in the hundreds place stays the same.

687	⟶	700
− 516	⟶	− 500
		200

Step 2 Write zeros for the tens and ones places.

So, 687 − 516 is about **200**.

Use rounding or compatible numbers to estimate the difference.

1. 92 − 43 ______ − ______ ______

2. 271 − 152 ______ − ______ ______

3. 517 − 249 ______ − ______ ______

4. 445 − 112 ______ − ______ ______

5. 92 − 65 ______ − ______ ______

6. 776 − 384 ______ − ______ ______

Name ______________________

Estimate Differences

Use rounding or compatible numbers to estimate the difference.

1. $\begin{array}{r} 40 \\ -\ 13 \\ \hline \end{array}$ $\begin{array}{r} 40 \\ -\ 10 \\ \hline 30 \end{array}$

2. $\begin{array}{r} 762 \\ -\ 332 \\ \hline \end{array}$ $\begin{array}{r} \_\_\_\_ \\ -\ \_\_\_\_ \\ \hline \end{array}$

3. $\begin{array}{r} 823 \\ -\ 242 \\ \hline \end{array}$ $\begin{array}{r} \_\_\_\_ \\ -\ \_\_\_\_ \\ \hline \end{array}$

4. $\begin{array}{r} 98 \\ -\ 49 \\ \hline \end{array}$ $\begin{array}{r} \_\_\_\_ \\ -\ \_\_\_\_ \\ \hline \end{array}$

5. $\begin{array}{r} 287 \\ -\ 162 \\ \hline \end{array}$ $\begin{array}{r} \_\_\_\_ \\ -\ \_\_\_\_ \\ \hline \end{array}$

6. $\begin{array}{r} 359 \\ -\ 224 \\ \hline \end{array}$ $\begin{array}{r} \_\_\_\_ \\ -\ \_\_\_\_ \\ \hline \end{array}$

7. $\begin{array}{r} 68 \\ -\ 31 \\ \hline \end{array}$ $\begin{array}{r} \_\_\_\_ \\ -\ \_\_\_\_ \\ \hline \end{array}$

8. $\begin{array}{r} 476 \\ -\ 155 \\ \hline \end{array}$ $\begin{array}{r} \_\_\_\_ \\ -\ \_\_\_\_ \\ \hline \end{array}$

9. $\begin{array}{r} 622 \\ -\ 307 \\ \hline \end{array}$ $\begin{array}{r} \_\_\_\_ \\ -\ \_\_\_\_ \\ \hline \end{array}$

10. 771 − 531

____ − ____ = ____

11. 299 − 61

____ − ____ = ____

Problem Solving REAL WORLD

12. Ben has a collection of 812 stamps. He gives his brother 345 stamps. About how many stamps does Ben have left?

____

13. Savannah's bakery sold 284 pies in September. In October the bakery sold 89 pies. About how many more pies did Savannah's bakery sell in September than in October?

____

Name ______________________________

Lesson 45

COMMON CORE STANDARD CC.3.NBT.2

Lesson Objective: Count by tens and ones, use a number line, make compatible numbers, or use friendly numbers to find sums mentally.

Mental Math Strategies for Addition

You can count by tens and ones to find a sum.

Find 58 + 15.

Step 1 Count on to the nearest ten. Start at 58. Count to 60.

Step 2 Count by tens. Start at 60. Count to 70.

Step 3 Then count by ones. Start at 70. Count to 73.

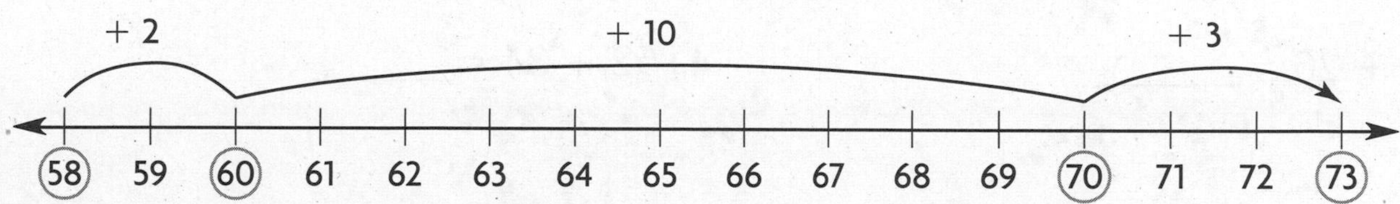

Think: **58 + 2 + 10 + 3 = 73**

So, 58 + 15 = **73**.

You can also count on by tens first and then by ones.

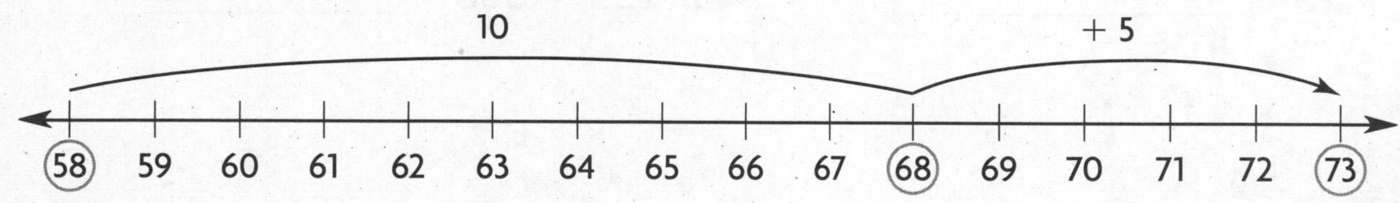

Think: **58 + 10 + 5 = 73**

So, 58 + 15 = **73**.

1. Count by tens and ones to find 54 + 26. Draw jumps and label the number line to show your thinking.

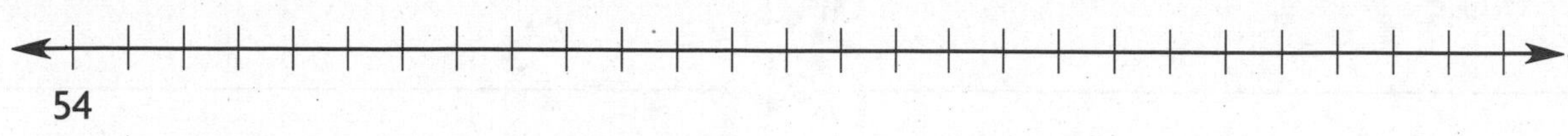

54 + 26 = _____

Name ____________________

Mental Math Strategies for Addition

**Count by tens and ones to find the sum.
Use the number line to show your thinking.**

1. 29 + 14 = 43

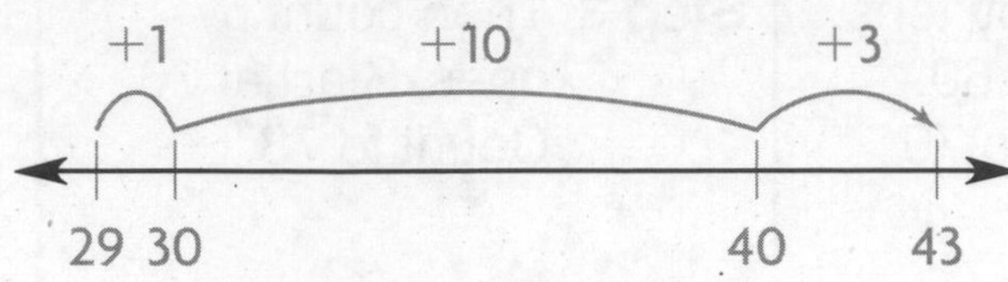

2. 36 + 28 = ______

3. 45 + 26 = ______

4. 52 + 34 = ______

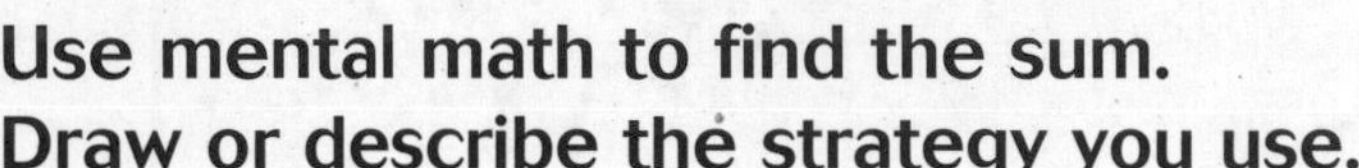

**Use mental math to find the sum.
Draw or describe the strategy you use.**

5. 52 + 19 = ____________

6. 122 + 306 = ____________

Problem Solving REAL WORLD

7. Shelley spent 17 minutes washing the dishes. She spent 38 minutes cleaning her room. **Explain** how you can use mental math to find how long Shelley spent on the two tasks.

____
____
____
____

8. It took Marty 42 minutes to write a book report. Then he spent 18 minutes correcting his report. **Explain** how you can use mental math to find how long Marty spent on his book report.

____
____
____
____

Name ______________________________

Lesson 46

COMMON CORE STANDARD CC.3.NBT.2

Lesson Objective: Use the Commutative and Associative Properties of Addition to add more than two addends.

Algebra • Use Properties to Add

You can use addition properties and strategies to help you add.

Find 3 + 14 + 21.	Find 7 + (3 + 22).
The **Commutative Property of Addition** states that you can add numbers in any order and still get the same sum.	The **Associative Property of Addition** states that you can group addends in different ways and still get the same sum.
Step 1 Look for numbers that are easy to add. **Think:** Make doubles. 3 + 1 = 4 and 4 + 4 = 8.	**Step 1** Look for numbers that are easy to add. **Think:** Make a ten. 7 + 3 = 10
Step 2 Use the Commutative Property to change the order. 3 + 14 + 21 = 3 + 21 + 14	**Step 2** Use the Associative Property to change the grouping. 7 + (3 + 22) = (7 + 3) + 22
Step 3 Add. 3 + 21 + 14 = 24 + 14 24 + 14 = 30 + 8	**Step 3** Add. (7 + 3) + 22 = 10 + 22 10 + 22 = 32
So, 3 + 14 + 21 = 38.	So, 7 + (3 + 22) = 32.

Use addition properties and strategies to find the sum.

1. 2 + 15 + 8 = _____
2. 19 + 36 + 1 = _____
3. 25 + 44 + 5 = _____
4. 12 + 36 + 18 + 14 = _____
5. 23 + 14 + 23 = _____
6. 11 + 15 + 19 + 14 = _____

Name ___________________________

Use Properties to Add

Lesson 46
CC.3.NBT.2

Use addition properties and strategies to find the sum.

1. 34 + 62 + 51 + 46 = **193**

34, 46 → 10
10 ← 46, 62
  34
  46
  62
+ 51
193

2. 27 + 68 + 43 = ______

3. 42 + 36 + 18 = ______

4. 74 + 35 + 16 + 45 = ______

5. 41 + 26 + 149 = ______

6. 52 + 64 + 28 + 44 = ______

Problem Solving REAL WORLD

7. A pet shelter has 26 dogs, 37 cats, and 14 gerbils. How many of these animals are in the pet shelter in all?

____

8. The pet shelter bought 85 pounds of dog food, 50 pounds of cat food, and 15 pounds of gerbil food. How many pounds of animal food did the pet shelter buy?

____

Name ____________________

COMMON CORE STANDARD CC.3.NBT.2

Lesson Objective: Use the break apart strategy to add 3-digit numbers.

Use the Break Apart Strategy to Add

You can use the break apart strategy to add.

Add. 263 + 215

Think and Record

Step 1 Estimate. Round to the nearest hundred.

300 + 200 = **500**

Step 2 Start with the hundreds. Break apart the addends. Then add each place value.

263 = 200 + 60 + 3
215 = 200 + 10 + 5
400 + 70 + 8

Step 3 Add the sums.

400 + 70 + 8 = **478**

So, 263 + 215 = **478**.

Model

263 = 2 hundreds + 6 tens + 3 ones

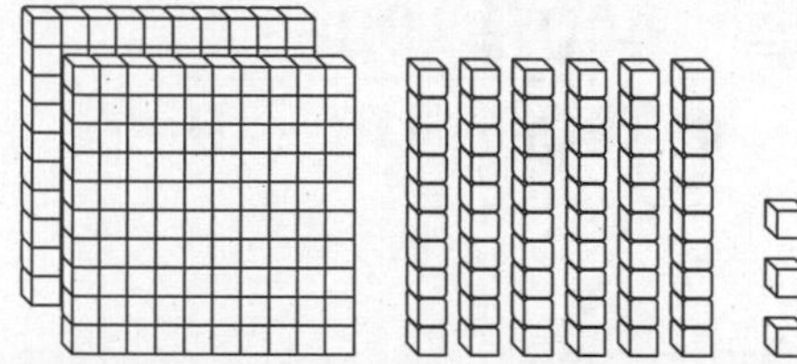

215 = 2 hundreds + 1 ten + 5 ones

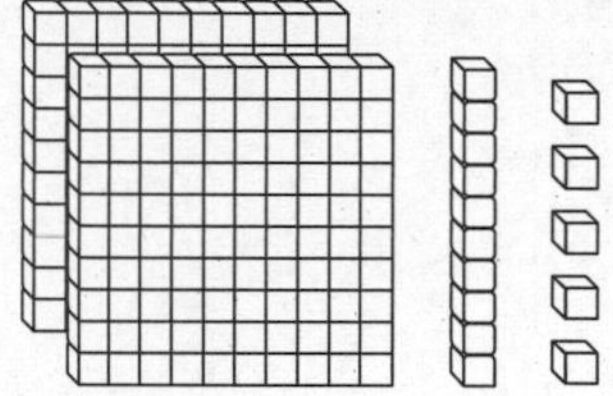

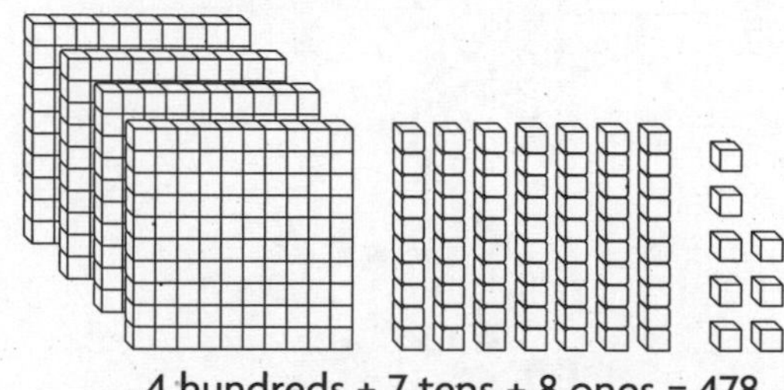

4 hundreds + 7 tens + 8 ones = 478

Estimate. Then use the break apart strategy to find the sum.

1. Estimate: ______
   242 =
   + 536 = ____________

2. Estimate: ______
   469 =
   + 413 = ____________

3. Estimate: ______
   385 =
   + 519 = ____________

4. Estimate: ______
   527 =
   + 266 = ____________

Name ______________________

Lesson 47
CC.3.NBT.2

Use the Break Apart Strategy to Add

Estimate. Then use the break apart strategy to find the sum.

1. Estimate: 800

325 = 300 + 20 + 5
\+ 494 = 400 + 90 + 4
700 + 110 + 9

2. Estimate: ______

518 =
\+ 372 =

3. Estimate: ______

473 =
\+ 123 =

4. Estimate: ______

208 =
\+ 569 =

5. Estimate: ______

731 =
\+ 207 =

6. Estimate: ______

495 =
\+ 254 =

Problem Solving REAL WORLD

Use the table for 7–8.

7. Laura is making a building using Set A and Set C. How many blocks can she use in her building?

____

8. Clark is making a building using Set B and Set C. How many blocks can he use in his building?

____

Build-It Blocks

Set	Number of Blocks
A	165
B	188
C	245

Name ______________________

Lesson 48

COMMON CORE STANDARD CC.3.NBT.2

Lesson Objective: Use place value to add 3-digit numbers.

Use Place Value to Add

You can use place value to add 3-digit numbers.

Add. 268 + 195 **Estimate.** 300 + 200 = 500

Step 1 Add the ones. If there are 10 or more ones, regroup as tens and ones.

$$\begin{array}{r} {}^{1} \\ 268 \\ +\ 195 \\ \hline 3 \end{array}$$

8 ones + **5** ones = 13 ones

13 ones = 1 ten 3 ones

Step 2 Add the tens. Regroup the tens as hundreds and tens.

$$\begin{array}{r} {}^{1\,1} \\ 268 \\ +\ 195 \\ \hline 63 \end{array}$$

1 ten + **6** tens + **9** tens = 16 tens

16 tens = 1 hundred 6 tens

Step 3 Add the hundreds.

$$\begin{array}{r} {}^{1\,1} \\ 268 \\ +\ 195 \\ \hline 463 \end{array}$$

1 hundred + **2** hundreds + **1** hundred = 4 hundreds

So, 268 + 195 = 463.

Estimate. Then find the sum.

1. Estimate: ______

$$\begin{array}{r} 156 \\ +\ 323 \\ \hline \end{array}$$

2. Estimate: ______

$$\begin{array}{r} 347 \\ +\ 390 \\ \hline \end{array}$$

3. Estimate: ______

$$\begin{array}{r} 472 \\ +\ 108 \\ \hline \end{array}$$

4. Estimate: ______

$$\begin{array}{r} 239 \\ +\ 570 \\ \hline \end{array}$$

5. Estimate: ______

$$\begin{array}{r} 110 \\ +\ 576 \\ \hline \end{array}$$

6. Estimate: ______

$$\begin{array}{r} 258 \\ +\ 324 \\ \hline \end{array}$$

7. Estimate: ______

$$\begin{array}{r} 471 \\ +\ 269 \\ \hline \end{array}$$

8. Estimate: ______

$$\begin{array}{r} 585 \\ +\ 309 \\ \hline \end{array}$$

Name ______________________

Use Place Value to Add

Estimate. Then find the sum.

1. Estimate: 600

$$\begin{array}{r} \overset{1}{3}24 \\ +\ 285 \\ \hline 609 \end{array}$$

2. Estimate: ______

$$\begin{array}{r} 519 \\ +\ 347 \\ \hline \end{array}$$

3. Estimate: ______

$$\begin{array}{r} 323 \\ +\ 151 \\ \hline \end{array}$$

4. Estimate: ______

$$\begin{array}{r} 169 \\ +\ 354 \\ \hline \end{array}$$

5. Estimate: ______

$$\begin{array}{r} 148 \\ +\ 285 \\ \hline \end{array}$$

6. Estimate: ______

$$\begin{array}{r} 270 \\ +\ 453 \\ \hline \end{array}$$

7. Estimate: ______

$$\begin{array}{r} 275 \\ +\ 116 \\ \hline \end{array}$$

8. Estimate: ______

$$\begin{array}{r} 157 \\ +\ 141 \\ \hline \end{array}$$

9. Estimate: ______

$$\begin{array}{r} 127 \\ +\ 290 \\ \hline \end{array}$$

10. Estimate: ______

$$\begin{array}{r} 258 \\ +\ 565 \\ \hline \end{array}$$

11. Estimate: ______

$$\begin{array}{r} 311 \\ +\ 298 \\ \hline \end{array}$$

12. Estimate: ______

$$\begin{array}{r} 534 \\ +\ 256 \\ \hline \end{array}$$

Problem Solving REAL WORLD

13. Mark has 215 baseball cards. Emily has 454 baseball cards. How many baseball cards do Mark and Emily have altogether?

____

14. Jason has 330 pennies. Richie has 268 pennies. Rachel has 381 pennies. Which two students have more than 700 pennies combined?

____

Name ______________________

Lesson 49

COMMON CORE STANDARD CC.3.NBT.2

Lesson Objective: Use a number line, friendly numbers, or the break apart strategy to find differences mentally.

Mental Math Strategies for Subtraction

You can count up on a number line to find a difference.

Find 53 – 27.

Step 1 Count up by tens. Start at 27. Count up to 47.

Step 2 Count up by ones. Start at 47. Count up to 53.

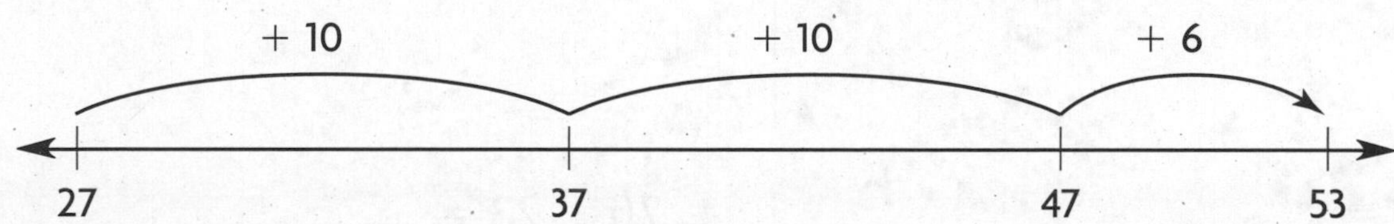

Think: 10 + 10 + 6 = 26.

So, 53 – 27 = 26.

You can take away tens and ones to find a difference.

Step 1 Take away tens. Start at 53.

Step 2 Take away ones. Start at 33.

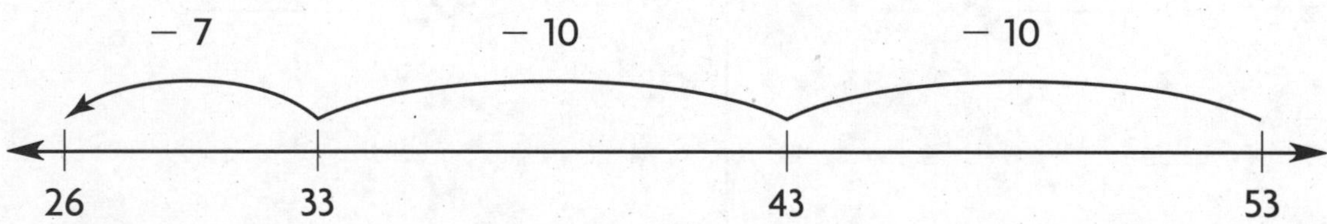

Think: 53 – 10 – 10 – 7 = 26.

So, 53 – 27 = 26.

1. Find 92 – 65. Draw jumps and label the number line to show your thinking.

92 – 65 = ______.

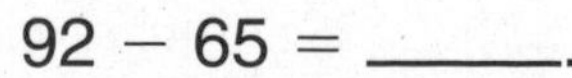

Name ___________________________

Mental Math Strategies for Subtraction

Use mental math to find the difference. Draw or describe the strategy you use.

1. 74 − 39 = **35**

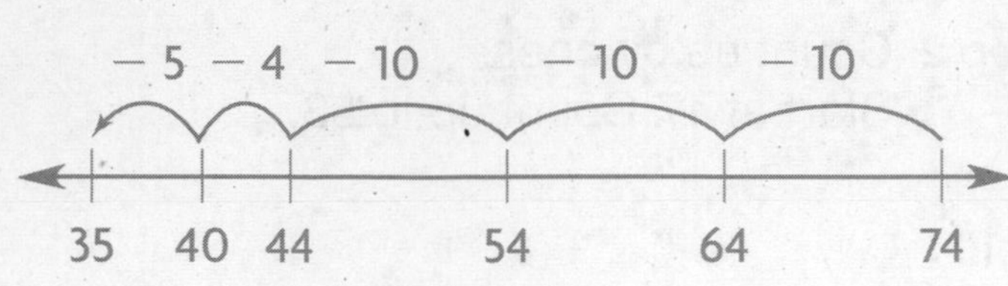

2. 93 − 28 = ________

3. 51 − 9 = ________

4. 76 − 23 = ________

5. 357 − 214 = ________

6. 285 − 99 = ________

Problem Solving REAL WORLD

7. Ruby has 78 books. Thirty-one of the books are on shelves. The rest are still packed in boxes. How many of Ruby's books are still in boxes?

____

8. Kyle has 130 pins in his collection. He has 76 of the pins displayed on his wall. The rest are in a drawer. How many of Kyle's pins are in a drawer?

____

Name ______________________________

Lesson 50

COMMON CORE STANDARD CC.3.NBT.2

Lesson Objective: Use place value to subtract 3-digit numbers.

Use Place Value to Subtract

You can use place value to subtract 3-digit numbers.

Subtract. 352 − 167 **Estimate.** 400 − 200 = 200

Step 1 Subtract the ones.

```
   4 12
  3 5 2
- 1 6 7
-------
      5
```

Are there enough ones to subtract 7?
There are not enough ones.
Regroup **5** tens **2** ones as 4 tens 12 ones.
12 ones − 7 ones = 5 ones

Step 2 Subtract the tens.

```
    14
  2 4 12
  3 5 2
- 1 6 7
-------
    8 5
```

Are there enough tens to subtract 6?
There are not enough tens.
Regroup **3** hundreds **4** tens as 2 hundreds 14 tens.
14 tens − 6 tens = 8 tens

Step 3 Subtract the hundreds.

```
    14
  2 4 12
  3 5 2
- 1 6 7
-------
  1 8 5
```

2 hundreds − **1** hundred = 1 hundred

So, 352 − 167 = 185.

Estimate. Then find the difference.

1. Estimate: ______

$$\begin{array}{r} 537 \\ -123 \\ \hline \end{array}$$

2. Estimate: ______

$$\begin{array}{r} 268 \\ -157 \\ \hline \end{array}$$

3. Estimate: ______

$$\begin{array}{r} 426 \\ -218 \\ \hline \end{array}$$

4. Estimate: ______

$$\begin{array}{r} 785 \\ -549 \\ \hline \end{array}$$

5. Estimate: ______

$$\begin{array}{r} 354 \\ -206 \\ \hline \end{array}$$

6. Estimate: ______

$$\begin{array}{r} 679 \\ -482 \\ \hline \end{array}$$

7. Estimate: ______

$$\begin{array}{r} 787 \\ -378 \\ \hline \end{array}$$

8. Estimate: ______

$$\begin{array}{r} 843 \\ -675 \\ \hline \end{array}$$

Name ____________________

Use Place Value to Subtract

Estimate. Then find the difference.

1. Estimate: 500

   7 15
   585
   − 119

2. Estimate: ______

   738
   − 227

3. Estimate: ______

   651
   − 376

4. Estimate: ______

   815
   − 281

5. Estimate: ______

   487
   − 290

6. Estimate: ______

   936
   − 329

7. Estimate: ______

   270
   − 128

8. Estimate: ______

   364
   − 177

9. Estimate: ______

   627
   − 253

10. Estimate: ______

    862
    − 419

11. Estimate: ______

    726
    − 148

12. Estimate: ______

    543
    − 358

Problem Solving

13. Mrs. Cohen has 427 buttons. She uses 195 buttons to make puppets. How many buttons does Mrs. Cohen have left?

    ____

14. There were 625 ears of corn and 247 tomatoes sold at a farm stand. How many more ears of corn were sold than tomatoes?

    ____

Name ______________________

Lesson 51

COMMON CORE STANDARD CC.3.NBT.2

Lesson Objective: Use the combine place values strategy to subtract 3-digit numbers.

Combine Place Values to Subtract

You can combine place values to subtract. Think of two digits next to each other as one number.

Subtract. 354 − 248

Estimate. 350 − 250 = **100**

Step 1 Look at the digits in the ones place.	**Step 2** Combine the tens and ones places.	**Step 3** Subtract the hundreds.
Think: 8 > 4, so combine place values.	**Think:** There are 54 ones and 48 ones. Subtract the ones. Write 0 for the tens.	
354 − 248	354 − 248 **06**	354 − 248 **106**

So, 354 − 248 = **106**.

Remember: You can also combine hundreds and tens to subtract.

Estimate. Then find the difference.

1. Estimate: ______	**2.** Estimate: ______	**3.** Estimate: ______	**4.** Estimate: ______
485 −376	657 −424	347 −198	623 −397

5. Estimate: ______	**6.** Estimate: ______	**7.** Estimate: ______	**8.** Estimate: ______
443 −207	500 −338	835 −548	712 −289

Name ______________________

Lesson 51
CC.3.NBT.2

Combine Place Values to Subtract

Estimate. Then find the difference.

1. Estimate: 200

$$\begin{array}{r} 476 \\ -\ 269 \\ \hline \end{array}$$

2. Estimate: ______

$$\begin{array}{r} 615 \\ -\ 342 \\ \hline \end{array}$$

3. Estimate: ______

$$\begin{array}{r} 508 \\ -\ 113 \\ \hline \end{array}$$

4. Estimate: ______

$$\begin{array}{r} 716 \\ -\ 229 \\ \hline \end{array}$$

5. Estimate: ______

$$\begin{array}{r} 700 \\ -\ 326 \\ \hline \end{array}$$

6. Estimate: ______

$$\begin{array}{r} 325 \\ -\ 179 \\ \hline \end{array}$$

7. Estimate: ______

$$\begin{array}{r} 935 \\ -\ 813 \\ \hline \end{array}$$

8. Estimate: ______

$$\begin{array}{r} 358 \\ -\ 292 \\ \hline \end{array}$$

9. Estimate: ______

$$\begin{array}{r} 826 \\ -\ 617 \\ \hline \end{array}$$

10. Estimate: ______

$$\begin{array}{r} 900 \\ -\ 158 \\ \hline \end{array}$$

11. Estimate: ______

$$\begin{array}{r} 607 \\ -\ 568 \\ \hline \end{array}$$

12. Estimate: ______

$$\begin{array}{r} 973 \\ -\ 869 \\ \hline \end{array}$$

Problem Solving REAL WORLD

13. Bev scored 540 points. This was 158 points more than Ike scored. How many points did Ike score?

____

14. A youth group earned $285 washing cars. The group's expenses were $79. How much profit did the group make washing cars?

____

Name ______________________

Lesson 52

COMMON CORE STANDARD CC.3.NBT.3

Lesson Objective: Solve multiplication problems by using the strategy *draw a diagram.*

Problem Solving • Use the Distributive Property

There are 6 rows of singers in a performance. There are 20 singers in each row. How many singers are in the performance?

Read the Problem	Solve the Problem
What do I need to find? I need to find how many singers are in the performance	**Record the steps you used to solve the problem.** 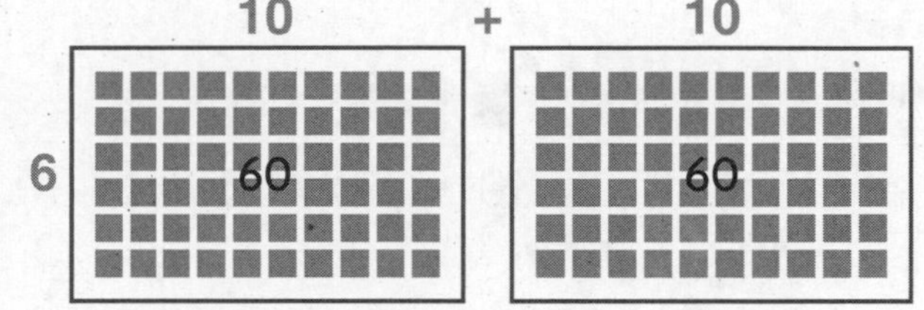 First, I draw and label a diagram to show __6__ rows of __20__ singers.
What information do I need to use? There are __6__ rows of singers. Each row has __20__ singers.	Next, I break apart 20 into 10 + 10 and find the products of the two smaller rectangles. $6 \times 10 =$ ____ $6 \times 10 =$ ____
How will I use the information? I can draw a diagram and use the Distributive Property to break apart the factor 20 into $10 + 10$ to use facts I know.	Then, I find the sum of the two products. ____ + ____ = ____ $6 \times 20 =$ ____ So, there are ____ singers.

1. Eight teams play in a Little League series. Each team has 20 players. How many players are in the series?

   ____

2. The assembly room has 6 rows with 30 chairs in each row. If third graders fill 3 rows, how many third graders are in the room?

   ____

Name ________________________________

Problem Solving • Use the Distributive Property

Read each problem and solve.

1. Each time a student turns in a perfect spelling test, Ms. Ricks puts an achievement square on the bulletin board. There are 6 rows of squares on the bulletin board. Each row has 30 squares. How many perfect spelling tests have been turned in?

   Think: $6 \times 30 = 6 \times (10 + 10 + 10)$

   $= 60 + 60 + 60 = 180$

   180 spelling tests

2. Norma practices violin for 50 minutes every day. How many minutes does Norma practice violin in 7 days?

   ____

3. A kitchen designer is creating a new backsplash for the wall behind a kitchen sink. The backsplash will have 5 rows of tiles. Each row will have 20 tiles. How many tiles are needed for the entire backsplash?

   ____

4. A bowling alley keeps shoes in rows of cubbyholes. There are 9 rows of cubbyholes, with 20 cubbyholes in each row. If there is a pair of shoes in every cubbyhole, how many pairs of shoes are there?

   ____

5. The third-grade students are traveling to the science museum in 8 buses. There are 40 students on each bus. How many students are going to the museum?

   ____

Name ______________________

Lesson 53

COMMON CORE STANDARD CC.3.NBT.3

Lesson Objective: Use base-ten blocks, a number line, or place value to multiply with multiples of 10.

Multiplication Strategies with Multiples of 10

You can use place value to multiply with multiples of 10.

Find 5 × 20.

Step 1 Use a multiplication fact you know.

Think: 5 × 2 = 10, so
5 × 2 ones = **10** ones

Step 2 Use place value to find the product.

Think: 5 × 2 tens = **10** tens,
or **100**

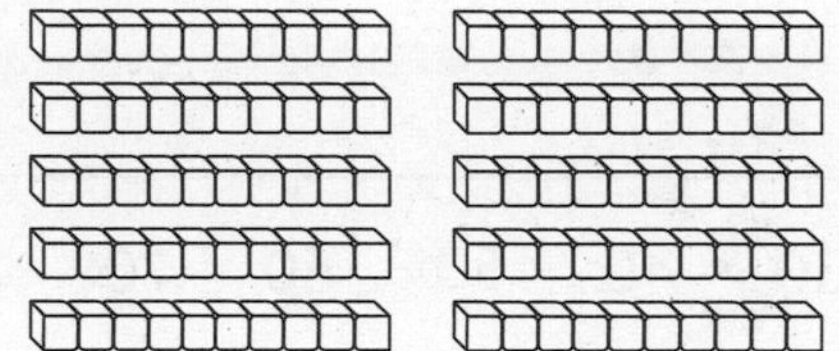

So, 5 × 20 = **100**.

You can also use a number line to multiply with multiples of 10.

Find 4 × 30.

Think: There are 4 groups of 30. Draw **4** jumps of 30.

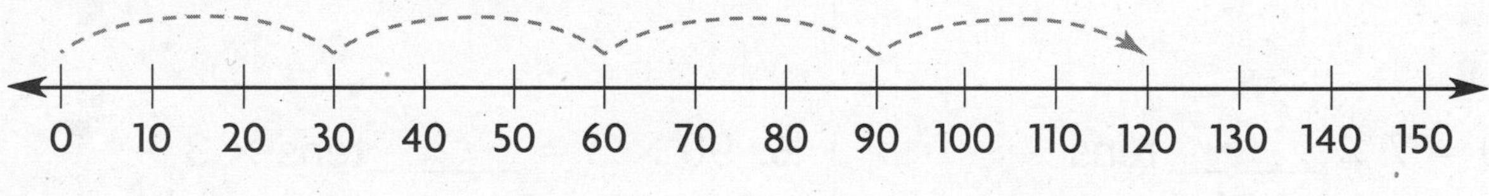

So, 4 × 30 = **120**.

Use place value to find the product.

1. 6 × 40 = 6 × _____ tens
= _____ tens = _____

2. 50 × 7 = _____ tens × 7
= _____ tens = _____

3. Use a number line to find the product. 3 × 50 = _____

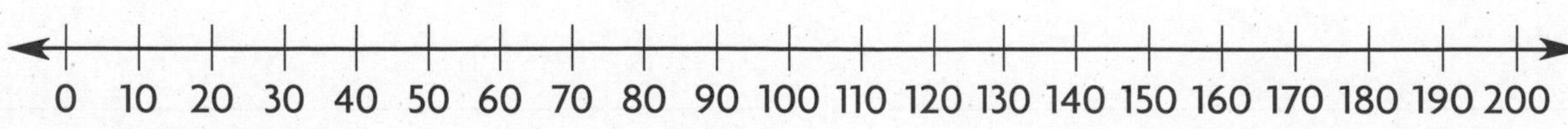

Name ______________________

Lesson 53

CC.3.NBT.3

Multiplication Strategies with Multiples of 10

Use a number line to find the product.

1. $2 \times 40 =$ 80

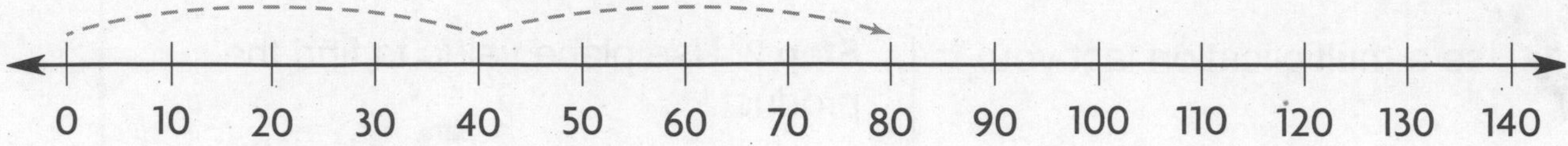

2. $4 \times 30 =$ ______

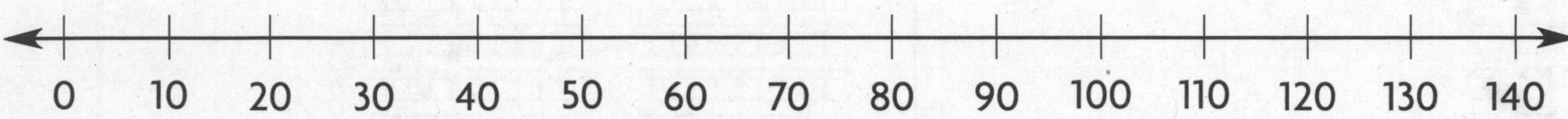

Use place value to find the product.

3. $5 \times 70 = 5 \times$ ______ tens

   $=$ ______ tens $=$ ______

4. $60 \times 4 =$ ______ tens $\times 4$

   $=$ ______ tens $=$ ______

5. $7 \times 30 = 7 \times$ ______ tens

   $=$ ______ tens $=$ ______

6. $90 \times 3 =$ ______ tens $\times 3$

   $=$ ______ tens $=$ ______

Problem Solving REAL WORLD

7. One exhibit at the aquarium has 5 fish tanks. Each fish tank holds 50 gallons of water. How much water do the 5 tanks hold in all?

   ____

8. In another aquarium display, there are 40 fish in each of 7 large tanks. How many fish are in the display in all?

   ____

Name ______________________

Lesson 54

COMMON CORE STANDARD CC.3.NBT.3

Lesson Objective: Model and record multiplication with multiples of 10.

Multiply Multiples of 10 by 1-Digit Numbers

You can use place value and regrouping to multiply multiples of 10.

Find 3 × 40.

	THINK	RECORD
Step 1 Use quick pictures to draw 3 groups of 40.	Multiply the ones. 3 × 0 ones = 0 ones.	$\begin{array}{r} 40 \\ \times\ 3 \\ \hline 0 \end{array}$
Step 2 Regroup the 12 tens.	Multiply the tens. 3 × 4 tens = 12 tens Regroup the 12 tens as 1 hundred 2 tens	$\begin{array}{r} 40 \\ \times\ 3 \\ \hline 120 \end{array}$

So, 3 × 40 = 120.

Find the product. Draw a quick picture.

1. 4 × 50 = ______

2. 7 × 30 = ______

3. ______ = 9 × 20

4. 6 × 70 = ______

Name ______________________

Multiply Multiples of 10 by 1-Digit Numbers

Find the product. Use base-ten blocks or draw a quick picture.

1. $4 \times 50 =$ 200

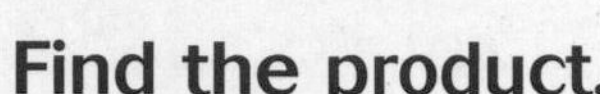

2. $60 \times 3 =$ ______

3. ______ $= 60 \times 5$

Find the product.

4. $\begin{array}{r} 30 \\ \times\ 8 \\ \hline \end{array}$

5. $\begin{array}{r} 50 \\ \times\ 2 \\ \hline \end{array}$

6. $\begin{array}{r} 60 \\ \times\ 7 \\ \hline \end{array}$

7. $\begin{array}{r} 70 \\ \times\ 4 \\ \hline \end{array}$

8. $6 \times 90 =$ ____

9. $9 \times 70 =$ ____

10. $8 \times 90 =$ ____

11. ____ $= 6 \times 80$

Problem Solving REAL WORLD

12. Each model car in a set costs $4. There are 30 different model cars in the set. How much would it cost to buy all the model cars in the set?

____

13. Amanda exercises for 50 minutes each day. How many minutes will she exercise in 7 days?

____

Name ________________________________

COMMON CORE STANDARD CC.3.NF.1

Lesson Objective: Explore and identify equal parts of a whole.

Equal Parts of a Whole

When you divide a shape into **equal parts**, each part must be exactly the same size.

This rectangle is divided into **2** equal parts, or **halves**.

This rectangle is divided into **3** equal parts, or **thirds**.

This rectangle is divided into **4** equal parts, or **fourths**.

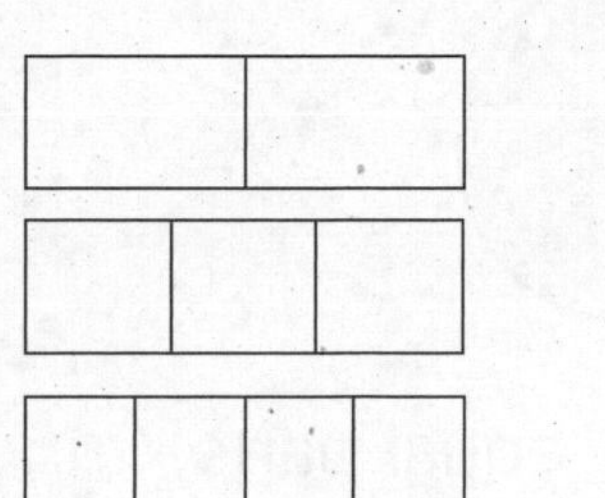

Write the number of equal parts. Then write the name for the parts.

1. 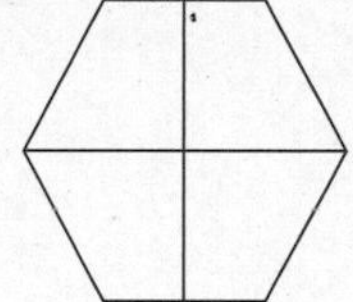

____ equal parts

____

2. 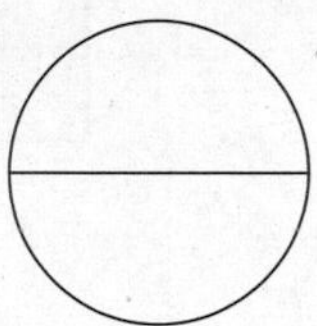

____ equal parts

____

3. 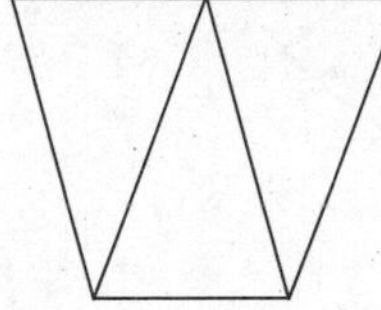

____ equal parts

____

Write whether each shape is divided into *equal* parts or *unequal* parts.

4. 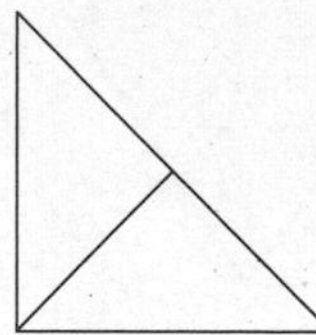

______________ parts

5. 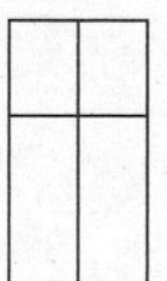

______________ parts

6. 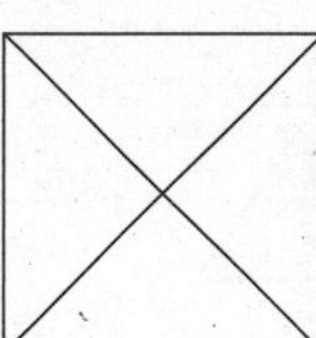

______________ parts

Draw lines to divide the squares into equal parts.

7. 3 thirds

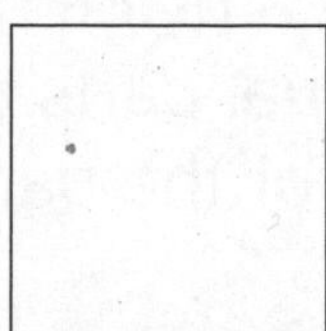

8. 6 sixths

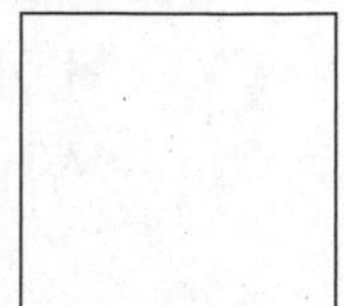

9. 8 eighths

Name ______________________________

Lesson 55

CC.3.NF.1

Equal Parts of a Whole

Write the number of equal parts.
Then write the name for the parts.

1. 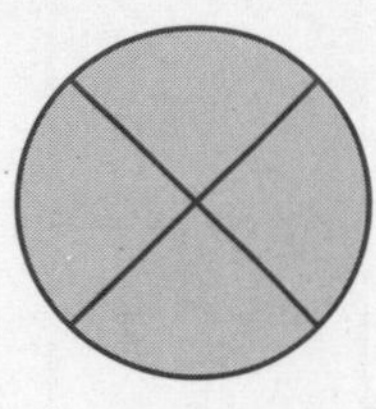

4 equal parts

fourths

2. 

_____ equal parts

____

3. 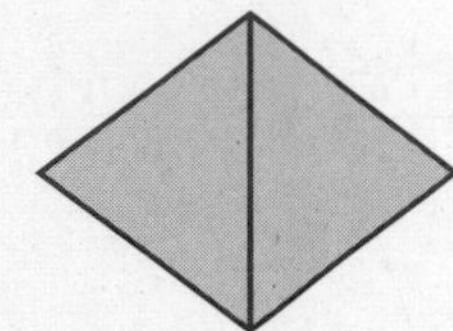

_____ equal parts

____

4. 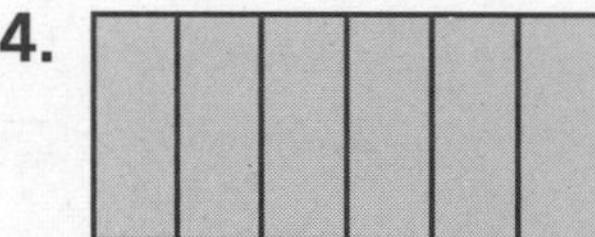

_____ equal parts

____

Write whether the shape is divided into *equal parts or unequal parts.*

5. 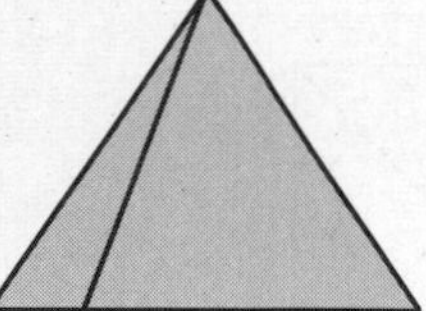

______________ parts

6. 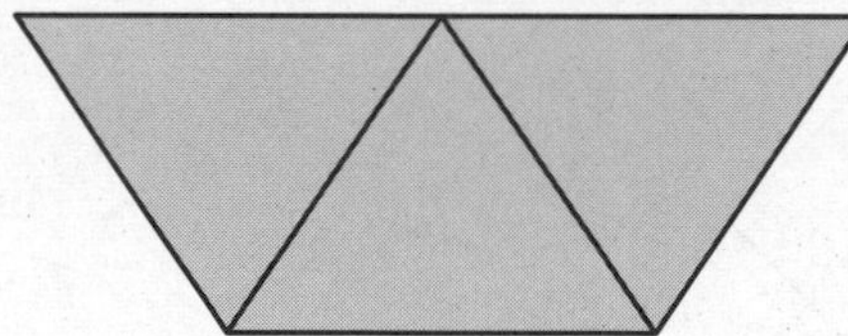

______________ parts

Problem Solving REAL WORLD

7. Diego cuts a round pizza into eight equal slices. What is the name for the parts?

____

8. Madison is making a place mat. She divides it into 6 equal parts to color. What is the name for the parts?

____

Name ______________________________

COMMON CORE STANDARD CC.3.NF.1

Lesson Objective: Divide models to make equal shares.

Equal Shares

Six brothers share 5 sandwiches equally. How much does each brother get? Draw to model the problem.

Step 1 Draw **5** squares for the sandwiches.

Step 2 There are **6** brothers. Draw lines to divide each sandwich into 6 equal parts.

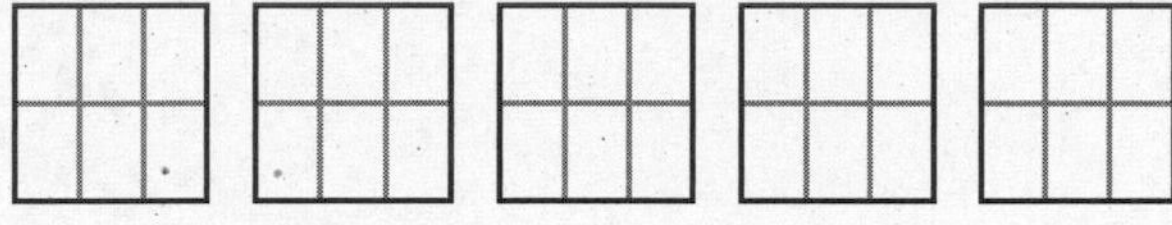

Step 3 Each brother will get 1 equal part from each sandwich.

So, each brother gets **5 sixths** of a sandwich.

Draw lines to show how much each person gets. Write the answer.

1. 4 sisters share 3 pies equally.

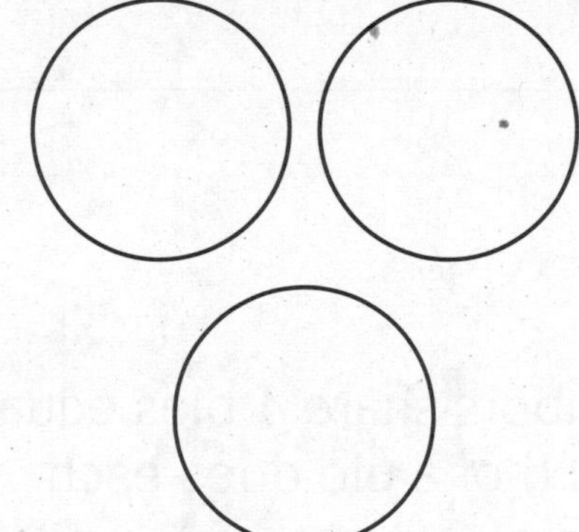

____

2. 6 friends share 3 fruit bars equally.

____

Name ______________________

Lesson 56

CC.3.NF.1

Equal Shares

For 1–2, draw lines to show how much each person gets. Write the answer.

1. 6 friends share 3 sandwiches equally.

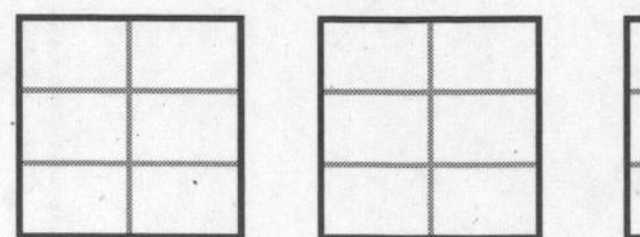

Possible answer: 1 half or 3 sixths of a sandwich

2. 8 classmates share 4 pizzas equally.

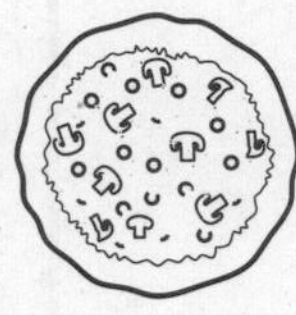 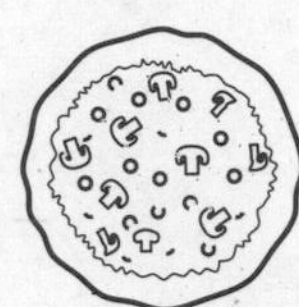 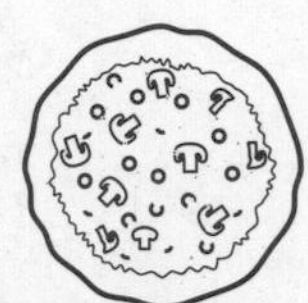 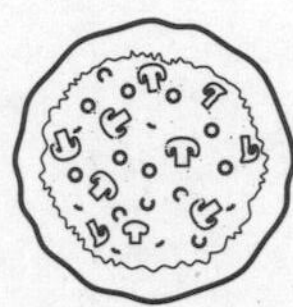

____

3. 4 teammates share 5 granola bars equally. Draw to show how much each person gets. Shade the amount that one person gets. Write the answer.

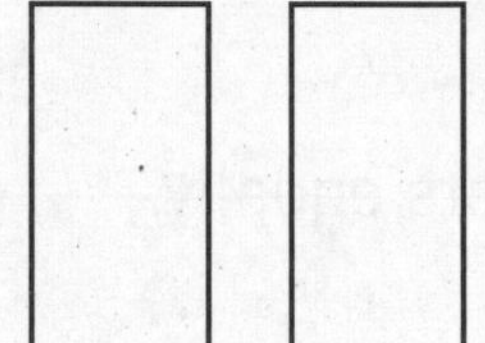  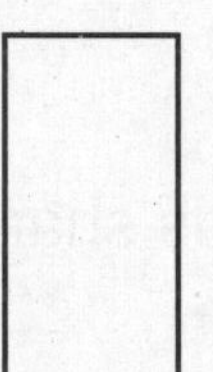 

____

Problem Solving REAL WORLD

4. Three brothers share 2 sandwiches equally. How much of a sandwich does each brother get?

____

____

5. Six neighbors share 4 pies equally. How much of a pie does each neighbor get?

____

____

Name ___________________________

Lesson 57

COMMON CORE STANDARD CC.3.NF.1

Lesson Objective: Use a fraction to name one part of a whole that is divided into equal parts.

Unit Fractions of a Whole

A **fraction** is a number. It names part of a whole or part of a group.

The top number tells how many equal parts are being counted.
The bottom number tells how many equal parts are in the whole.
A **unit fraction** names 1 equal part of a whole. It always has 1 as its top number.

How much is 1 part of a fruit bar that is cut into 8 equal parts?

Step 1 Use fraction strips. Make a strip showing 8 equal parts, or eighths.

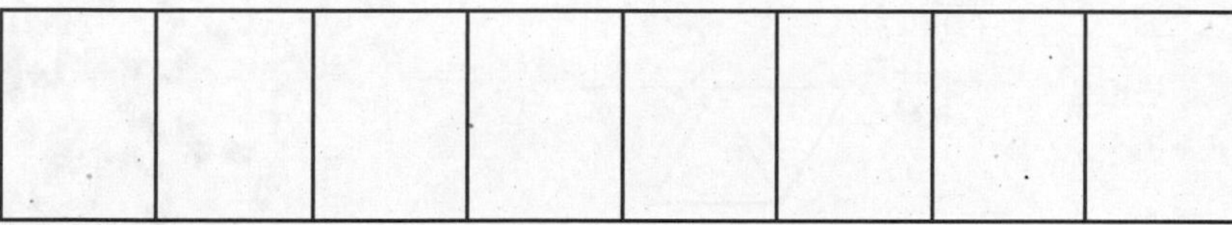

Step 2 Shade 1 of the parts and name it.

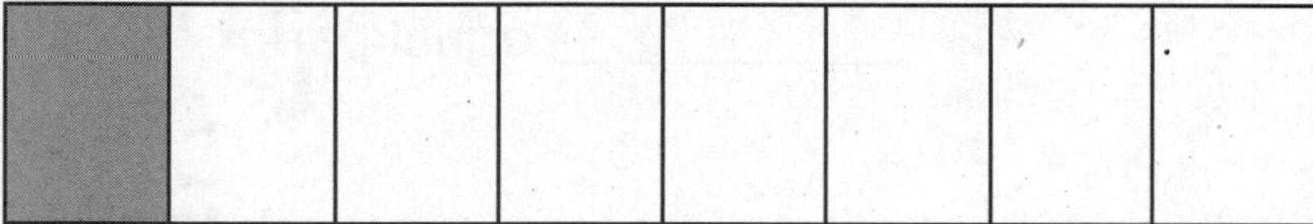

This fraction is called $\frac{1}{8}$.

So, 1 part of a fruit bar that can be divided into 8 equal parts is $\frac{1}{8}$.

Write the number of equal parts in the whole.
Then write the fraction that names the shaded part.

1. 

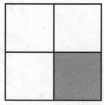

_____ equal parts

_____

2. 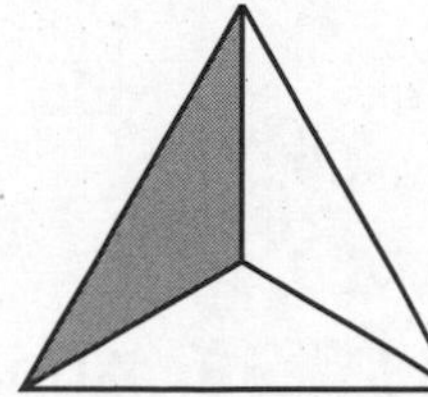

_____ equal parts

_____

3. 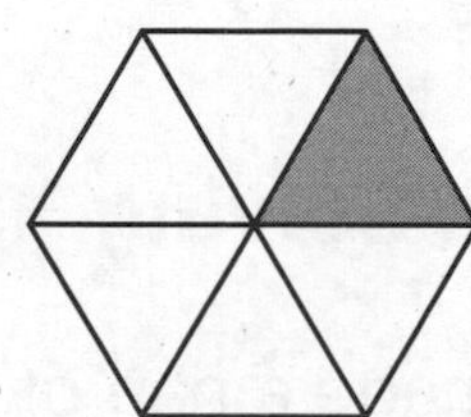

_____ equal parts

_____

Name ______________________

Lesson 57

CC.3.NF.1

Unit Fractions of a Whole

Write the number of equal parts in the whole. Then write the fraction that names the shaded part.

1. 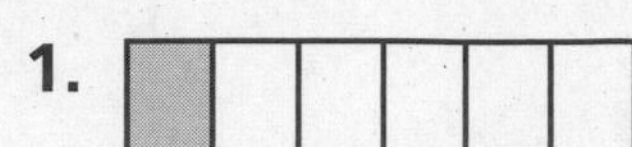

6 equal parts

$\frac{1}{6}$

2. 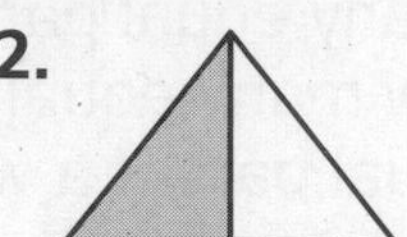

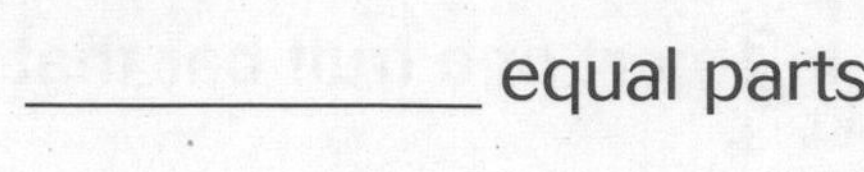

______ equal parts

______

3. 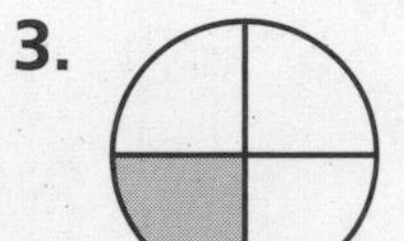

______ equal parts

______

4. 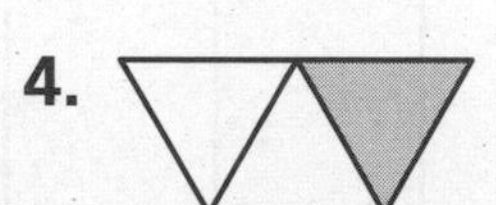

______ equal parts

______

Draw a picture of the whole.

5. $\frac{1}{3}$ is

6. $\frac{1}{8}$ is

Problem Solving REAL WORLD

7. Tyler made a pan of cornbread. He cut it into 8 equal pieces and ate 1 piece. What fraction of the cornbread did Tyler eat?

______

8. Anna cut an apple into 4 equal pieces. She gave 1 piece to her sister. What fraction of the apple did Anna give to her sister?

______

Name ____________________

COMMON CORE STANDARD CC.3.NF.1

Lesson Objective: Read, write, and model fractions that represent more than one part of a whole that is divided into equal parts.

Fractions of a Whole

Some shapes can be cut into equal parts.
A fraction can name more than 1 equal part of a whole.

Write a fraction in words and in numbers to name the shaded part.

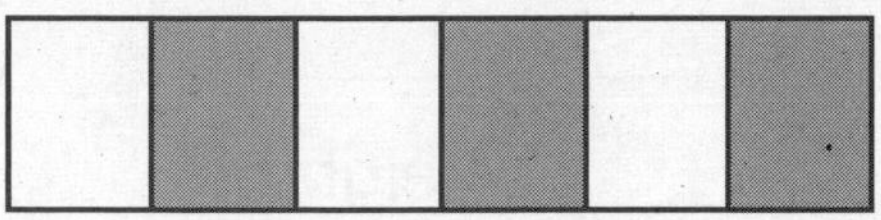

How many equal parts make up the whole shape? **6 equal parts**

How many parts are shaded? **3 parts**

So, 3 parts out of 6 equal parts are shaded. Read: **three sixths**. Write: $\frac{3}{6}$

1. Shade three parts out of eight equal parts. Write a fraction in words and in numbers to name the shaded part.

Read: ________ eighths

Write: ________

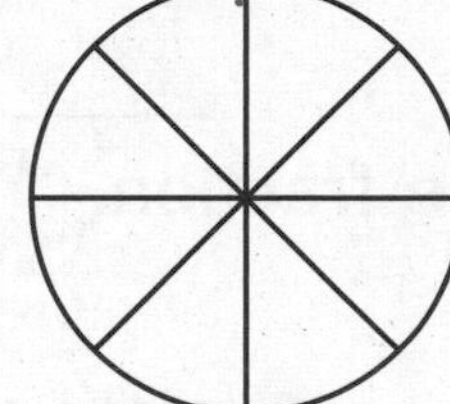

Write the fraction that names each part. Write a fraction in words and in numbers to name the shaded part.

2. 

Each part is ________.

________ sixths

____

3. 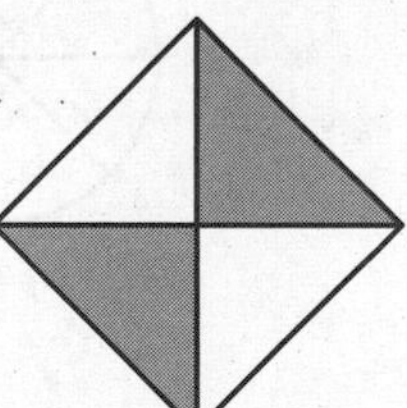

Each part is ________.

________ fourths

____

4. 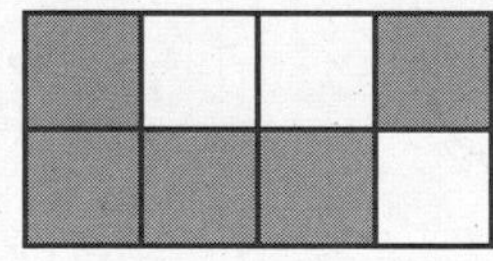

Each part is ________.

________ eighths

____

Name ________________________

Fractions of a Whole

Write the fraction that names each part. Write a fraction in words and in numbers to name the shaded part.

1. 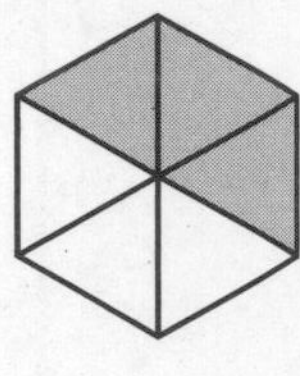

Each part is $\frac{1}{6}$.

three sixths

$\frac{3}{6}$

2. 

Each part is ________.

________ eighths

____

3. 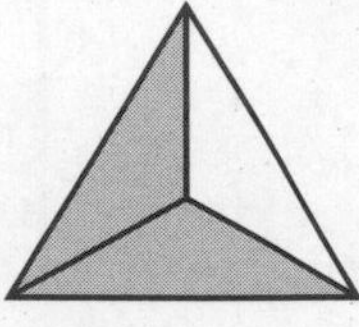

Each part is ________.

________ thirds

____

4. 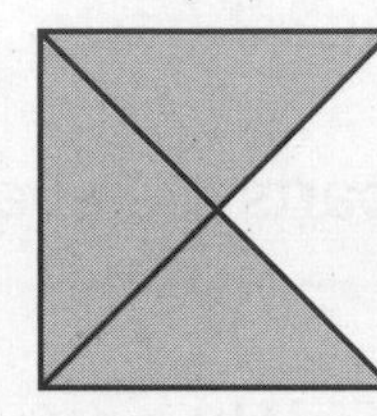

Each part is ________.

________ fourths

____

Shade the fraction circle to model the fraction. Then write the fraction in numbers.

5. four out of six

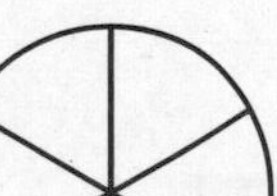

____

6. eight out of eight

____

Problem Solving REAL WORLD

7. Emma makes a poster for the school's spring concert. She divides the poster into 8 equal parts. She uses two of the parts for the title. What fraction of the poster does Emma use for the title?

____

8. Lucas makes a flag. It has 6 equal parts. Five of the parts are red. What fraction of the flag is red?

____

Name ________________________

COMMON CORE STANDARD CC.3.NF.1

Lesson Objective: Model, read, and write fractional parts of a group.

Fractions of a Group

Adam has a collection of cars.
What fraction names the shaded part of the collection?

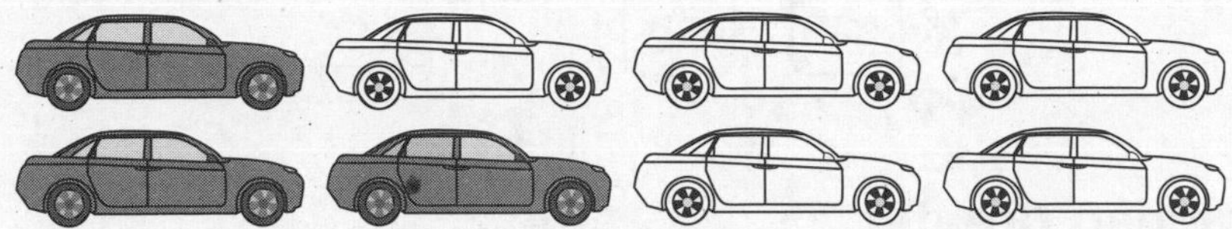

Step 1 Count how many cars are shaded. There are 3 shaded cars. This number will be the **numerator**, or the top number of the fraction.

Step 2 Count the total number of cars. 8 This number will be the **denominator**, or the bottom number of the fraction.

Step 3 Read the fraction: three eighths, or three out of eight.

So, $\frac{3}{8}$ of Adam's cars are shaded.

Write a fraction to name the shaded part of each group.

1. 

______

2. 

______

Write a whole number and a fraction greater than 1 to name the part filled.

3. 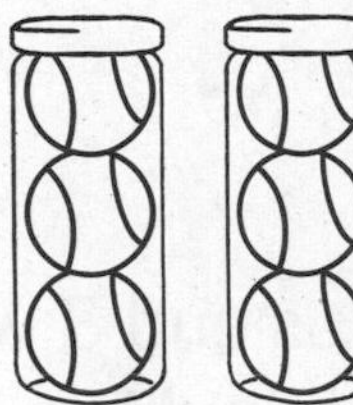

Think: 1 can = 1

______ ______

4. 

Think: 1 pan = 1

______ ______

Name ______________________

Fractions of a Group

Write a fraction to name the shaded part of each group.

1.  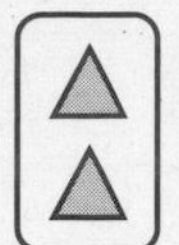  

$\frac{6}{8}$

2. 

______

Write a whole number and a fraction greater than 1 to name the part filled. Think: 1 container = 1

3. 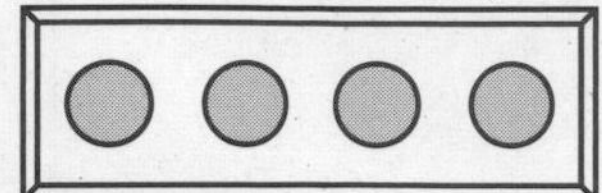 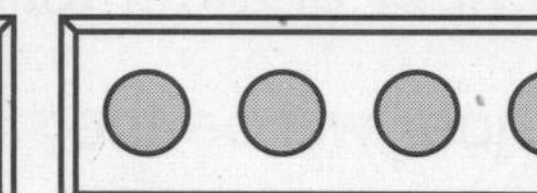

______ ______

4.   

______ ______

Draw a quick picture. Then, write a fraction to name the shaded part of the group.

5. Draw 4 circles.
Shade 2 circles.

______

6. Draw 6 circles.
Make 3 groups.
Shade 1 group.

______

Problem Solving

7. Brian has 3 basketball cards and 5 baseball cards. What fraction of Brian's cards are baseball cards?

______

8. Sophia has 3 pink tulips and 3 white tulips. What fraction of Sophia's tulips are pink?

______

Name ___________________________

Lesson 60

COMMON CORE STANDARD CC.3.NF.1

Lesson Objective: Find fractional parts of a group using unit fractions.

Find Part of a Group Using Unit Fractions

Lauren bought 12 stamps for postcards. She gave Brianna $\frac{1}{6}$ of them. How many stamps did Lauren give to Brianna?

Step 1 Find the total number of stamps. 12 stamps

Step 2 Since you want to find $\frac{1}{6}$ of the group, there should be 6 equal groups. Circle one of the groups to show $\frac{1}{6}$.

Step 3 Find $\frac{1}{6}$ of the stamps. How many stamps are in 1 group? 2 stamps

So, Lauren gave Brianna 2 stamps. $\frac{1}{6}$ of 12 = 2

Circle equal groups to solve. Count the number of shapes in 1 group.

1. $\frac{1}{4}$ of 8 = __________

2. $\frac{1}{3}$ of 9 = __________

3. $\frac{1}{4}$ of 16 = __________

4. $\frac{1}{6}$ of 18 = __________

Name ____________________

Find Part of a Group Using Unit Fractions

Circle equal groups to solve. Count the number of items in 1 group.

1. $\frac{1}{4}$ of 12 = 3

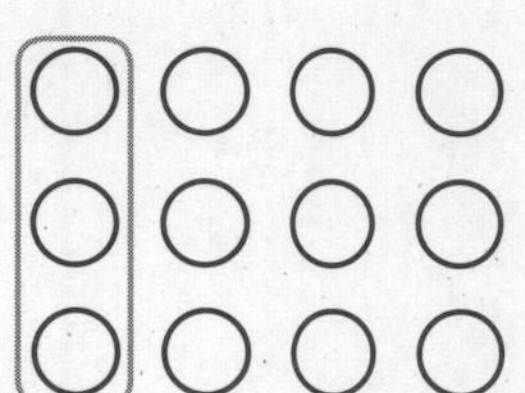

2. $\frac{1}{8}$ of 16 = ____

3. $\frac{1}{3}$ of 12 = ____

4. $\frac{1}{3}$ of 9 = ____

5. $\frac{1}{6}$ of 18 = ____

6. $\frac{1}{2}$ of 4 = ____

Problem Solving REAL WORLD

7. Marco drew 24 pictures. He drew $\frac{1}{6}$ of them in art class. How many pictures did Marco draw in art class?

____

8. Caroline has 16 marbles. One eighth of them are blue. How many of Caroline's marbles are blue?

____

Name ______________________________

COMMON CORE STANDARD CC.3.NF.1

Lesson Objective: Solve fraction problems by using the strategy *draw a diagram.*

Problem Solving • Find the Whole Group Using Unit Fractions

There are 3 apple juice boxes in the cooler. One fourth of the juice boxes in the cooler are apple juice. How many juice boxes are in the cooler?

Read the Problem	Solve the Problem
What do I need to find? I need to find <u>how many juice boxes</u> are in the cooler. **What information do I need to use?** There are <u>3</u> apple juice boxes. <u>One fourth</u> of the juice boxes are apple juice. **How will I use the information?** I will use the information in the problem to draw a diagram.	**Describe how to draw a diagram to solve.** The denominator in $\frac{1}{4}$ tells you that there are <u>4</u> parts in the whole group. Draw 4 circles to show <u>4</u> parts. Since 3 juice boxes are $\frac{1}{4}$ of the group, draw <u>3</u> counters in the first circle. Since there are <u>3</u> counters in the first circle, draw <u>3</u> counters in each of the remaining circles. Then count all of the counters. So, there are <u>12</u> juice boxes in the cooler. 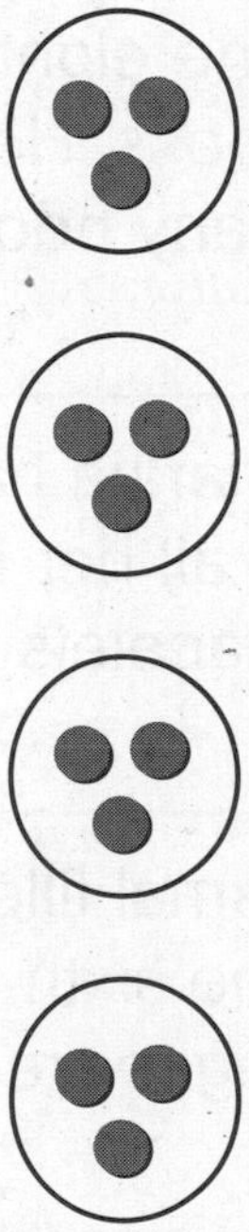

1. Max has 3 beta fish in his fish tank. One half of his fish are beta fish. How many fish does Max have in his tank?

____

2. Two boys are standing in line. One sixth of the students in line are boys. How many students are standing in line?

____

Name ______________________________

Problem Solving • Find the Whole Group Using Unit Fractions

Draw a quick picture to solve.

1. Katrina has 2 blue ribbons for her hair. One fourth of all her ribbons are blue. How many ribbons does Katrina have in all?

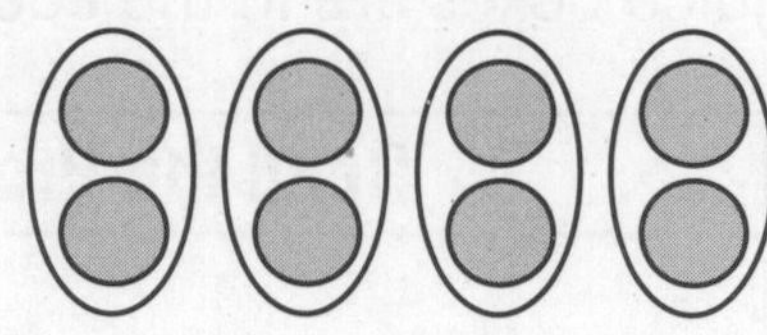

8 ribbons

2. One eighth of Tony's books are mystery books. He has 3 mystery books. How many books does Tony have in all?

____

3. Brianna has 4 pink bracelets. One third of all her bracelets are pink. How many bracelets does Brianna have?

____

4. Ramal filled 3 pages in a stamp album. This is one sixth of the pages in the album. How many pages are there in Ramal's stamp album?

____

5. Jeff helped repair one half of the bicycles in a bike shop last week. If Jeff worked on 5 bicycles, how many bicycles did the shop repair in all last week?

____

6. Layla collects postcards. She has 7 postcards from Europe. Her postcards from Europe are one third of her total collection. How many postcards in all does Layla have?

____

Name ______________________________

Lesson 64

COMMON CORE STANDARD CC.3.NF.3b

Lesson Objective: Generate equivalent fractions by using models.

Equivalent Fractions

Kaitlyn used $\frac{3}{4}$ of a sheet of wrapping paper.

Find a fraction that is equivalent to $\frac{3}{4}$. $\frac{3}{4} = \frac{\blacksquare}{8}$

Step 1 The top fraction strip is divided into 4 equal parts. Shade $\frac{3}{4}$ of the strip to show how much paper Kaitlyn used.

Step 2 The bottom strip is divided into 8 equal parts. Shade parts of the strip until the same amount is shaded as in the top strip.
6 parts of the bottom strip are shaded.

1/8	1/8	1/8	1/8	1/8	1/8	1/8	1/8

$\frac{3}{4} = \frac{6}{8}$

So, $\frac{6}{8}$ is equivalent to $\frac{3}{4}$.

Each shape is 1 whole. Shade the model to find the equivalent fraction.

1. 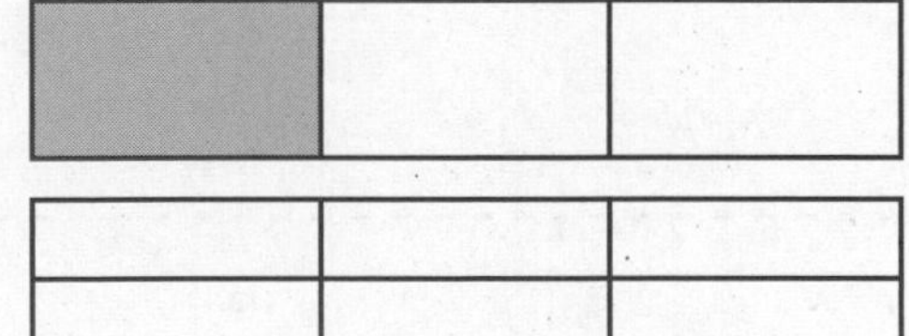

$\frac{1}{3} = \frac{\blacksquare}{6}$

2. 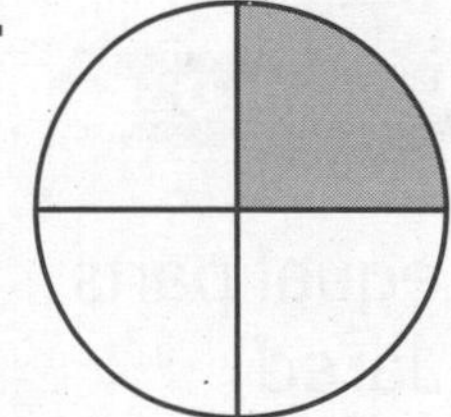 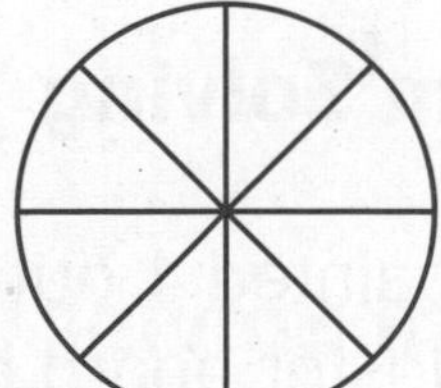

$\frac{1}{4} = \frac{\blacksquare}{8}$

3. 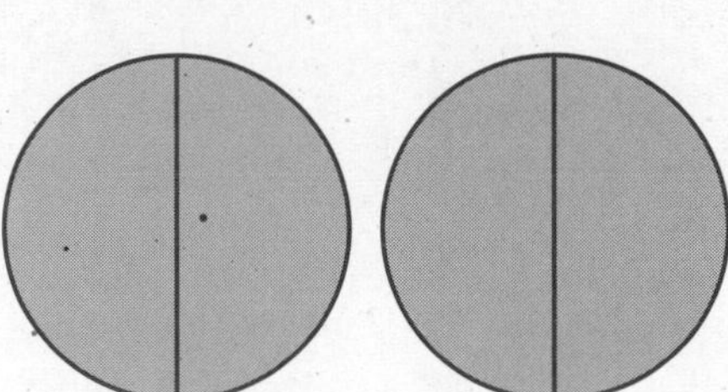 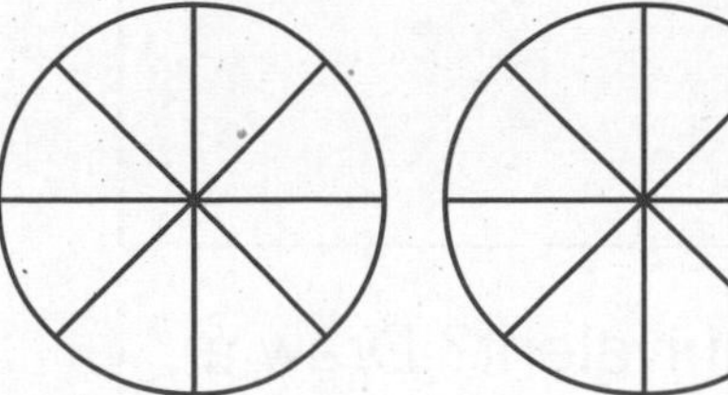

$\frac{4}{2} = \frac{\blacksquare}{8}$

Name ____________________

Lesson 64

CC.3.NF.3b

Equivalent Fractions

Each shape is 1 whole. Shade the model to find the equivalent fraction.

1.

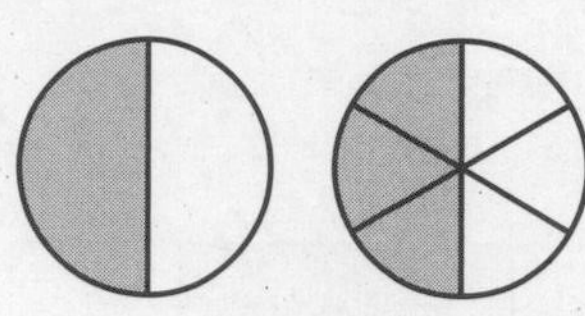

$\frac{1}{2} = \frac{3}{6}$

2.

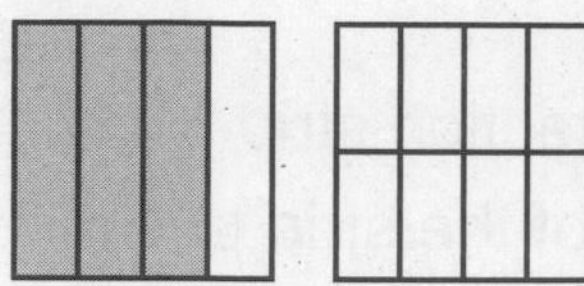

$\frac{3}{4} = \frac{6}{■}$

Circle equal groups to find the equivalent fraction.

3.

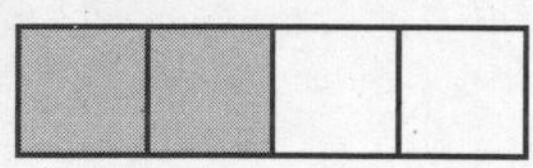

$\frac{2}{4} = \frac{■}{2}$

4.

$\frac{4}{6} = \frac{■}{3}$

roblem Solving REAL WORLD

May painted 4 out of 8 equal parts of a poster board blue. Jared ainted 2 out of 4 equal parts of a ame-size poster board red. Write actions to show which part of the ster board each person painted.

____

6. Ar e fractions equivalent? Draw a mc to explain.

____

Name ______________________

Lesson 66

COMMON CORE STANDARD CC.3.NF.3d

Lesson Objective: Solve comparison problems by using the strategy *act it out.*

Problem Solving • Compare Fractions

Nick walked $\frac{2}{4}$ mile to the gym. Then he walked $\frac{3}{4}$ mile to the store. Which distance is shorter?

Read the Problem

What do I need to find?

I need to find which distance is shorter.

What information do I need to use?

Nick walked $\frac{2}{4}$ mile to the gym. Then he walked $\frac{3}{4}$ mile to the store.

How will I use the information?

I will use fraction strips and compare the lengths of the models to find which distance is shorter.

Solve the Problem

1			
$\frac{1}{4}$	$\frac{1}{4}$	$\frac{1}{4}$	$\frac{1}{4}$
$\frac{1}{4}$	$\frac{1}{4}$	$\frac{1}{4}$	$\frac{1}{4}$

Compare the lengths.

$\frac{2}{4} < \frac{3}{4}$

The length of the $\frac{2}{4}$ model is less than the length of the $\frac{3}{4}$ model.

So, the distance to the gym is shorter.

1. Mariana and Shawn each had 6 pages to read. Mariana read $\frac{2}{3}$ of her pages. Shawn read $\frac{1}{3}$ of his pages. Who read more pages? **Explain.**

____

____

2. Carlos ran $\frac{3}{8}$ of the race course. Lori ran $\frac{3}{6}$ of the same race course. Who ran farther? **Explain.**

____

____

____

Name ______________________________

Problem Solving • Compare Fractions

Lesson 66
CC.3.NF.3d

Solve.

1. Luis skates $\frac{2}{3}$ mile from his home to school. Isabella skates $\frac{2}{4}$ mile to get to school. Who skates farther?

   Think: Use fraction strips to act it out.

   Luis

2. Sandra makes a pizza. She puts mushrooms on $\frac{2}{8}$ of the pizza. She adds green peppers to $\frac{5}{8}$ of the pizza. Which topping covers more of the pizza?

   ____

3. The jars of paint in the art room have different amounts of paint. The green paint jar is $\frac{4}{8}$ full. The purple paint jar is $\frac{4}{6}$ full. Which paint jar is less full?

   ____

4. Jan has a recipe for bread. She uses $\frac{2}{3}$ cup of flour and $\frac{1}{3}$ cup of chopped onion. Which ingredient does she use more of, flour or onion?

   ____

5. Edward walked $\frac{3}{4}$ mile from his home to the park. Then he walked $\frac{2}{4}$ mile from the park to the library. Which distance is shorter?

   ____

Name ______________________________

Lesson 67

COMMON CORE STANDARD CC.3.NF.3d

Lesson Objective: Compare fractions with the same denominator by using models and reasoning strategies.

Compare Fractions with the Same Denominator

Pete's Prize Pizzas makes a special pizza. Of the toppings, $\frac{1}{4}$ is peppers and $\frac{3}{4}$ is ham. Does the pizza have more peppers or ham?

Compare $\frac{1}{4}$ and $\frac{3}{4}$.

Step 1 The denominators of both fractions are the same, 4. Use fraction circles divided into fourths to model the fractions.

Step 2 Shade 1 part of the first circle to show $\frac{1}{4}$.

Shade 3 parts of the second circle to show $\frac{3}{4}$.

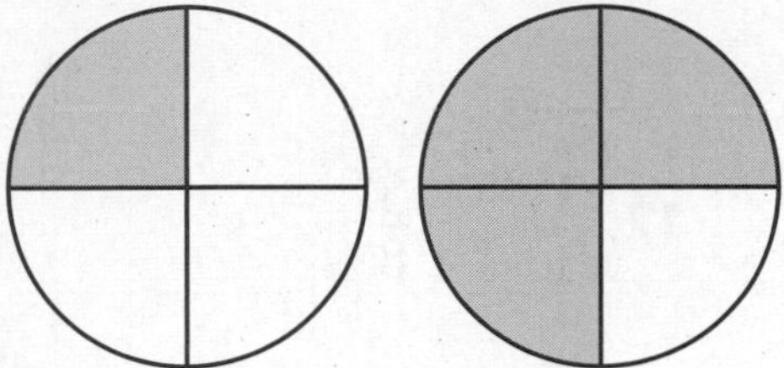

Step 3 Compare. 3 parts is more than 1 part.

$\frac{3}{4} > \frac{1}{4}$

So, the pizza has more **ham**.

Compare. Write <, >, or =.

1. 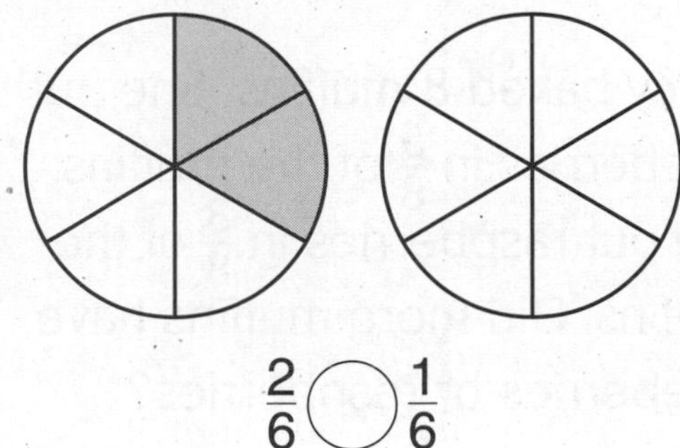

$\frac{2}{6}$ ◯ $\frac{1}{6}$

2. 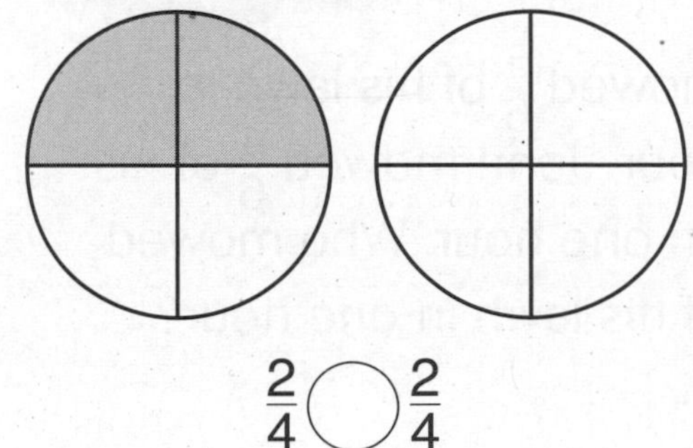

$\frac{2}{4}$ ◯ $\frac{2}{4}$

3. $\frac{1}{3}$ ◯ $\frac{2}{3}$

4. $\frac{5}{8}$ ◯ $\frac{3}{8}$

5. $\frac{1}{4}$ ◯ $\frac{3}{4}$

6. $\frac{4}{8}$ ◯ $\frac{4}{8}$

Name ______________________________

Lesson 67
CC.3.NF.3d

Compare Fractions with the Same Denominator

Compare. Write <, >, or =.

1. $\frac{3}{4}$ (>) $\frac{1}{4}$
2. $\frac{3}{6}$ ◯ $\frac{0}{6}$
3. $\frac{1}{2}$ ◯ $\frac{1}{2}$
4. $\frac{5}{6}$ ◯ $\frac{6}{6}$
5. $\frac{7}{8}$ ◯ $\frac{5}{8}$
6. $\frac{2}{3}$ ◯ $\frac{3}{3}$
7. $\frac{8}{8}$ ◯ $\frac{0}{8}$
8. $\frac{1}{6}$ ◯ $\frac{1}{6}$
9. $\frac{3}{4}$ ◯ $\frac{2}{4}$
10. $\frac{1}{6}$ ◯ $\frac{2}{6}$
11. $\frac{1}{2}$ ◯ $\frac{0}{2}$
12. $\frac{3}{8}$ ◯ $\frac{3}{8}$
13. $\frac{1}{4}$ ◯ $\frac{4}{4}$
14. $\frac{5}{8}$ ◯ $\frac{4}{8}$
15. $\frac{4}{6}$ ◯ $\frac{6}{6}$

Problem Solving REAL WORLD

16. Ben mowed $\frac{5}{6}$ of his lawn in one hour. John mowed $\frac{4}{6}$ of his lawn in one hour. Who mowed less of his lawn in one hour?

____

17. Darcy baked 8 muffins. She put blueberries in $\frac{5}{8}$ of the muffins. She put raspberries in $\frac{3}{8}$ of the muffins. Did more muffins have blueberries or raspberries?

____

Name ____________________

Lesson 68

COMMON CORE STANDARD CC.3.NF.3d

Lesson Objective: Compare fractions with the same numerator by using models and reasoning strategies.

Compare Fractions with the Same Numerator

Ryan takes a survey of his class. $\frac{1}{8}$ of the class has dogs, and $\frac{1}{3}$ of the class has cats. Are there more dog owners or cat owners in Ryan's class?

Compare the fractions. $\frac{1}{8}$ ● $\frac{1}{3}$

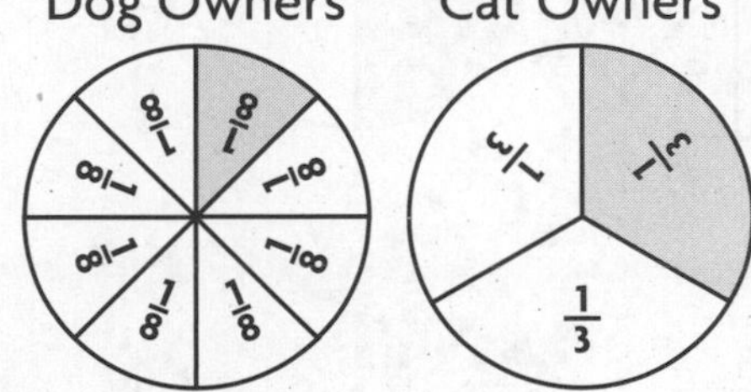

Step 1 Divide the first circle into 8 equal parts. Shade $\frac{1}{8}$ of the circle to show dog owners.

Step 2 Divide the second circle into 3 equal parts. Shade $\frac{1}{3}$ of the circle to show cat owners.

Step 3 Compare the shaded parts of the circles. Which shaded part is larger?

$\frac{1}{3}$ is larger than $\frac{1}{8}$. $\frac{1}{8} < \frac{1}{3}$

So, there are more **cat owners** than **dog owners** in Ryan's class.

Compare. Write <, >, or =.

1. $\frac{3}{4}$ ◯ $\frac{3}{6}$
2. $\frac{1}{8}$ ◯ $\frac{1}{6}$
3. $\frac{2}{4}$ ◯ $\frac{2}{6}$
4. $\frac{2}{3}$ ◯ $\frac{2}{6}$
5. $\frac{4}{6}$ ◯ $\frac{4}{8}$
6. $\frac{2}{8}$ ◯ $\frac{2}{4}$
7. $\frac{5}{6}$ ◯ $\frac{5}{8}$
8. $\frac{1}{3}$ ◯ $\frac{1}{4}$
9. $\frac{3}{6}$ ◯ $\frac{3}{4}$
10. $\frac{1}{3}$ ◯ $\frac{1}{3}$
11. $\frac{3}{3}$ ◯ $\frac{3}{4}$
12. $\frac{2}{8}$ ◯ $\frac{2}{6}$

Name ____________________

Compare Fractions with the Same Numerator

Compare. Write $<$, $>$, or $=$.

1. $\frac{1}{8}$ ($<$) $\frac{1}{2}$

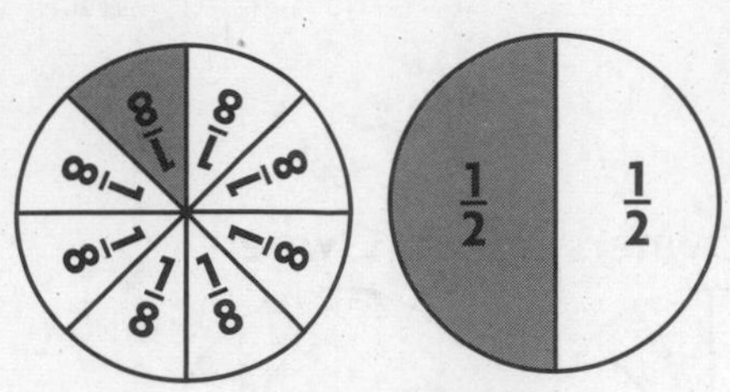

2. $\frac{3}{8}$ ◯ $\frac{3}{6}$

3. $\frac{2}{3}$ ◯ $\frac{2}{4}$

4. $\frac{2}{8}$ ◯ $\frac{2}{3}$

5. $\frac{3}{6}$ ◯ $\frac{3}{4}$

6. $\frac{1}{2}$ ◯ $\frac{1}{6}$

7. $\frac{5}{6}$ ◯ $\frac{5}{8}$

8. $\frac{4}{8}$ ◯ $\frac{4}{8}$

9. $\frac{6}{8}$ ◯ $\frac{6}{6}$

Problem Solving REAL WORLD

10. Javier is buying food in the lunch line. The tray of salad plates is $\frac{3}{8}$ full. The tray of fruit plates is $\frac{3}{4}$ full. Which tray is more full?

____

11. Rachel bought some buttons. Of the buttons, $\frac{2}{4}$ are yellow and $\frac{2}{8}$ are red. Rachel bought more of which color buttons?

____

Name ______________________________

COMMON CORE STANDARD CC.3.NF.3d

Lesson Objective: Compare fractions by using models and strategies involving the size of the pieces in the whole.

Compare Fractions

Mrs. Brown's recipe uses $\frac{2}{3}$ cup of flour. Mrs. Young's recipe uses $\frac{3}{4}$ cup of flour. Which recipe uses more flour?

Compare $\frac{2}{3}$ and $\frac{3}{4}$.

- You can compare fractions using fraction strips.

Step 1 Model each fraction.

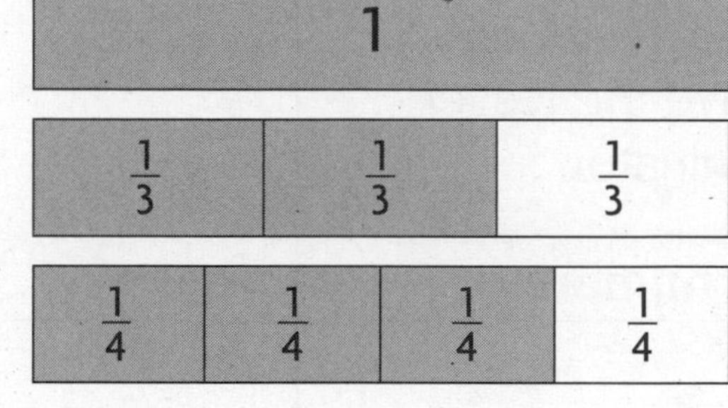

Step 2 Compare the lengths of the models. The length of the $\frac{3}{4}$ model is greater than the length of the $\frac{2}{3}$ model.

$\frac{3}{4}$ (>) $\frac{2}{3}$

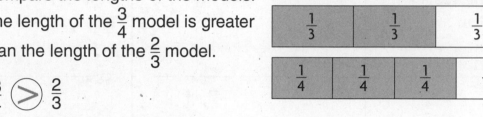

So, Mrs. Young's recipe uses more flour.

Compare $\frac{3}{6}$ and $\frac{4}{6}$. Which is greater?

- The denominators are the same, so compare the numerators.

$3 < 4$, so $\frac{3}{6} < \frac{4}{6}$.

So, $\frac{4}{6}$ is greater than $\frac{3}{6}$. $\frac{4}{6}$ (>) $\frac{3}{6}$

Compare. Write <, >, or =. Write the strategy you used.

1. $\frac{2}{8}$ ◯ $\frac{3}{8}$

____

2. $\frac{7}{8}$ ◯ $\frac{5}{6}$

____

3. $\frac{3}{4}$ ◯ $\frac{3}{6}$

____

4. $\frac{3}{6}$ ◯ $\frac{5}{6}$

____

Name ______________________________

Compare Fractions

Compare. Write <, >, or =. Write the strategy you used.

1. $\frac{3}{8}$ (<) $\frac{3}{4}$

   Think: The numerators are the same. Compare the denominators. The greater fraction will have the lesser denominator.

   same numerator

   ____

2. $\frac{2}{3}$ ◯ $\frac{7}{8}$

   ____

   ____

3. $\frac{3}{4}$ ◯ $\frac{1}{4}$

   ____

   ____

Name a fraction that is less than or greater than the given fraction. Draw to justify your answer.

4. greater than $\frac{1}{3}$ —

5. less than $\frac{3}{4}$ —

Problem Solving REAL WORLD

6. At the third-grade party, two groups each had their own pizza. The blue group ate $\frac{7}{8}$ pizza. The green group ate $\frac{2}{8}$ pizza. Which group ate more of their pizza?

   ____

7. Ben and Antonio both take the same bus to school. Ben's ride is $\frac{7}{8}$ mile. Antonio's ride is $\frac{3}{4}$ mile. Who has a longer bus ride?

   ____

Name ____________________

Lesson 70

COMMON CORE STANDARD CC.3.NF.3d

Lesson Objective: Compare and order fractions by using models and reasoning strategies.

Compare and Order Fractions

You can use a number line to compare and order fractions.

Order $\frac{5}{8}$, $\frac{2}{8}$, and $\frac{7}{8}$ from least to greatest.

Since you are comparing eighths, use a number line divided into eighths.

Step 1 Draw a point on the number line to show $\frac{5}{8}$.

Step 2 Repeat for $\frac{2}{8}$ and $\frac{7}{8}$.

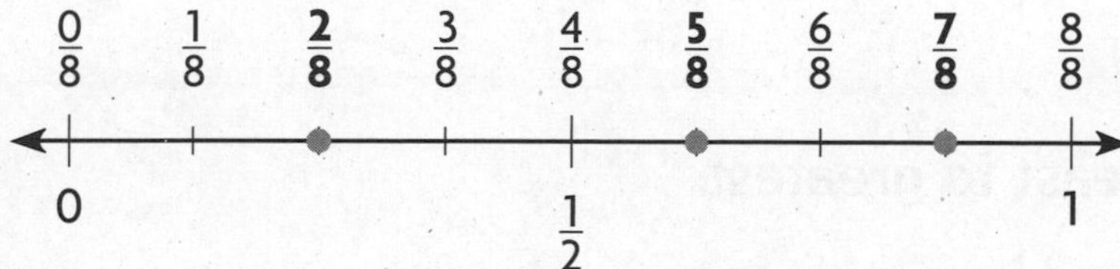

Step 3 Fractions increase in size as you move right on the number line. Write the fractions in order from left to right.

So, the order from least to greatest is $\frac{2}{8}$, $\frac{5}{8}$, $\frac{7}{8}$.

Write the fractions in order from least to greatest.

1. $\frac{4}{6}$, $\frac{6}{6}$, $\frac{3}{6}$

$\frac{0}{6}$ $\frac{1}{6}$ $\frac{2}{6}$ $\frac{3}{6}$ $\frac{4}{6}$ $\frac{5}{6}$ $\frac{6}{6}$

0 $\frac{1}{2}$ 1

____

2. $\frac{2}{3}$, $\frac{2}{6}$, $\frac{2}{4}$

Think: When the numerators are the same, look at the denominators to compare the size of the pieces.

____

3. $\frac{1}{4}$, $\frac{1}{8}$, $\frac{1}{2}$

____

4. $\frac{3}{4}$, $\frac{0}{4}$, $\frac{2}{4}$

____

Name ____________________

Compare and Order Fractions

Write the fractions in order from greatest to least.

1. $\frac{4}{4}, \frac{1}{4}, \frac{3}{4}$ $\frac{4}{4}$, $\frac{3}{4}$, $\frac{1}{4}$

Think: The denominators are the same, so compare the numerators: $4 > 3 > 1$.

2. $\frac{2}{8}, \frac{5}{8}, \frac{1}{8}$ ______, ______, ______

3. $\frac{1}{3}, \frac{1}{6}, \frac{1}{2}$ ______, ______, ______

4. $\frac{2}{3}, \frac{2}{6}, \frac{2}{8}$ ______, ______, ______

Write the fractions in order from least to greatest.

5. $\frac{2}{4}, \frac{4}{4}, \frac{3}{4}$ ______, ______, ______

6. $\frac{4}{6}, \frac{5}{6}, \frac{2}{6}$ ______, ______, ______

7. $\frac{7}{8}, \frac{0}{8}, \frac{3}{8}$ ______, ______, ______

8. $\frac{3}{4}, \frac{3}{6}, \frac{3}{8}$ ______, ______, ______

Problem Solving REAL WORLD

9. Mr. Jackson ran $\frac{7}{8}$ mile on Monday. He ran $\frac{3}{8}$ mile on Wednesday and $\frac{5}{8}$ mile on Friday. On which day did Mr. Jackson run the shortest distance?

____

10. Delia has three pieces of ribbon. Her red ribbon is $\frac{2}{4}$ foot long. Her green ribbon is $\frac{2}{3}$ foot long. Her yellow ribbon is $\frac{2}{6}$ foot long. She wants to use the longest piece for a project. Which color ribbon should Delia use?

____

Name ___________________________

Lesson 71

COMMON CORE STANDARD CC.3.MD.1

Lesson Objective: Read, write, and tell time on analog and digital clocks to the nearest minute.

Time to the Minute

Tommy wants to know what time the clock shows. He also wants to know one way to write the time.

Step 1 Where is the hour hand pointing? What is the hour?
It points just after the 6, so the hour is 6.

Step 2 Where is the minute hand pointing?
It points just after the 3.

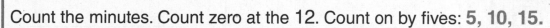

Count the minutes. Count zero at the 12. Count on by fives: **5, 10, 15.**

Then count on by ones: **16, 17.**

So, the time is **6:17**, or **seventeen minutes after six**.

Write the time. Write one way you can read the time.

1.

____

____

____

2.

____

____

____

3.

____

____

____

4.

____

____

____

Name ___

Time to the Minute

Lesson 71
CC.3.MD.1

Write the time. Write one way you can read the time.

1. 

1:16; sixteen minutes after one

2. 

3. 

4. 

5. 

6. 

Write the time another way.

7. 23 minutes after 4

8. 18 minutes before 11

9. 10 minutes before 9

10. 7 minutes after 1

Problem Solving REAL WORLD

11. What time is it when the hour hand is a little past the 3 and the minute hand is pointing to the 3?

12. Pete began practicing at twenty-five minutes before eight. What is another way to write this time?

Name ______________________________

Lesson 72

COMMON CORE STANDARD CC.3.MD.1

Lesson Objective: Decide when to use A.M. and P.M. when telling time to the nearest minute.

A.M. and P.M.

Lori and her father went shopping at the time shown on the clock at the right. How should Lori write the time?
Use A.M. or P.M.

Step 1 Read the time on the clock. **11:30**

Step 2 Decide if the time is A.M. or P.M.

REMEMBER

Write **P.M.** for times after noon and before midnight.

Write **A.M.** for times after midnight and before noon.

Noon is 12:00 in the daytime.

Midnight is 12:00 at night.

Think: Most people go shopping **during the day**.

So, Lori should write the time as **11:30 A.M.**

Write the time for the activity. Use A.M. or P.M.

1. leave school

____

2. eat dinner

____

3. arrive at school

____

4. Mackenzie's violin lesson starts at the time shown on the clock. Write the time using A.M. or P.M.

____

5. The diner opens for breakfast at the time shown on the clock. Write the time using A.M. or P.M.

____

Name ______________________

A.M. and P.M.

Write the time for the activity. Use A.M. or P.M.

1. eat lunch

12:20 P.M.

2. go home after school

3. see the sunrise

4. go for a walk

5. go to school

6. get ready for art class

Write the time. Use A.M. or P.M.

7. 13 minutes after 5:00 in the morning

8. 19 minutes before 9:00 at night

9. quarter before midnight

10. one-half hour after 4:00 in the morning

Problem Solving REAL WORLD

11. Jaime is in math class. What time is it? Use A.M. or P.M.

12. Pete began practicing his trumpet at fifteen minutes past three. Write this time using A.M. or P.M.

Name ______________________

COMMON CORE STANDARD CC.3.MD.1

Lesson Objective: Use a number line or an analog clock to measure time intervals in minutes.

Measure Time Intervals

Julia starts her homework at 4:20 P.M. She finishes at 5:00 P.M. How much time does Julia spend doing homework?

Elapsed time is the amount of time that passes from the start of an activity to the end of the activity.

Use a number line to find elapsed time.

Step 1 Begin with the start time, **4:20**.

Step 2 Skip count **by tens** to count the minutes from 4:20 to 5:00.

Step 3 Label the number line. Draw jumps for every 10 minutes until you get to 5:00.

10 + 10 + 10 + 10 = 40 minutes

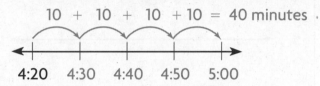

4:20 4:30 4:40 4:50 5:00

Step 4 Add the minutes that have elapsed. **40 minutes**

So, Julia spends **40 minutes** doing homework.

Use the number line to find the elapsed time.

1. Start: 3:15 P.M. End: 3:45 P.M.

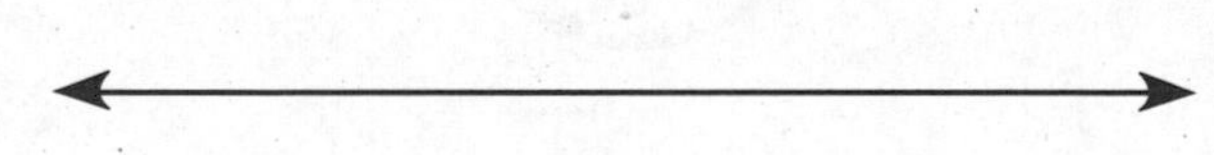

____

2. Start: 11:05 A.M. End: 11:56 A.M.

____

Find the elapsed time.

3. Start: 4:10 P.M. End: 4:46 P.M.

____

4. Start: 10:30 A.M. End: 10:59 A.M.

____

Name ______________________________

Lesson 73
CC.3.MD.1

Measure Time Intervals

Find the elapsed time.

1. Start: 8:10 A.M. End: 8:45 A.M.

35 minutes

2. Start: 6:45 P.M. End: 6:54 P.M.

____

3. Start: 3:00 P.M. End: 3:37 P.M.

____

4. Start: 10:05 A.M. End: 10:21 A.M.

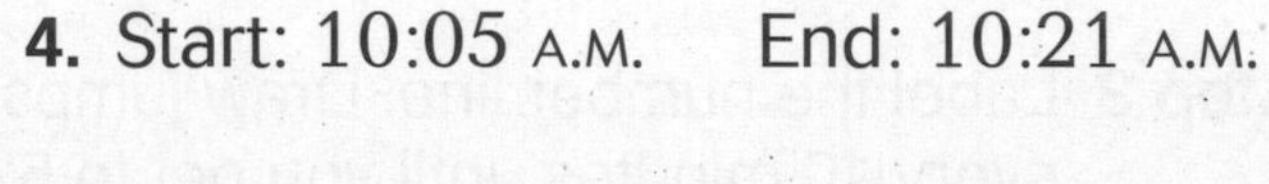

____

5. Start: 7:30 A.M. End: 7:53 A.M.

____

6. Start: 5:20 A.M. End: 5:47 A.M.

____

Problem Solving

7. A show at the museum starts at 7:40 P.M. and ends at 7:57 P.M. How long is the show?

____

8. The first train leaves the station at 6:15 A.M. The second train leaves at 6:55 A.M. How much later does the second train leave the station?

____

Name ___________________________________

Lesson 74

COMMON CORE STANDARD CC.3.MD.1

Lesson Objective: Use a number line or an analog clock to add or subtract time intervals to find starting times or ending times.

Use Time Intervals

You can use a number line to find the starting time when you know the ending time and the elapsed time.

The ending time is 4:05 P.M. Use the number line to find the starting time if the elapsed time is 35 minutes.

Step 1

Find the ending time on the number line.

Think: The ending time is 4:05 P.M.

Step 2

Jump back 5 minutes.

Think: Jump back 5 minutes to get to the hour.

You jump back to **4:00 P.M.**

Step 3

Jump back 30 minutes.

Think: Jump back 30 minutes to get to a total of 35 minutes.

You jump back to **3:30 P.M.**

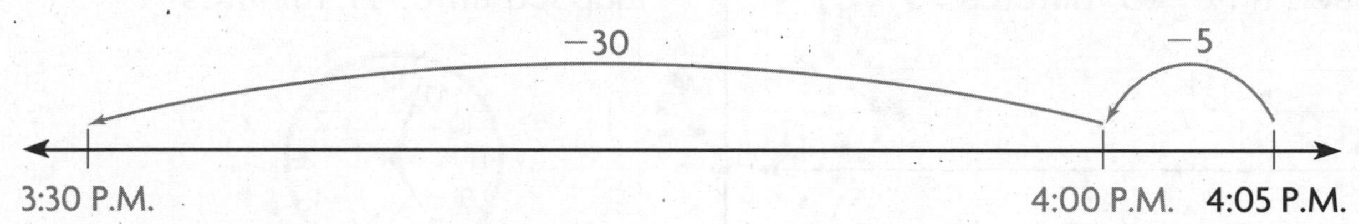

So, the starting time is **3:30 P.M.**

1. Use the number line to find the starting time if the elapsed time is 25 minutes. ____________

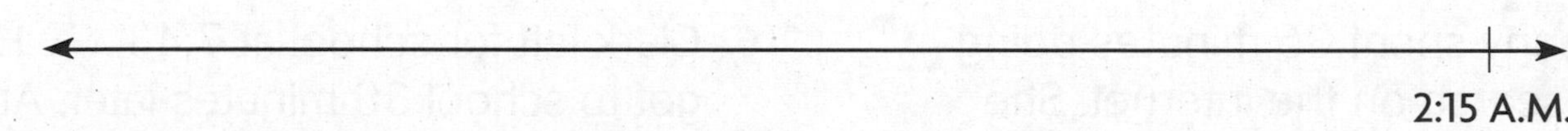

2. Use the number line to find the starting time if the elapsed time is 45 minutes. ____________

6:00 P.M.

Name ______________________

Use Time Intervals

Find the starting time.

1. Ending time: 4:29 P.M.
   Elapsed time: 55 minutes

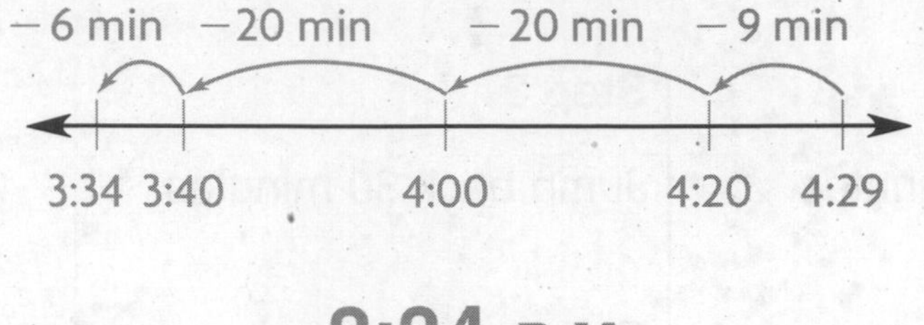

3:34 P.M.

2. Ending time: 10:08 A.M.
   Elapsed time: 30 minutes

____

Find the ending time.

3. Starting time: 2:15 A.M.
   Elapsed time: 45 minutes

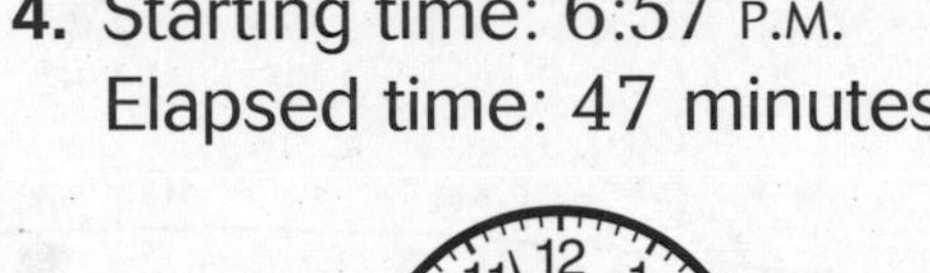

____

4. Starting time: 6:57 P.M.
   Elapsed time: 47 minutes

____

Problem Solving

5. Jenny spent 35 minutes doing research on the Internet. She finished at 7:10 P.M. At what time did Jenny start her research?

____

6. Clark left for school at 7:43 A.M. He got to school 36 minutes later. At what time did Clark get to school?

____

Name ______________________

Lesson 75

COMMON CORE STANDARD CC.3.MD.1

Lesson Objective: Solve problems involving addition and subtraction of time intervals by using the strategy *draw a diagram*.

Problem Solving • Time Intervals

As soon as Carter got home, he worked on his book report for 45 minutes. Then he did chores for 30 minutes. He finished at 5:15 P.M. At what time did Carter get home?

Read the Problem	Solve the Problem
What do I need to find? I need to find what <u>time</u> Carter got <u>home</u>.	• Find Carter's 5:15 P.M. finishing time on the number line. • Count back 30 minutes using two 15-minute jumps to find the time Carter started his chores. <u>4:45 P.M.</u> −15 min −15 min 4:45 5:00 5:15 P.M.
What information do I need to use? Carter worked for <u>45 minutes</u> on his report. He did chores for <u>30 minutes</u>. He finished at <u>5:15 P.M.</u>.	• Count back 45 minutes for the time Carter worked on his report. The jumps end at <u>4:00 P.M.</u> −45 min −15 min −15 min 4:00 4:45 5:00 5:15 P.M.
How will I use the information? I will use a number line and count back to find the time Carter got home.	So, Carter got home at <u>4:00 P.M.</u>

1. Kiera must be at school at 7:45 A.M. The ride to school takes 15 minutes. She needs 45 minutes to eat breakfast and get ready. At what time should Kiera get up?

____

2. Jack and his family go to the movies. First, they eat lunch at 1:30 P.M. It takes them 40 minutes to eat. Then they drive 25 minutes to get to the movie theater. At what time do Jack and his family get to the theater?

____

Name ______________________

Problem Solving • Time Intervals

Solve each problem. Show your work.

1. Hannah wants to meet her friends downtown. Before leaving home, she does chores for 60 minutes and eats lunch for 20 minutes. The walk downtown takes 15 minutes. Hannah starts her chores at 11:45 A.M. At what time does she meet her friends?

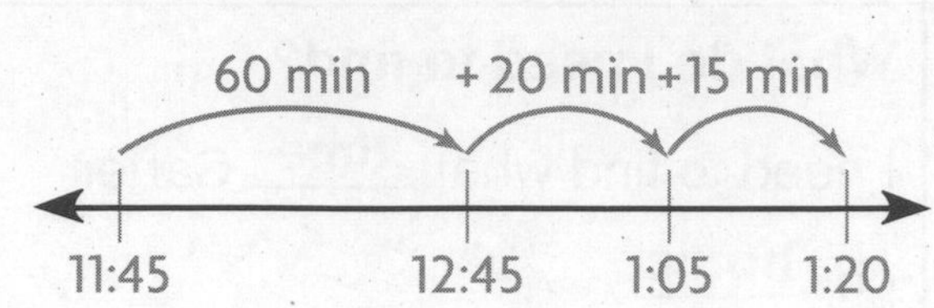

1:20 P.M.

2. Katie practiced the flute for 45 minutes. Then she ate a snack for 15 minutes. Next, she watched television for 30 minutes, until 6:00 P.M. At what time did Katie start practicing the flute?

____

3. Nick gets out of school at 2:25 P.M. He has a 15-minute ride home on the bus. Next, he goes on a 30-minute bike ride. Then he spends 55 minutes doing homework. At what time does Nick finish his homework?

____

4. The third-grade class is going on a field trip by bus to the museum. The bus leaves the school at 9:45 A.M. The bus ride takes 47 minutes. At what time does the bus arrive at the museum?

____

Name ______________________________

COMMON CORE STANDARD CC.3.MD.2

Lesson Objective: Estimate and measure liquid volume in liters.

Estimate and Measure Liquid Volume

Liquid volume is the amount of liquid in a container. You can measure liquid volume using the metric unit **liter** (L).

A water bottle holds about 1 liter. Estimate how much liquid a plastic cup and a fish bowl will hold. Then write the containers in order from the greatest to least liquid volume.

A plastic cup holds **less than 1 liter**.

A water bottle holds about 1 liter.

A fish bowl holds **more than 1 liter**.

Think: A plastic cup is *smaller* than a water bottle.

Think: A fish bowl is *larger* than a water bottle.

So, the order of the containers from greatest to least liquid volume is **fish bowl**, **water bottle**, **plastic cup**.

1. A wading pool is filled with water. Is the amount *more than 1 liter, about 1 liter,* or *less than 1 liter*?

____

Estimate how much liquid volume there will be when the container is filled. Write *more than 1 liter*, *about 1 liter*, or *less than 1 liter*.

2. vase

____

3. mug

____

4. bathtub

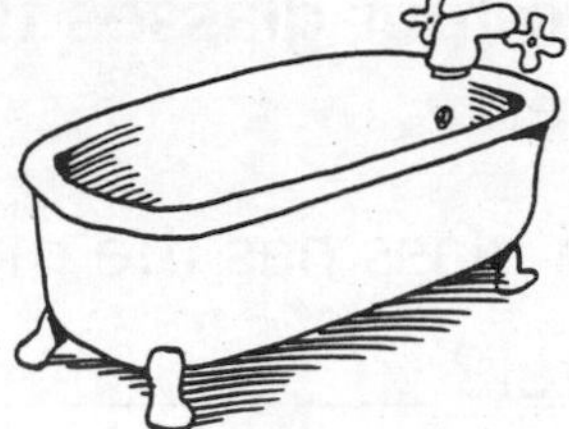

____

Name ________________________________

Estimate and Measure Liquid Volume

Estimate how much liquid volume there will be when the container is filled. Write *more than 1 liter, about 1 liter,* or *less than 1 liter.*

1. large milk container

more than 1 liter

2. small milk container

____

3. water bottle

____

4. spoonful of water

____

5. bathtub filled halfway

____

6. filled eyedropper

____

Problem Solving REAL WORLD

Use the pictures for 7–8. Alan pours water into four glasses that are the same size.

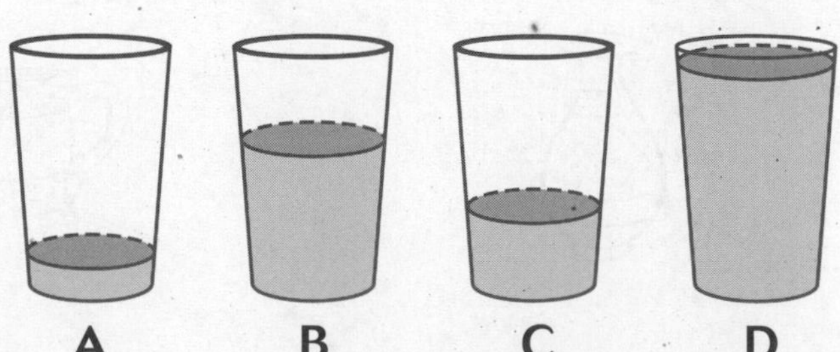

7. Which glass has the most amount of water? ____________

8. Which glass has the least amount of water? ____________

Name ______________________________

Lesson 78

COMMON CORE STANDARD CC.3.MD.2

Lesson Objective: Add, subtract, multiply, or divide to solve problems involving liquid volumes or masses.

Solve Problems About Liquid Volume and Mass

You can use a model or write an equation to solve problems about liquid volume and mass.

Tina's watering can holds 4 liters of water. Todd's watering can holds 6 liters of water. What is the total liquid volume of both watering cans?

Tina's Watering Can

Todd's Watering Can

Use a bar model.

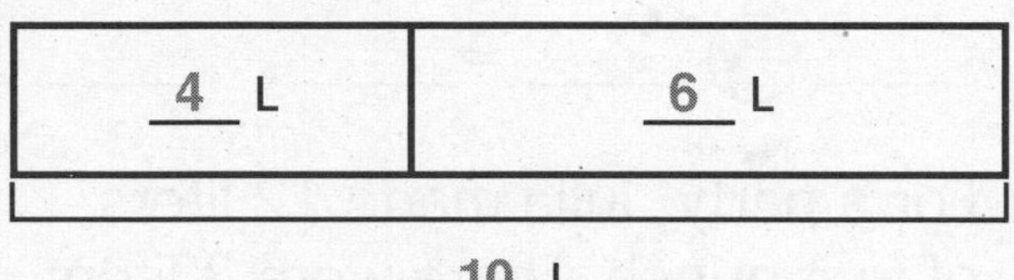

Think: Add to find the total.

4 L + 6 L = **10** L

So, the total liquid volume is 10 L.

Write an equation.

Think: I can write an addition equation to find the sum of the liquid volumes.

4 (+) 6 = 10

So, the total liquid volume is 10 L.

Write an equation and solve the problem.

1. Kyra has a small bucket that holds 3 liters of water and a large bucket that holds 5 liters of water. Altogether, how many liters of water do the two buckets hold?

2. Rick's recipe calls for 25 grams of raisins and 40 grams of nuts. How many more grams of nuts than raisins does the recipe call for?

___ ◯ ___ = ___ __________

Name ______________________________

Lesson 78

CC.3.MD.2

Solve Problems About Liquid Volume and Mass

Write an equation and solve the problem.

1. Luis was served 145 grams of meat and 217 grams of vegetables at a meal. What was the total mass of the meat and the vegetables?

Think: Add to find how much in all.

145 (+) 217 = _____ _______

2. The gas tank of a riding mower holds 5 liters of gas. How many 5-liter gas tanks can you fill from a full 20-liter gas can?

_____ ◯ _____ = _____ _______

3. To make a lemon-lime drink, Mac mixed 4 liters of lemonade with 2 liters of limeade. How much lemon-lime drink did Mac make?

_____ ◯ _____ = _____ _______

4. A nickel has a mass of 5 grams. There are 40 nickels in a roll of nickels. What is the mass of a roll of nickels?

_____ ◯ _____ = _____ _______

5. Four families share a basket of 16 kilograms of apples equally. How many kilograms of apples does each family get?

_____ ◯ _____ = _____ _______

6. For a party, Julia made 12 liters of fruit punch. There were 3 liters of fruit punch left after the party. How much fruit punch did the people drink at the party?

_____ ◯ _____ = _____ _______

Problem Solving REAL WORLD

7. Zoe's fish tank holds 27 liters of water. She uses a 3-liter container to fill the tank. How many times does she have to fill the 3-liter container in order to fill her fish tank?

____

8. Adrian's backpack has a mass of 15 kilograms. Theresa's backpack has a mass of 8 kilograms. What is the total mass of both backpacks?

____

Name ______________________________

Lesson 79

COMMON CORE STANDARD CC.3.MD.3

Lesson Objective: Organize data in tables and solve problems using the strategy *make a table.*

Problem Solving • Organize Data

One way to show data is in a tally table. Another way to show data is in a frequency table. A **frequency table** uses numbers to record data.

The students in Jake's class voted for their favorite sport. How many more students chose soccer than chose baseball?

Favorite Sport	
Sport	**Tally**
Soccer	𝍸 IIII
Baseball	𝍸 I
Football	IIII

Read the Problem	Solve the Problem
What do I need to find? **How many more students chose soccer than chose baseball?** **What information do I need to use?** **the data about favorite sport from the tally table** **How will I use the information?** **I will count the tally marks. Then I will write the number of tally marks for each sport in the frequency table.** **Next, I will subtract to compare the votes for soccer and the votes for baseball.**	Count the tally marks for each sport. Write the numbers in the frequency table. **Think:** I = 1 vote 𝍸 = 5 votes Soccer has **1** 𝍸 and **4** I, so write 9 in the frequency table. **Favorite Sport** Sport — Number Soccer — 9 Baseball — 6 Football — 4 Subtract to find how many more students chose soccer than chose baseball. 9 − 6 = **3** So, **3** more students chose soccer than chose baseball as their favorite sport.

1. How many students chose football and baseball combined?

   ____

2. How many fewer students chose football than chose soccer?

   ____

Name ____________________

Problem Solving • Organize Data

Use the Favorite School Subject tables for 1–4.

1. The students in two third-grade classes recorded their favorite school subject. The data are in the tally table. How many fewer students chose science than chose social studies as their favorite school subject?

Favorite School Subject	
Subject	**Tally**
Math	~~IIII~~ ~~IIII~~ I
Science	~~IIII~~
Language Arts	~~IIII~~ II
Reading	~~IIII~~ IIII
Social Studies	~~IIII~~ ~~IIII~~ II

Think: Use the data in the tally table to record the data in the frequency table. Then solve the problem.

social studies: 12 students

science: 5 students

12 – 5 = 7

So, 7 fewer students chose science.

Favorite School Subject	
Subject	**Number**
Math	
Science	5
Language Arts	
Reading	
Social Studies	12

2. What subject did the least number of students choose?

____

3. How many more students chose math than language arts as their favorite subject?

_____ more students

4. Suppose 3 students changed their vote from math to science. Describe how the frequency table would change.

____

____

____

____

____

Name ________________________

Lesson 80

COMMON CORE STANDARD CC.3.MD.3

Lesson Objective: Read and interpret data in a scaled picture graph.

Use Picture Graphs

A **picture graph** shows information using small pictures or symbols.

A **key** tells what the symbol stands for. A symbol can stand for more than 1.

Which state in the picture graph below has 9 national park areas?

The key for the picture graph shows that each 🌲 = **6** national park areas.

Count the number of 🌲 next to each state.

Oregon has one tree picture and half of a tree picture.

Think:
🌲 = 6 park areas
half 🌲 = 3 park areas

National Park Areas

Michigan	🌲
Minnesota	🌲
Missouri	🌲 🌲
New York	🌲 🌲 🌲 🌲 🌲
Oregon	🌲 half 🌲

Key: Each 🌲 = 6 national park areas.

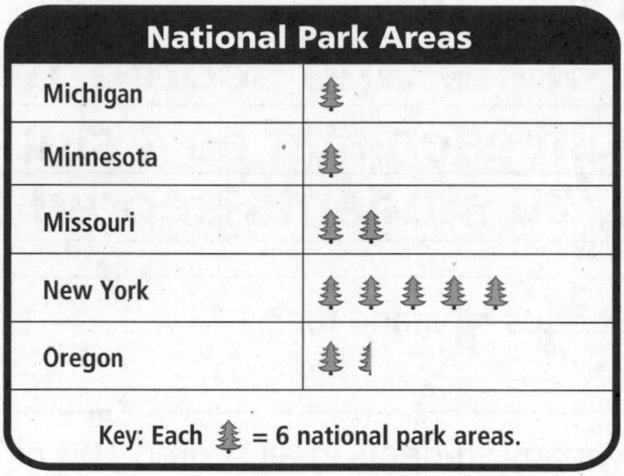

So, **Oregon** has 9 national park areas.

Use the Favorite Ice Pop Flavor picture graph for 1–4.

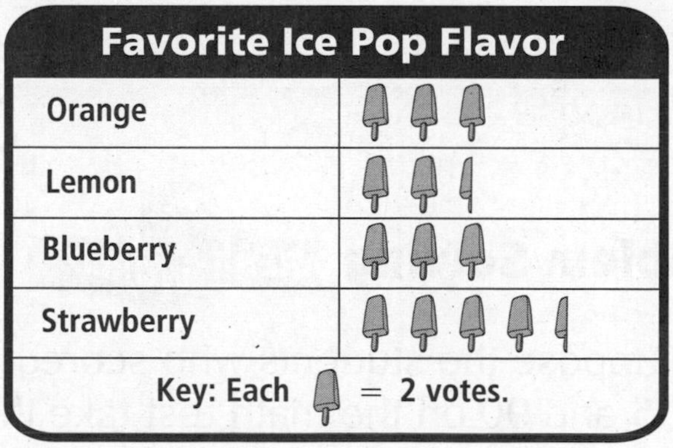

Favorite Ice Pop Flavor

Orange	🍦 🍦 🍦
Lemon	🍦 🍦 half 🍦
Blueberry	🍦 🍦 🍦
Strawberry	🍦 🍦 🍦 🍦 half 🍦

Key: Each 🍦 = 2 votes.

1. How many people chose orange?

____

2. How many people chose lemon?

____

3. How many fewer people chose lemon than chose strawberry?

____

4. How many people in all were surveyed?

____

Name ______________________

Use Picture Graphs

Use the Math Test Scores picture graph for 1–7.

Mrs. Perez made a picture graph of her students' scores on a math test.

Math Test Scores	
100	★★★★★
95	★★★
90	★★★½
85	★
Key: Each ★ = 4 students.	

1. How many students scored 100? How can you find the answer?

To find the number of students who scored 100, count each star as 4 students. So, 20 students scored 100.

2. What does ½★ stand for?

____

3. How many students in all scored 100 or 95?

____

4. How many more students scored 90 than 85?

____

5. How many students in all took the test?

____

Problem Solving

6. Suppose the students who scored 85 and 90 on the math test take the test again and score 95. How many stars would you have to add to the picture graph next to 95?

____

7. If 2 more students took the math test and both made a score of 80, what would the picture graph look like?

____

Name ___________________________

Lesson 81

COMMON CORE STANDARD CC.3.MD.3

Lesson Objective: Draw a scaled picture graph to show data in a table.

Make Picture Graphs

Use the data in this table to make a picture graph.

Number of Ball Caps Sold	
Basketball Game	**Caps**
Falcons and Mustangs	20
Sharks and Bulldogs	30
Hawks and Comets	5
Rams and Cardinals	15

Step 1 Write the title.

Step 2 Write the names of the games.

Step 3 Decide what number each picture will represent. You can count by fives to find the number of caps sold, so let each [cap] represent 5 caps.

Step 4 Draw one cap for every 5 caps sold during each game. There were 20 caps sold during the Falcons and Mustangs game. Count to 20 by fives. 5, 10, 15, 20. So, 4 caps should be drawn. Draw the caps for the rest of the games.

Number of Ball Caps Sold	
Falcons and Mustangs	[cap] [cap] [cap] [cap]
Sharks and Bulldogs	
Hawks and Comets	
Rams and Cardinals	

Key: Each [cap] = 5 caps.

Use your picture graph above for 1–3.

1. During which game were the most ball caps sold?

____

2. How many pictures would you draw if 45 ball caps were sold in a game?

____

3. During which two games were a total of 25 caps sold?

____

Name ______________________

Make Picture Graphs

Ben asked his classmates about their favorite kind of TV show. He recorded their responses in a frequency table. Use the data in the table to make a picture graph.

Favorite TV Show	
Type	**Number**
Cartoons	9
Sports	6
Movies	3

Follow the steps to make a picture graph.

Step 1 Write the title at the top of the graph.

Step 2 Look at the numbers in the table. Tell how many students each picture represents for the key.

Step 3 Draw the correct number of pictures for each type of show.

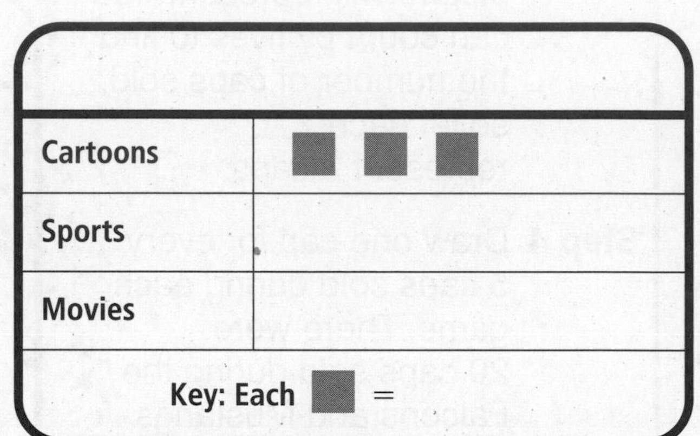

Use your picture graph for 1–5.

1. What title did you give the graph?

____

2. What key did you use?

____

3. How many pictures did you use to represent sports?

____

Problem Solving REAL WORLD

4. How many pictures would you draw if 12 students chose game shows as their favorite kind of TV show?

____

5. What key would you use if 10 students chose cartoons?

____

Name ______________________________

COMMON CORE STANDARD CC.3.MD.3

Lesson Objective: Read and interpret data in a scaled bar graph.

Use Bar Graphs

How many Olympic medals did Norway win in the 2008 Summer Olympics?

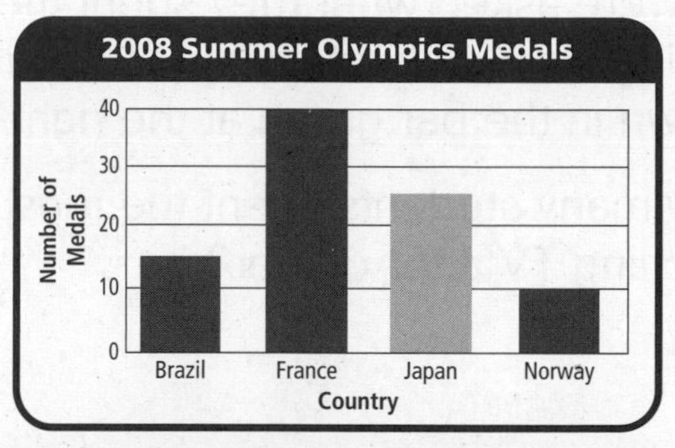

- Both bar graphs show the same data about Olympic medals. The top graph is a **vertical bar graph**. The bottom graph is a **horizontal bar graph**.

- Find Norway on the vertical bar graph and follow the bar to its end. Then follow the end across to the scale to find the number of medals. 10 medals.

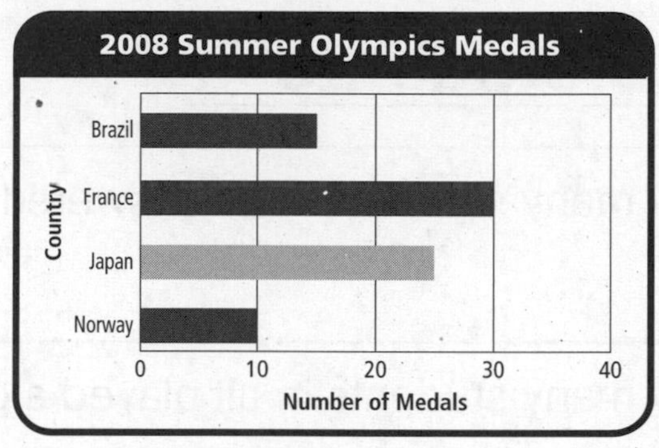

- Find Norway on the horizontal bar graph and follow the bar to its end. Then follow the end down to the scale to find the number of medals. 10 medals.

So, Norway won 10 medals.

Use the Favorite Type of Book bar graph for 1–4.

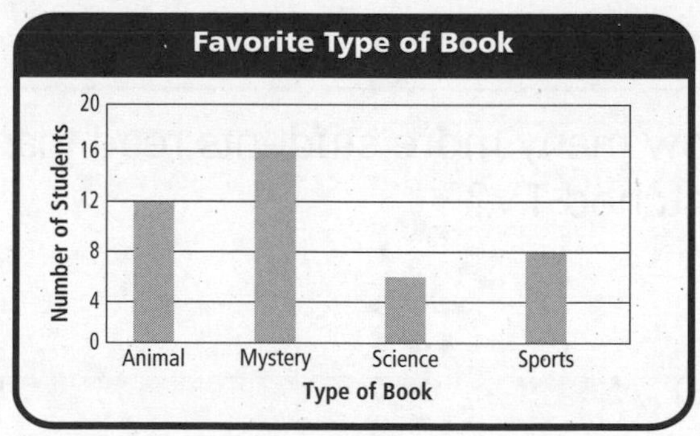

1. Which type of book did the most students choose?

____

2. Which type of book received 4 fewer votes than mystery?

____

3. Did more students choose books about mystery or books about science and sports together?

____

4. How many students in all answered the survey?

____

Name ____________________

Use Bar Graphs

Lesson 82
CC.3.MD.3

Use the After-Dinner Activities bar graph for 1–6.

The third-grade students at Case Elementary School were asked what they spent the most time doing last week after dinner. The results are shown in the bar graph at the right.

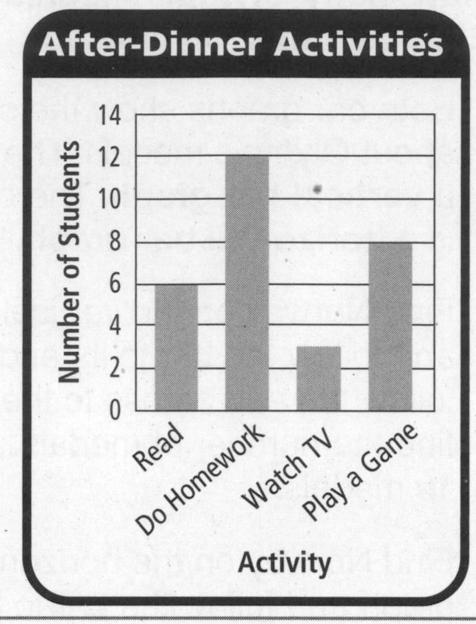

1. How many students spent the most time watching TV after dinner?

3 students

2. How many students in all answered the survey? ____________

3. How many students in all played a game or read? ____________

4. How many fewer students read than did homework? ____________

5. How many more students read than watched TV? ____________

Problem Solving REAL WORLD

6. Suppose 3 students changed their answers to reading instead of doing homework. Where would the bar for reading end?

____

Name ______________________________

Lesson Objective: Draw a scaled bar graph to show data in a table or picture graph.

Make Bar Graphs

Use data in a table to make a bar graph.

Favorite Winter Activity	
Sport	**Number of Votes**
Ice Skating	17
Skiing	14
Sledding	12
Snowboarding	3

Step 1 Write the title for the bar graph.

Step 2 Label the side and the bottom.

Step 3 Write the names of the sports.

Step 4 Choose a scale for your graph.

- The scale must be able to show the least number, 3, and the greatest number, 17.
- The numbers must be equally spaced. Start with 0 and count by twos until you reach 18.

Step 5 Draw the bar for ice skating. The bar will end halfway between 16 and 18 at 17.

Step 6 Then use the results in the table to draw the rest of the bars.

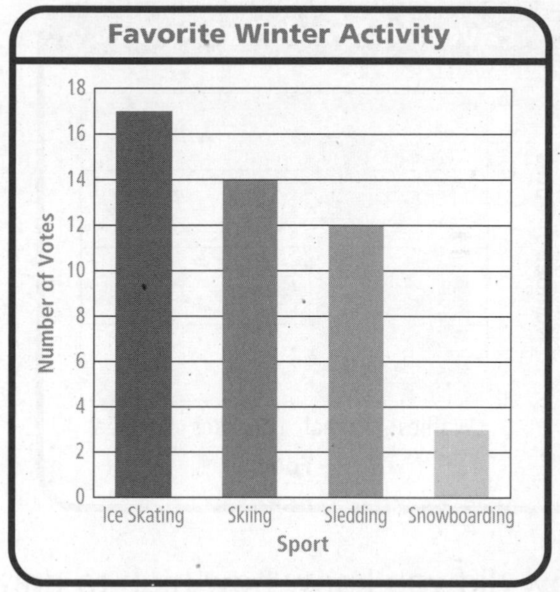

Use the results in the table to make a bar graph.

Favorite Summer Sport	
Sport	**Number of Votes**
Swimming	15
Inline Skating	10
Cycling	20

Name ____________________

Lesson 83
CC.3.MD.3

Make Bar Graphs

Ben asked some friends to name their favorite breakfast food. He recorded their choices in the frequency table at the right.

Favorite Breakfast Food	
Food	**Number of Votes**
Waffles	8
Cereal	14
Pancakes	12
Oatmeal	4

1. Complete the bar graph by using Ben's data.

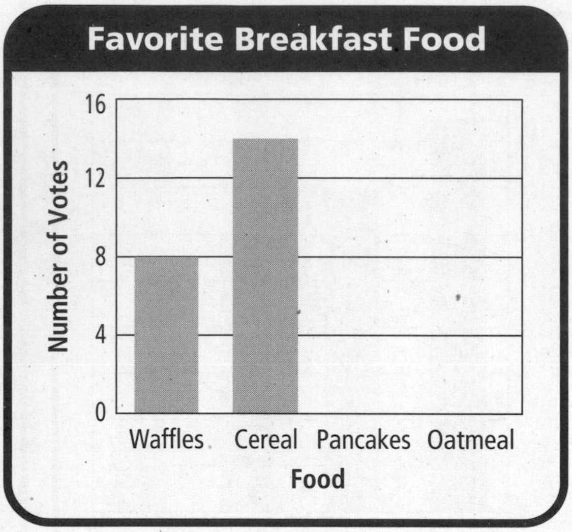

Use your bar graph for 2–5.

2. Which food did the most people choose as their favorite breakfast food?

____

3. How many people chose waffles as their favorite breakfast food?

____

4. How did you know how high to draw the bar for pancakes?

____

____

____

5. Suppose 6 people chose oatmeal as their favorite breakfast food. How would you change the bar graph?

____

____

____

____

Name ______________________________

Lesson 84

COMMON CORE STANDARD CC.3.MD.3

Lesson Objective: Solve one- and two-step compare problems using data represented in scaled bar graphs.

Solve Problems Using Data

You can use a model or write a number sentence to help you answer questions about data.

The bar graph shows the different ways students use the computer center after school. How many more students use the computer center for projects than for games?

One Way Use a model.

Find the bar for projects. The bar ends at 12. So, **12** students use the computer center for projects.

Find the bar for games. The bar ends halfway between 4 and 6. So, **5** students use the computer center for games. Count back along the scale from 12 to 5 to find the difference. The difference is 7 students.

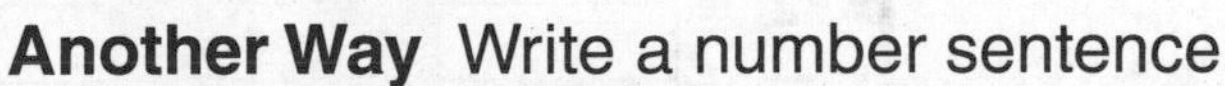

Another Way Write a number sentence.

Subtract to compare the number of students.
Think: There are 12 students who work on projects.
There are 5 students who play games.

$12 - 5 = 7$

So, **7** more students use the computer center for projects than for games.

Use the Computer Center bar graph for 1–3.

1. How many more students use the computer center for homework than for email? _____ more students

2. How many fewer students use the computer center for games than for homework? _____ fewer students

3. Do more students use the computer center for projects or for email and games combined? **Explain.** ______________________________

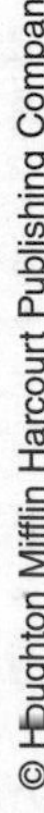

Name ______________________

Solve Problems Using Data

Use the Favorite Hot Lunch bar graph for 1–3.

1. How many more students chose pizza than chose grilled cheese?

   Think: Subtract the number of students who chose grilled cheese, 2, from the number of students who chose pizza, 11.

   $11 - 2 = 9$ _____ more students

2. How many students did not choose chicken patty? _____ students

3. How many fewer students chose grilled cheese than chose hot dog?

   _____ fewer students

Use the Ways to Get to School bar graph for 4–7.

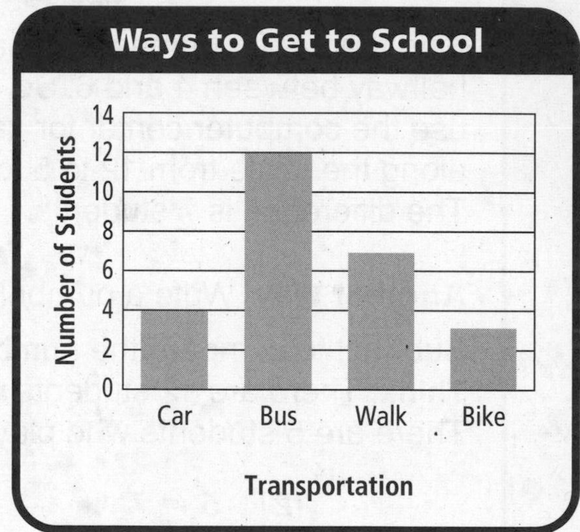

4. How many more students walk than ride in a car to get to school?

   _____ more students

5. How many students walk and ride a bike combined?

   _____ students

Problem Solving REAL WORLD

6. Is the number of students who get to school by car and bus greater than or less than the number of students who get to school by walking and biking? **Explain.**

   ____

   ____

7. **What if** 5 more students respond that they get to school by biking? Would more students walk or ride a bike to school? **Explain.**

   ____

   ____

   ____

Name ______________________

COMMON CORE STANDARD CC.3.MD.4

Lesson Objective: Read and interpret data in a line plot and use data to make a line plot.

Use and Make Line Plots

A **line plot** uses marks to record each piece of data above a number line.

Louise measured the heights of tomato plants in her garden. She recorded the height of each plant.

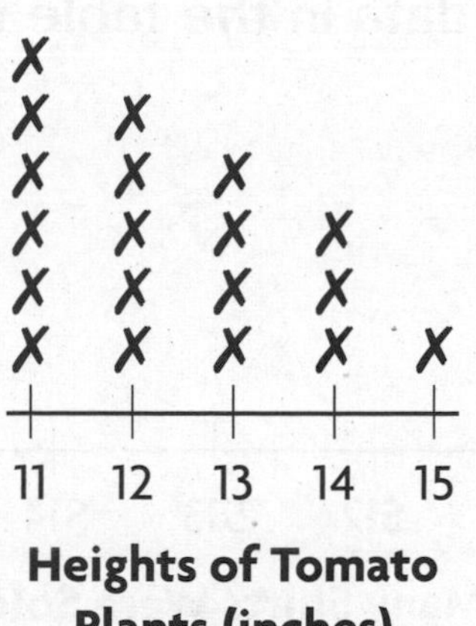

How many tomato plants are there?

Each ✗ stands for 1 plant.

Count all the ✗s. There are 19 in all.

This tells the total number of plants.

How many plants are taller than 13 inches?

Add the number of ✗s for 14 and 15.

3 plants are 14 inches tall. 1 plant is 15 inches tall.

$3 + 1 = 4$ So, 4 plants are taller than 13 inches.

Use the Spelling Test Scores line plot for 1–3.

1. Which test score did the most students receive?

____

2. How many more students scored 90 than 100?

____

3. How many students in all took the spelling test?

____

Name ______________________

Use and Make Line Plots

Lesson 85
CC.3.MD.4

Use the data in the table to make a line plot.

How Many Shirts Were Sold at Each Price?	
Price	**Number Sold**
$11	1
$12	4
$13	6
$14	4
$15	0
$16	2

$11 $12 $13 $14 $15 $16

How Many Shirts Were Sold at Each Price?

1. How many shirts sold for $12?

   4 shirts

2. At which price were the most shirts sold?

   ____

3. How many shirts in all were sold?

   ____

4. How many shirts were sold for $13 or more?

   ____

Problem Solving REAL WORLD

Use the line plot above for 5–6.

5. Were more shirts sold for less than $13 or more than $13? **Explain.**

   ____

6. Is there any price for which there are no data? **Explain.**

   ____

   ____

Name ______________________

Lesson 86

COMMON CORE STANDARD CC.3.MD.4

Lesson Objective: Measure length to the nearest half or fourth inch and use measurement data to make a line plot.

Measure Length

You can measure length to the nearest half or fourth inch.

Use a ruler to measure lines A–C to the nearest half inch.

A

B

C

Step 1 Line up the left end of Line A with the zero mark on the ruler.

Step 2 The right end of Line A is between the half-inch marks for $\underline{1}$ and $\underline{1\frac{1}{2}}$.

The mark that is closest to the right end is for $\underline{1\frac{1}{2}}$ inches.

So, the length of Line A to the nearest half inch is $\underline{1\frac{1}{2}}$ inches.

Repeat Steps 1 and 2 for lines B and C.

The length of Line B to the nearest half inch is $\underline{2\frac{1}{2}}$ inches.

The length of Line C to the nearest half inch is $\underline{3}$ inches.

Measure the length to the nearest half inch. Is the crayon closest to $1\frac{1}{2}$ inches, 2 inches, or $2\frac{1}{2}$ inches?

1. ______ inches

2. ______ inches

Name ________________________

Measure Length

Measure the length to the nearest half inch.

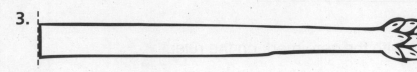

1. $1\frac{1}{2}$ inches

2. ______ inches

3. ______ inches

Measure the length to the nearest fourth inch.

4. ______ inches

5. ______ inches

6. ______ inch

7. ______ inches

Problem Solving

Use a separate sheet of paper for 8.

8. Draw 8 lines that are between 1 inch and 3 inches long. Measure each line to the nearest fourth inch, and make a line plot.

9. The tail on Alex's dog is $5\frac{1}{4}$ inches long. This length is between which two inch-marks on a ruler?

____

Name ______________________

Lesson 87

COMMON CORE STANDARDS CC.3.MD.5, CC.3.MD.5a

Lesson Objective: Explore perimeter and area as attributes of polygons.

Understand Area

A **unit square** is a square with a side length of 1 unit. **Area** is the measure of the number of unit squares needed to cover a surface. A **square unit** is used to measure area.

What is the area of the shape?

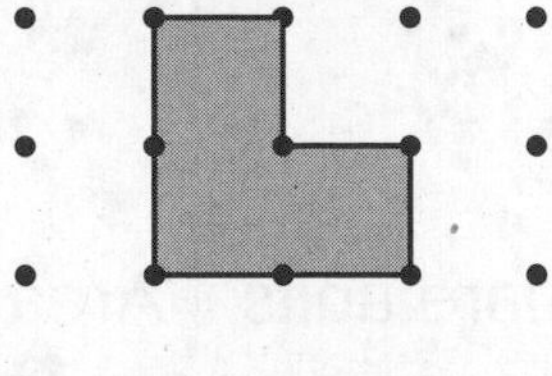

Step 1 Draw lines to show each unit square in the shape.

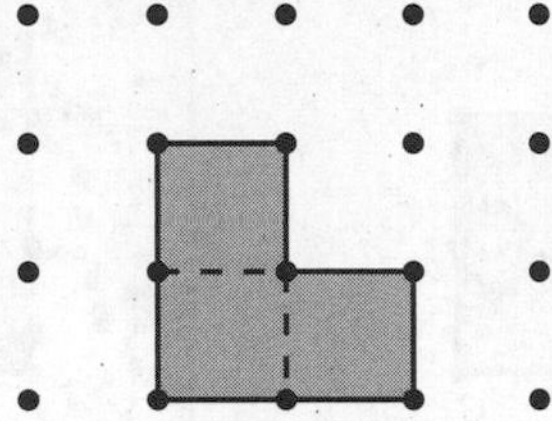

Step 2 Count the number of unit squares to find the area.

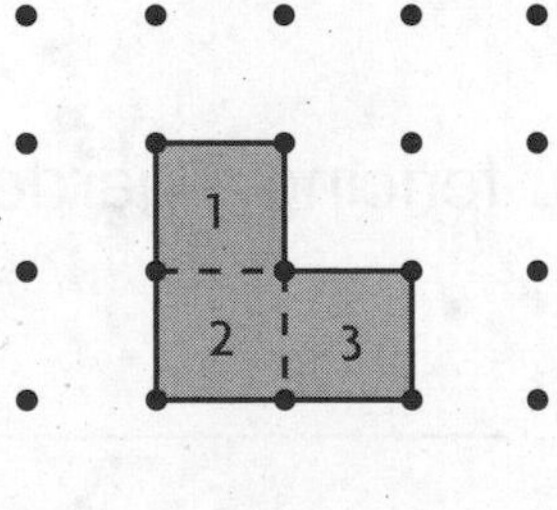

The area of the shape is **3** square units.

Count to find the area of the shape.

1.

Area = ____ square units

2.

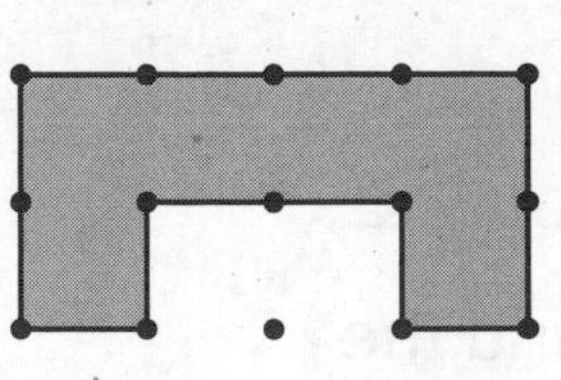

Area = ____ square units

3.

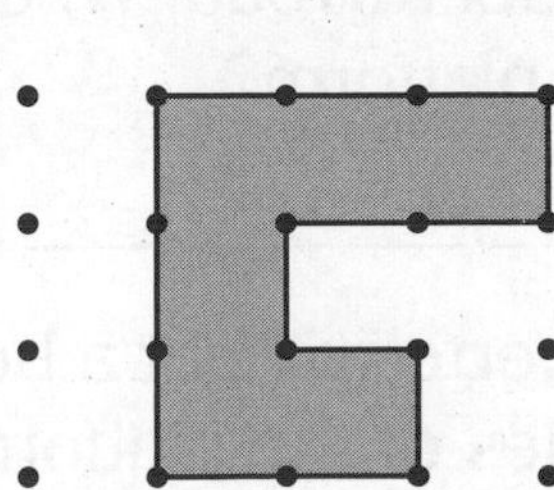

Area = ____ square units

Name ______________________

Understand Area

Count to find the area of the shape.

1. 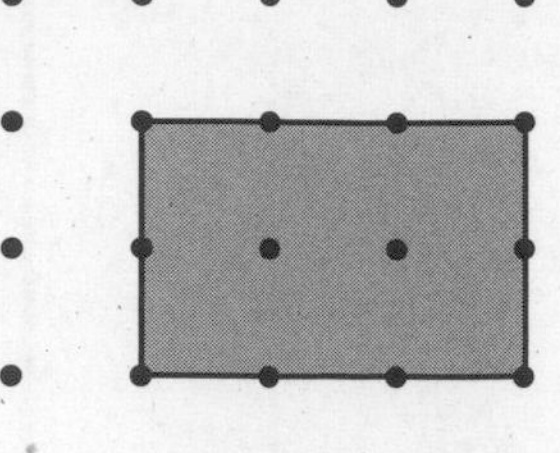

Area = 6 square units

2. 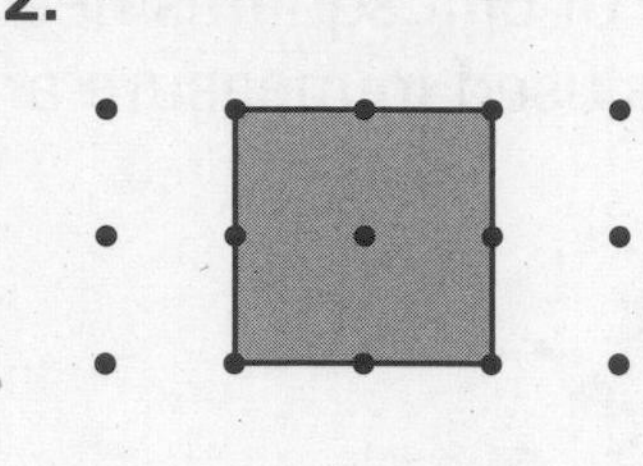

Area = ____ square units

3. 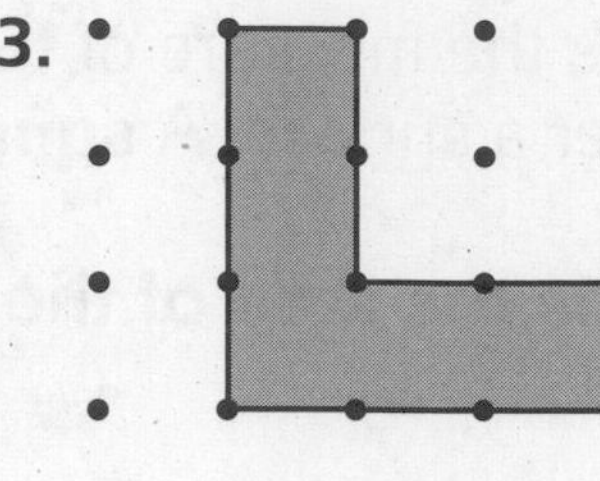

Area = ____ square units

4. 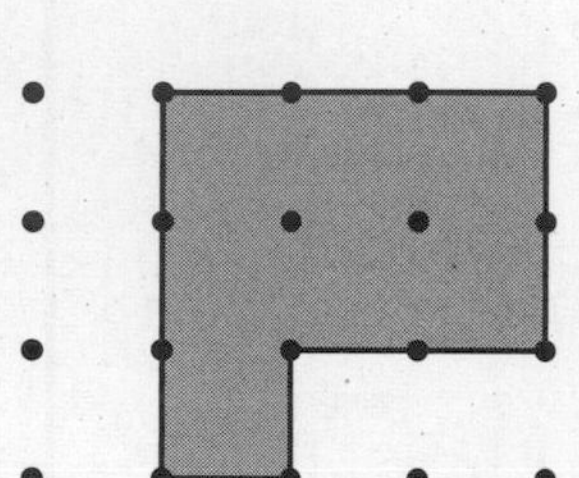

Area = ____ square units

5. 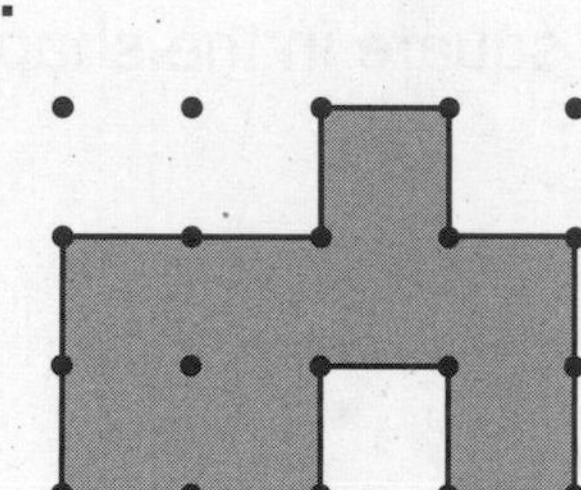

Area = ____ square units

6. 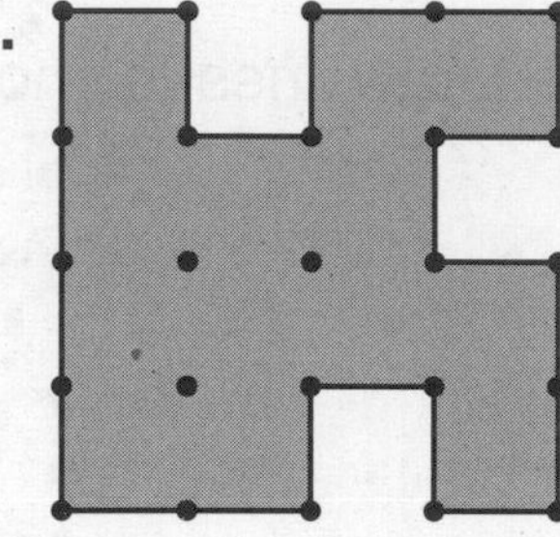

Area = ____ square units

Write *area* or *perimeter* for each situation.

7. carpeting a floor

____

8. fencing a garden

____

Problem Solving REAL WORLD

Use the diagram for 9–10.

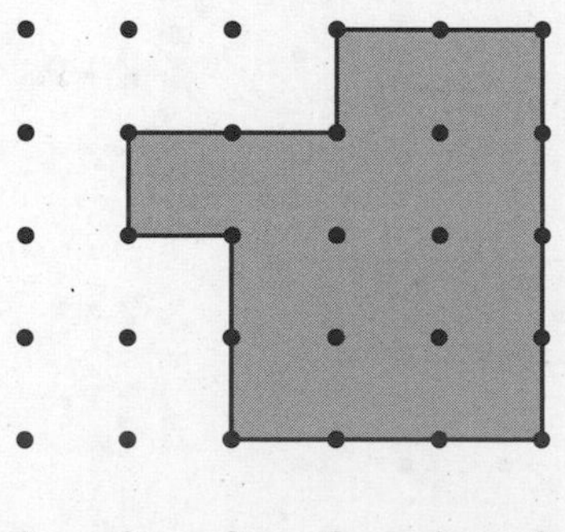

9. Roberto is building a platform for his model railroad. What is the area of the platform?

____

10. Roberto will put a border around the edges of the platform. How much border will he need?

____

Name ______________________________

COMMON CORE STANDARDS CC.3.MD.5b, CC.3.MD.6

Lesson Objective: Estimate and measure area of plane shapes by counting unit squares.

Measure Area

Find the area of the shape. Each unit square is 1 square inch.

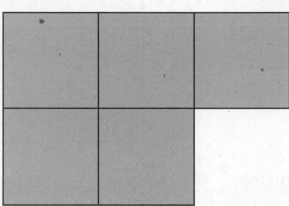

Think: How many unit squares are needed to cover this flat surface?

Step 1 Use 1-inch square tiles. Cover the surface of the shape with the tiles. Make sure there are no gaps (space between the tiles). Do not overlap the tiles.

Step 2 Count the tiles you used.
5 tiles are needed to cover the shape.

So, the area of the shape is 5 square inches.

Count to find the area of the shape.
Each square is 1 square inch.

1.

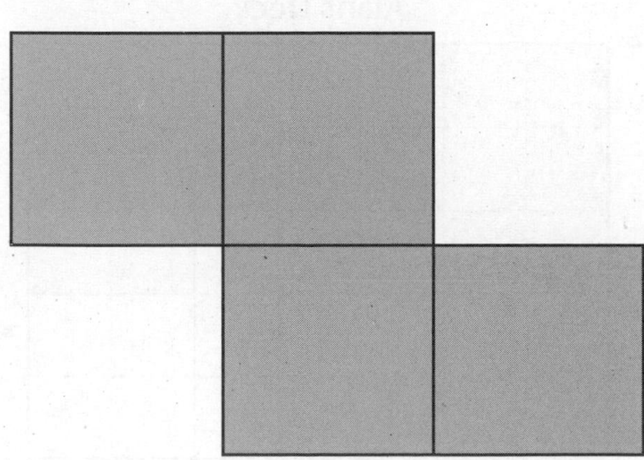

Area = _____ square inches

2.

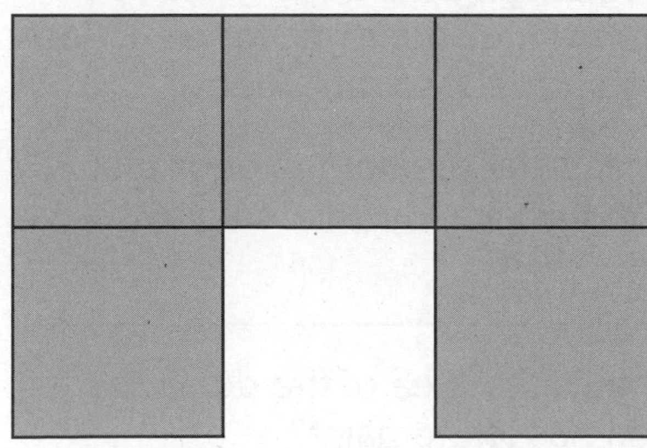

Area = _____ square inches

Name ______________________________

Measure Area

**Count to find the area of the shape.
Each unit square is 1 square centimeter.**

1. 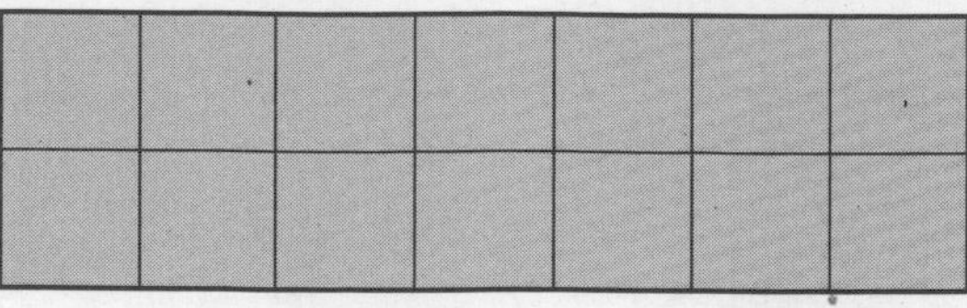

Area = 14 square centimeters

2. 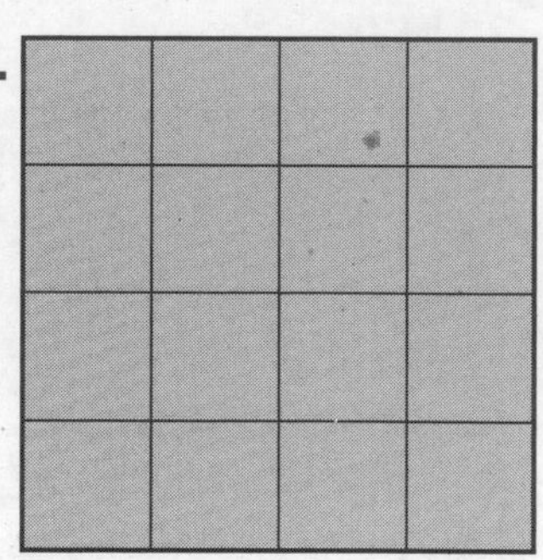

Area = ______ square centimeters

3. 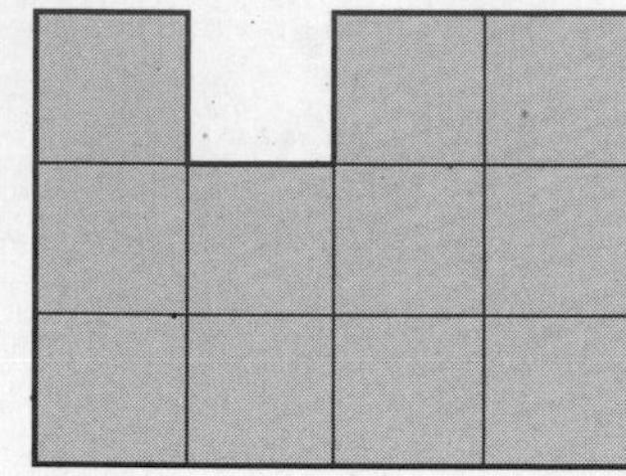

Area = ______ square centimeters

4. 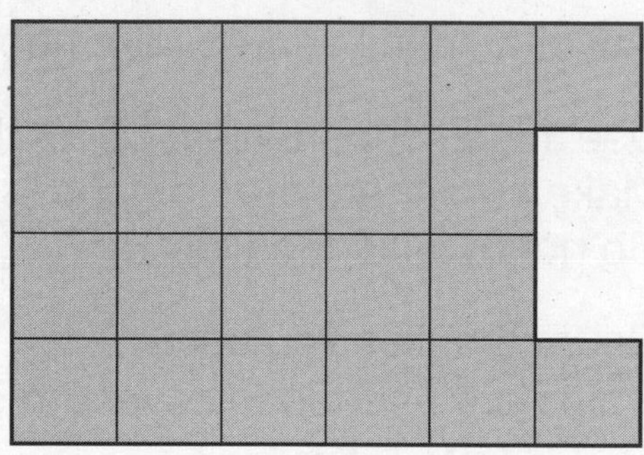

Area = ______ square centimeters

Problem Solving

Alan is painting his deck gray. Use the diagram at the right for 5–6. Each unit square is 1 square meter.

Alan's Deck

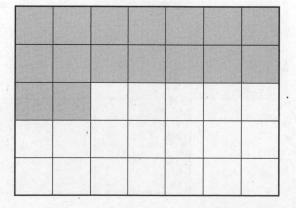

5. What is the area of the deck that Alan has already painted gray?

____

6. What is the area of the deck that Alan has left to paint?

____

Name ______________________________

Lesson 90

COMMON CORE STANDARD CC.3.MD.7b

Lesson Objective: Solve area problems by using the strategy *find a pattern.*

Problem Solving • Area of Rectangles

Mrs. Wilson wants to plant a garden, so she drew plans for some sample gardens. She wants to know how the areas of the gardens are related. How will the areas of Gardens A and B change? How will the areas of Gardens C and D change?

6 ft; 2 ft; A
3 ft; 2 ft; C
6 ft; 4 ft; B
3 ft; 4 ft; D

Use the graphic organizer to help you solve the problem.

Read the Problem

What do I need to find?	What information do I need to use?	How will I use the information?
I need to know how the areas will change from *A* to *B* and from C to D.	I need to use the length and width of each garden to find its area.	I will record the areas in a table. Then I will look for a pattern to see how the areas will change.

Solve the Problem

	Length	Width	Area		Length	Width	Area
Garden A	2 ft	6 ft	12 sq ft	Garden C	2 ft	3 ft	6 sq ft
Garden B	4 ft	6 ft	24 sq ft	Garden D	4 ft	3 ft	12 sq ft

From the table, I see that the lengths will be doubled and the widths will be the same.

The areas in square feet will change from 12 to 24 and from 6 to 12.

So, the area will be doubled.

Solve.

1. Mrs. Rios made a flower garden that is 8 feet long and 2 feet wide. She made a vegetable garden that is 4 feet long and 2 feet wide. How do the areas change?

____

____

Name ______________________

Lesson 10
CC.3.MD.7b

Problem Solving • Area of Rectangles

Use the information for 1–3.

An artist makes rectangular murals in different sizes. Below are the available sizes. Each unit square is 1 square meter.

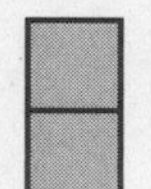
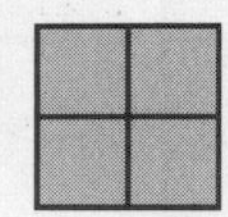
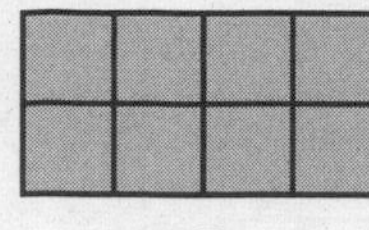
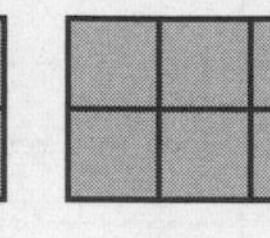
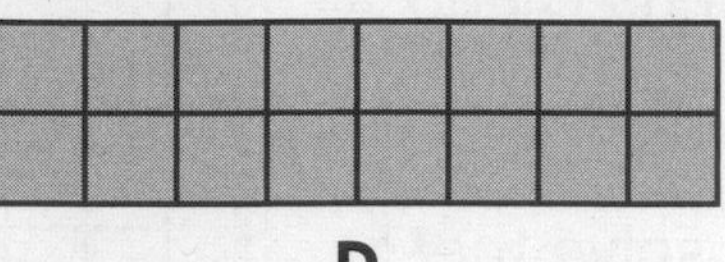

A **B** **C** **D**

1. Complete the table to find the area of each mural.

Mural	Length (in meters)	Width (in meters)	Area (in square meters)
A	2	1	2
B	2	2	4
C	2		
D	2		

2. Find and describe a pattern of how the length changes and how the width changes for murals A through D.

____

____

3. How do the areas of the murals change when the width changes?

____

4. Dan built a deck that is 5 feet long and 5 feet wide. He built another deck that is 5 feet long and 7 feet wide. He built a third deck that is 5 feet long and 9 feet wide. How do the areas change?

____

Name ______________________________

COMMON CORE STANDARDS CC.3.MD.7c, CC.3.MD.7d

Lesson Objective: Apply the Distributive Property to area models and to find the area of combined rectangles.

Area of Combined Rectangles

You can break apart a shape into rectangles to find the total area of the shape.

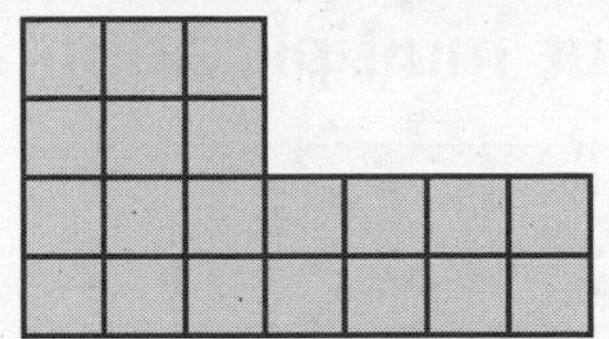

Step 1 Draw a line to break apart the shape into two rectangles.

Step 2 Count the number of unit squares in each rectangle.

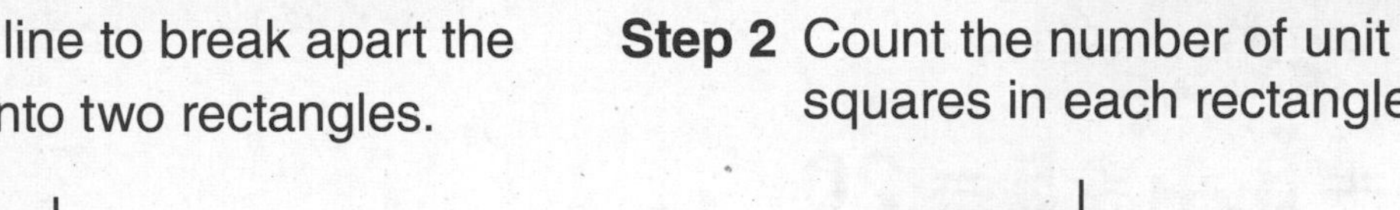

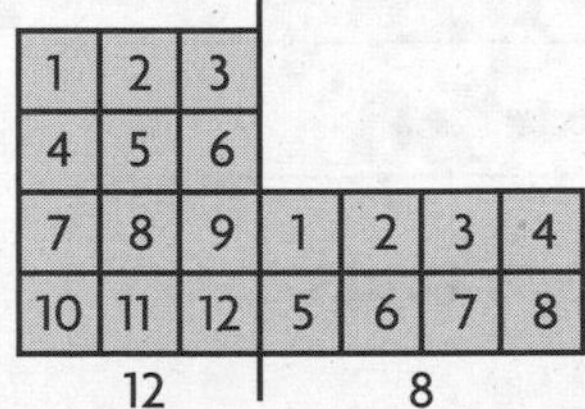

Step 3 Add the number of unit squares in each rectangle to find the total area.

12 + **8** = **20** unit squares

So, the area of the shape is **20** square units.

Draw a line to break apart the shape into rectangles. Find the area of the shape.

1.

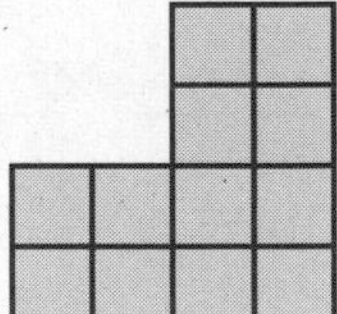

____

2.

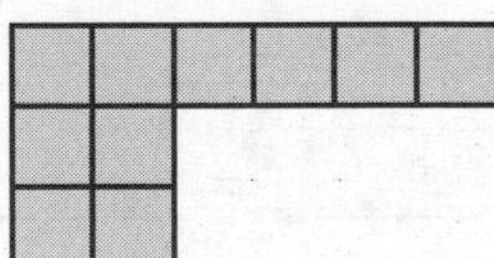

____

3.

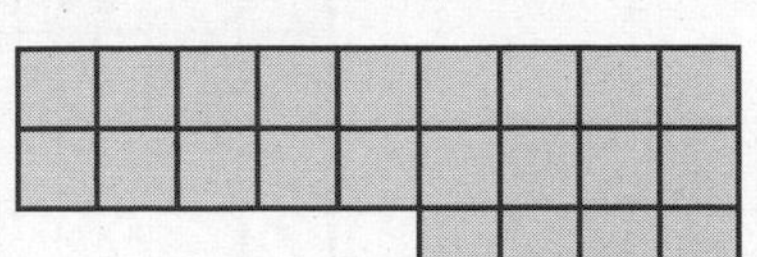

____

4.

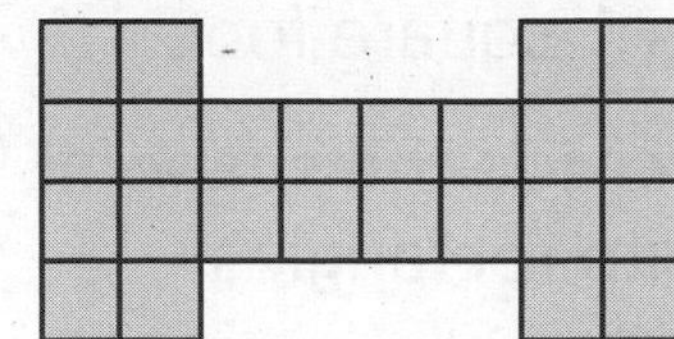

____

Name ______________________________

Lesson 91

CC.3.MD.7c, CC.3.MD.7d

Area of Combined Rectangles

Use the Distributive Property to find the area. Show your multiplication and addition equations.

1.

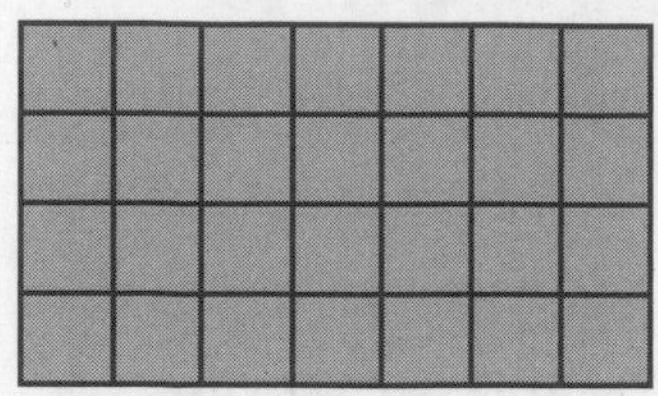

$4 \times 2 = 8, 4 \times 5 = 20$

$8 + 20 = 28$

28 square units

2.

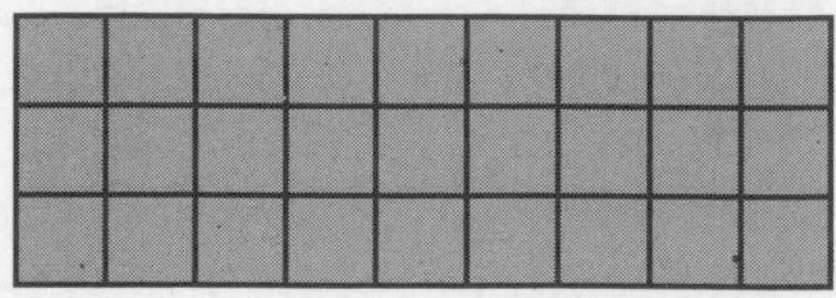

____

____

______ square units

Draw a line to break apart the shape into rectangles. Find the area of the shape.

3.

Rectangle 1: _____ × _____ = _____

Rectangle 2: _____ × _____ = _____

_____ + _____ = _____ square units

4.

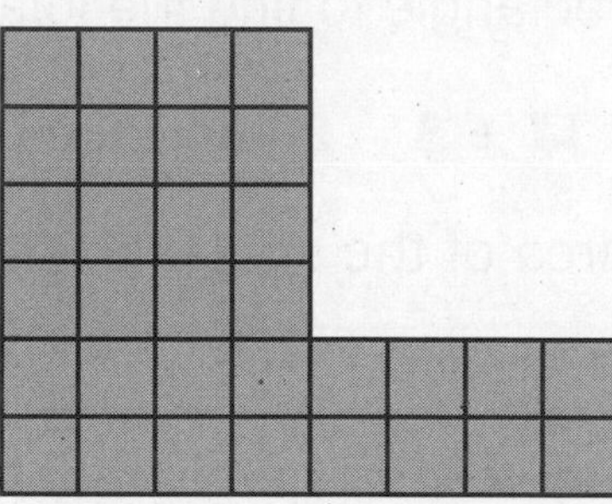

Rectangle 1: _____ × _____ = _____

Rectangle 2: _____ × _____ = _____

_____ + _____ = _____ square units

Problem Solving REAL WORLD

A diagram of Frank's room is at right. Each unit square is 1 square foot.

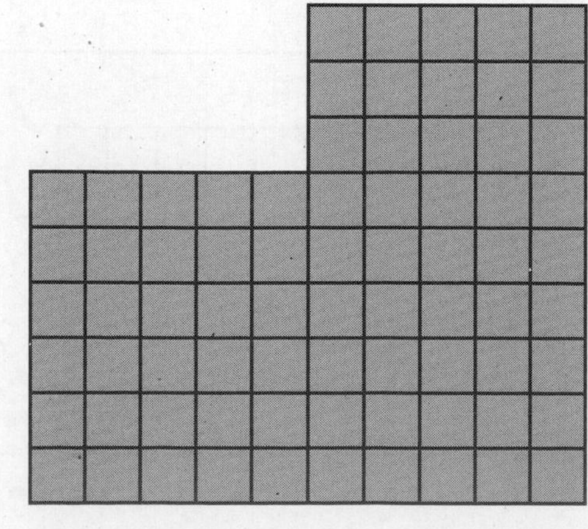

5. Draw a line to divide the shape of Frank's room into rectangles.

6. What is the total area of Frank's room?

______ square feet

Name ______________________________

Lesson 13

COMMON CORE STANDARD CC.3.MD.8

Lesson Objective: Estimate and measure perimeter of polygons using inch and centimeter rulers.

Find Perimeter

Kelsey wants to know the perimeter of the shape below. She can use an inch ruler to find the perimeter.

Step 1 Choose one side of the shape to measure. Place the zero mark of the ruler on the end of the side. Measure to the nearest inch. Write the length.

Step 2 Use the ruler to measure the other three sides. Write the lengths.

Step 3 Add the lengths of all the sides.
1 + 1 + 2 + 1 = 5

So, the perimeter of the shape is 5 inches.

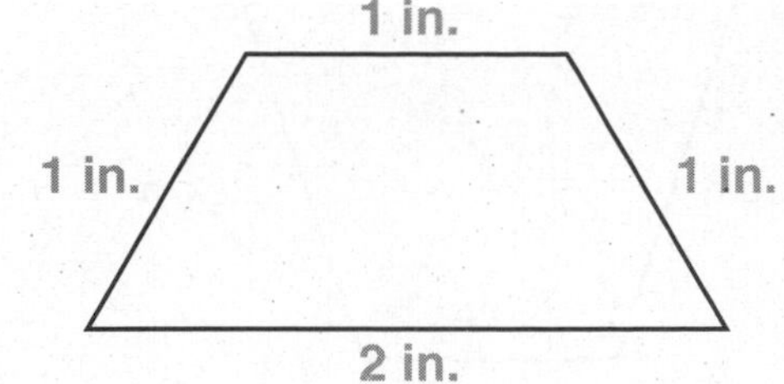

Use an inch ruler to find the perimeter.

1.

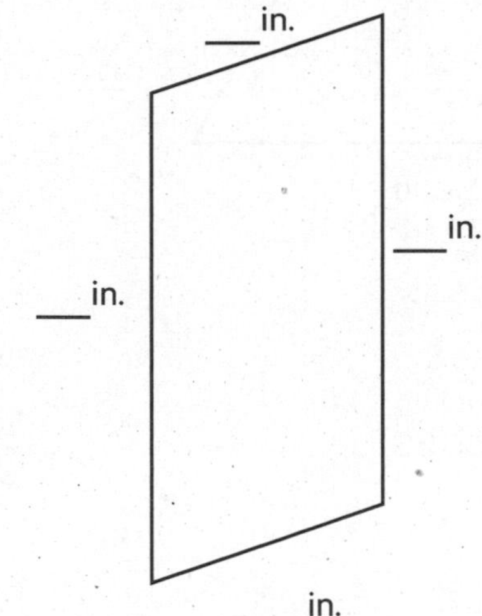

____________ inches

2.

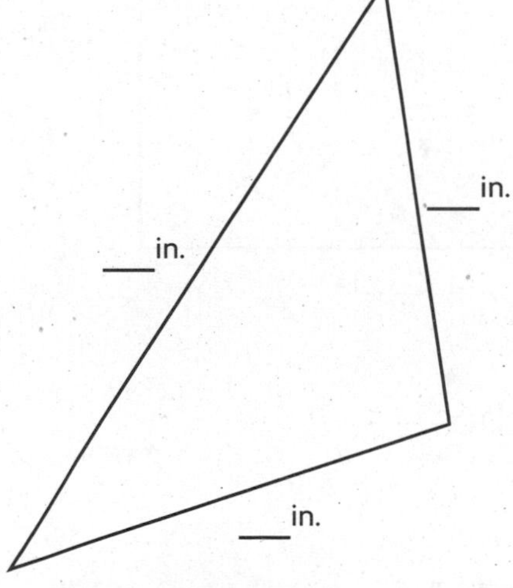

____________ inches

Name ______________________

Lesson 93

CC.3.MD.8

Find Perimeter

Use a ruler to find the perimeter.

1.

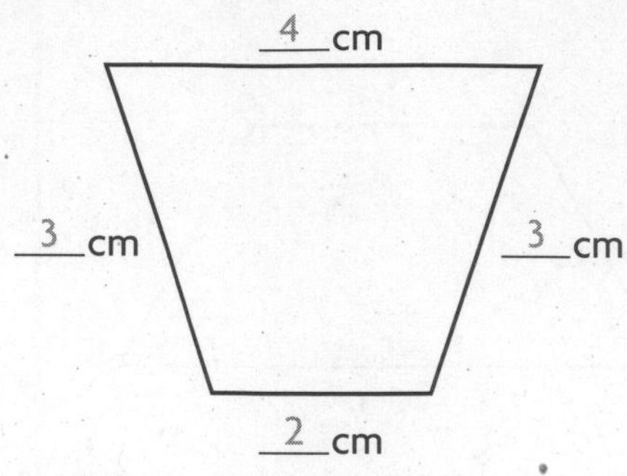

12 centimeters

2.

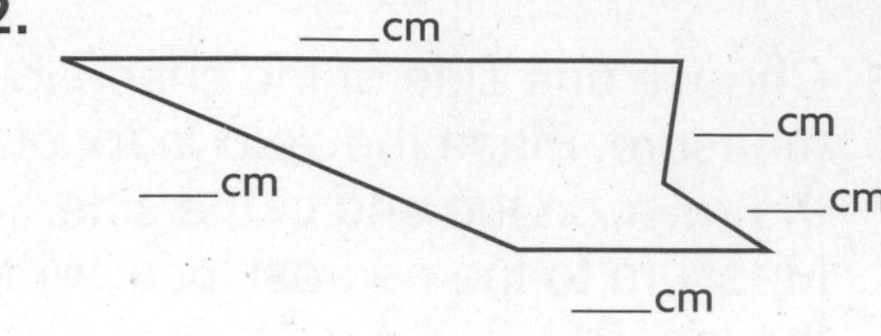

______ centimeters

3.

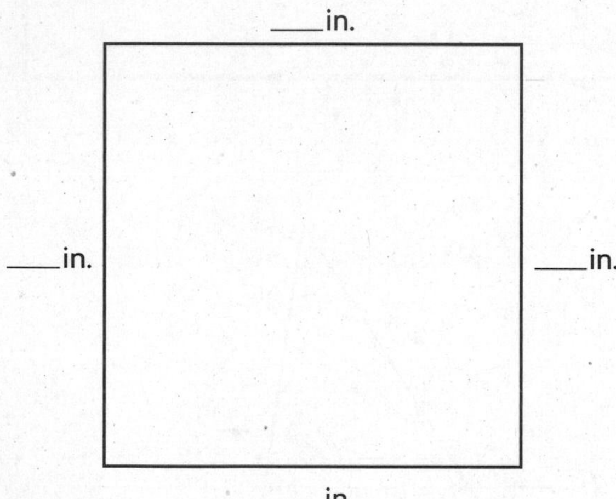

______ inches

4.

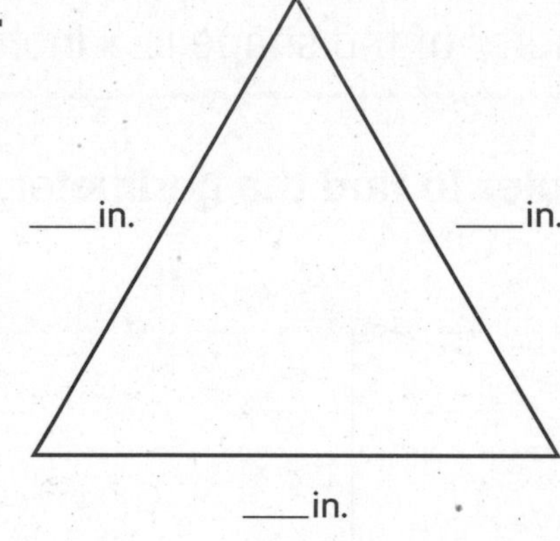

______ inches

Problem Solving REAL WORLD

Draw a picture to solve 5–6.

5. Evan has a square sticker that measures 5 inches on each side. What is the perimeter of the sticker?

____

6. Sophie draws a shape that has 6 sides. Each side is 3 centimeters. What is the perimeter of the shape?

____

Name ______________________________

COMMON CORE STANDARD CC.3.MD.8

Lesson Objective: Compare areas of rectangles that have the same perimeter.

Same Perimeter, Different Areas

You can use perimeter and area to compare rectangles.

Compare the perimeters of Rectangle *A* and Rectangle *B*.

A

B

Find the number of units around each rectangle.

Rectangle *A*: $3 + 2 + 3 + 2 =$ **10** units

Rectangle *B*: $4 + 1 + 4 + 1 =$ **10** units

Compare: **10** units = **10** units

So, Rectangle *A* has the same perimeter as Rectangle *B*.

Compare the areas of Rectangle *A* and Rectangle *B*.

A

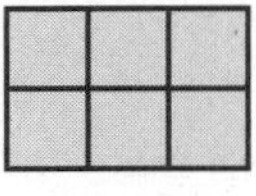

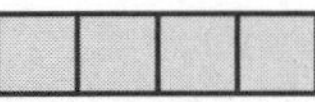

Find the number of unit squares needed to cover each rectangle.

Rectangle *A*: **2** rows of **3** $= 2 \times 3$, or **6** square units

Rectangle *B*: **1** row of **4** $= 1 \times 4$, or **4** square units

Compare: **6** square units > **4** square units

So, Rectangle *A* has a greater area than Rectangle *B*.

Find the perimeter and the area. Tell which rectangle has a greater area.

1. *A* *B*

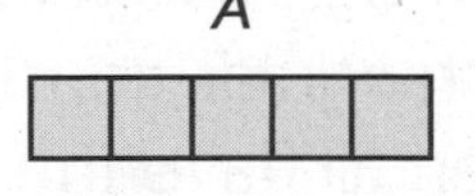

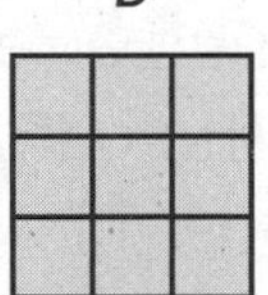

A: Perimeter = ____________;

Area = ____________

B: Perimeter = ____________;

Area = ____________

Rectangle _____ has a greater area.

2. *A* *B*

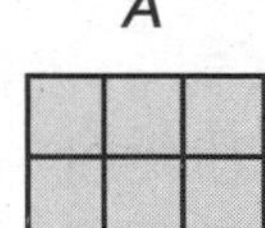

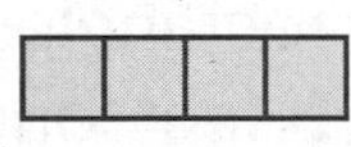

A: Perimeter = ____________;

Area = ____________

B: Perimeter = ____________;

Area = ____________

Rectangle _____ has a greater area.

Name ___________________________

Lesson 95

CC.3.MD.8

Same Perimeter, Different Areas

Find the perimeter and the area.
Tell which rectangle has a greater area.

1.

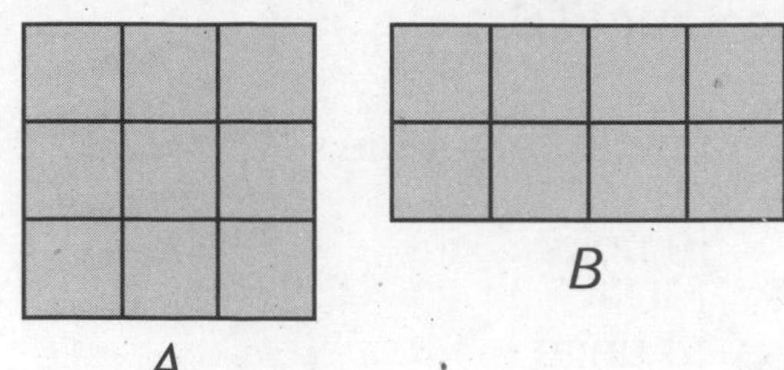

A: Perimeter = **12 units**;

Area = **9 square units**

B: Perimeter = ___________;

Area = ___________

Rectangle ______ has a greater area.

2.

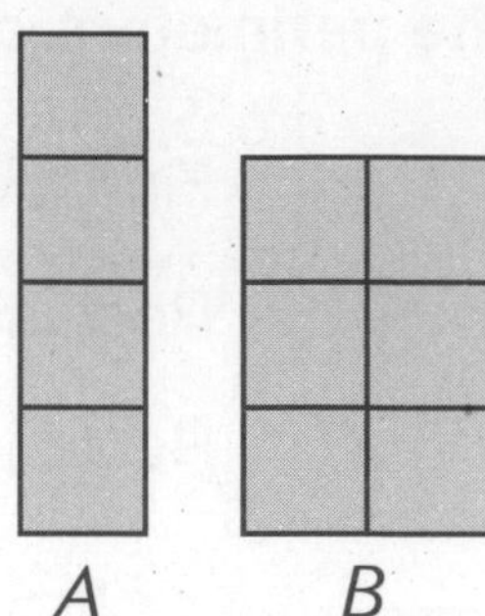

A: Perimeter = ___________;

Area = ___________

B: Perimeter = ___________;

Area = ___________

Rectangle ______ has a greater area.

Problem Solving REAL WORLD

3. Tara's and Jody's bedrooms are shaped like rectangles. Tara's bedroom is 9 feet long and 8 feet wide. Jody's bedroom is 7 feet long and 10 feet wide. Whose bedroom has the greater area? **Explain.**

____

____

____

4. Mr. Sanchez has 16 feet of fencing to put around a rectangular garden. He wants the garden to have the greatest possible area. How long should the sides of the garden be?

____

____

Name ______________________________

COMMON CORE STANDARD CC.3.MD.8

Lesson Objective: Compare perimeters of rectangles that have the same area.

Same Area, Different Perimeters

Find the perimeter and area of Rectangles *A* and *B*. Tell which rectangle has a greater perimeter.

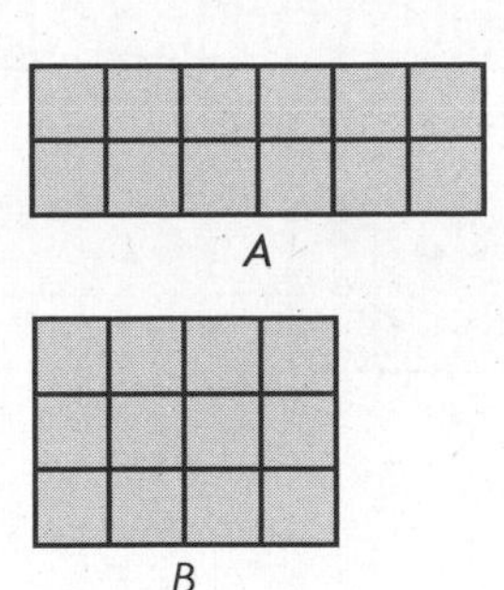

Step 1 Find the area of each rectangle. You can multiply the number of unit squares in each row by the number of rows.

Rectangle *A*: $2 \times 6 = 12$ square units

Rectangle *B*: $3 \times 4 = 12$ square units

Step 2 Find the perimeter of each rectangle. You can add the sides.

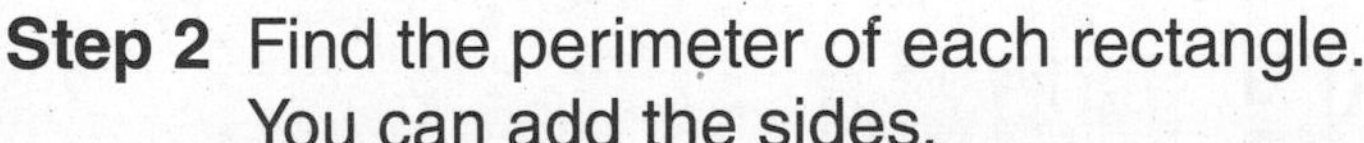

Rectangle *A*: $6 + 2 + 6 + 2 = 16$ units

Rectangle *B*: $4 + 3 + 4 + 3 = 14$ units

Step 3 Compare the perimeters. 16 units > 14 units.

So, Rectangle ***A*** has a greater perimeter.

Find the perimeter and the area. Tell which rectangle has a greater perimeter.

1.

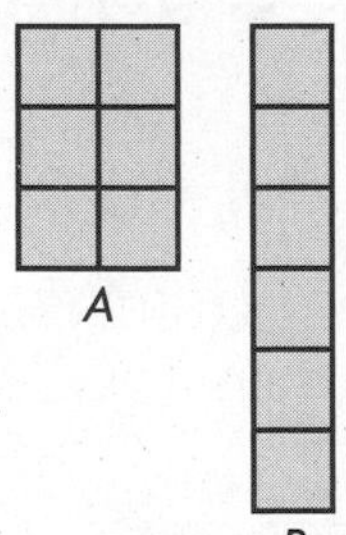

B

A: Area = ______________________;

Perimeter = ____________

B: Area = ______________________;

Perimeter = ____________

Rectangle _____ has a greater perimeter.

2.

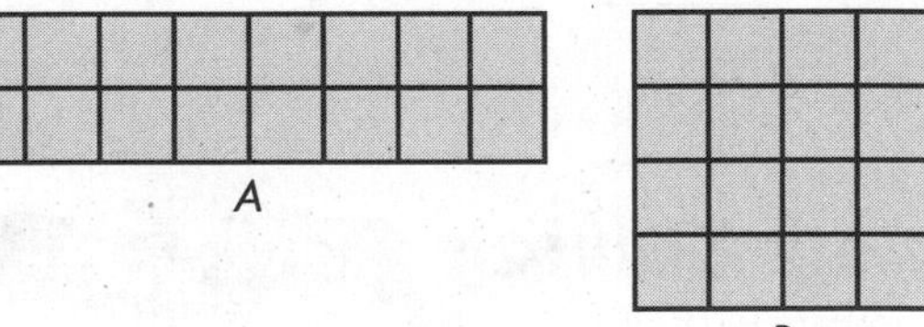

B

A: Area = ______________________,

Perimeter = ____________

B: Area = ______________________,

Perimeter = ____________

Rectangle _____ has a greater perimeter.

Name ______________________

Lesson 96
CC.3.MD.8

Same Area, Different Perimeters

Find the perimeter and the area. Tell which rectangle has a greater perimeter.

1. A

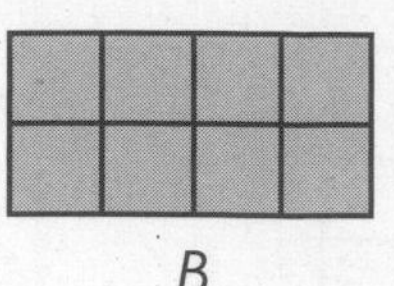

B

A: Area = **8 square units**;

Perimeter = **18 units**

B: Area = ______________;

Perimeter = ______________

Rectangle ____ has a greater perimeter.

2.

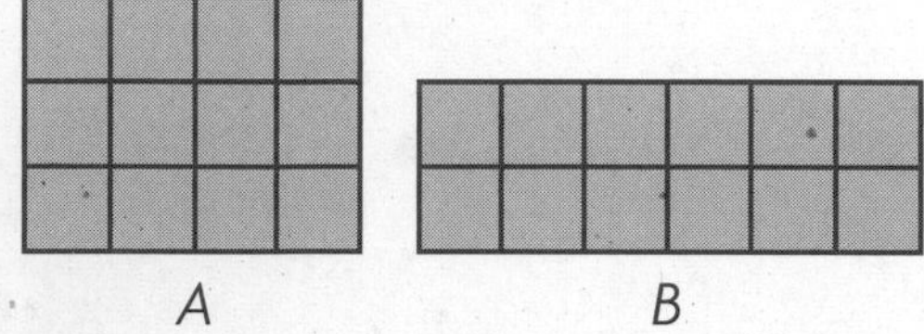

A B

A: Area = ______________;

Perimeter = ______________

B: Area = ______________;

Perimeter = ______________

Rectangle ____ has a greater perimeter.

3.

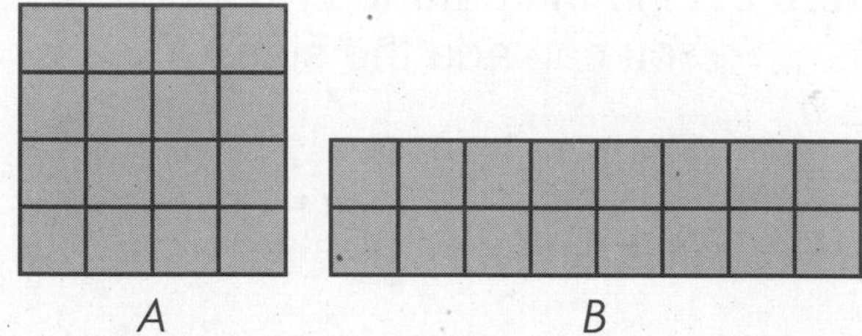

A B

A: Area = ______________;

Perimeter = ______________

B: Area = ______________;

Perimeter = ______________

Rectangle ____ has a greater perimeter.

Problem Solving

Use the tile designs for 4–5.

Beth's Tile Designs

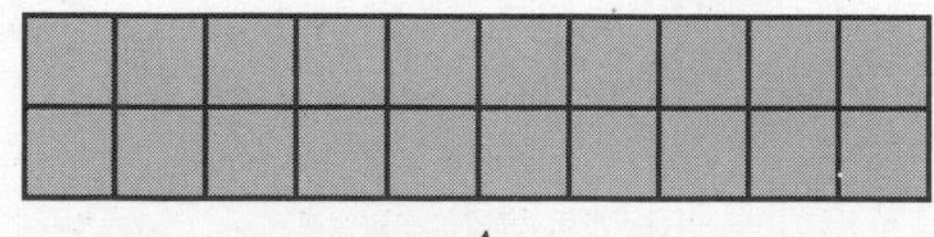

A

B

4. Compare the areas of Design A and Design B.

____

____

5. Compare the perimeters. Which design has the greater perimeter?

____

Name ________________________________

Lesson 100

COMMON CORE STANDARD CC.3.G.1

Lesson Objective: Determine if lines or line segments are intersecting, perpendicular, or parallel.

Describe Sides of Polygons

There are different types of line segments in polygons.

- **Intersecting lines** are lines that cross or meet. Intersecting lines form angles.

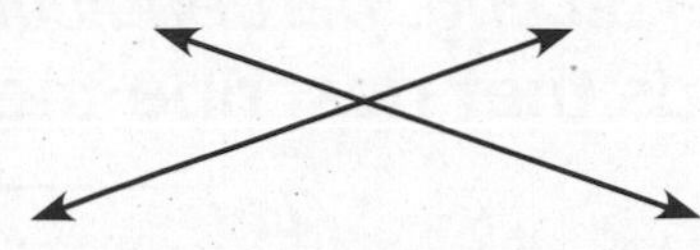

- **Perpendicular lines** are intersecting lines that cross or meet to form right angles.

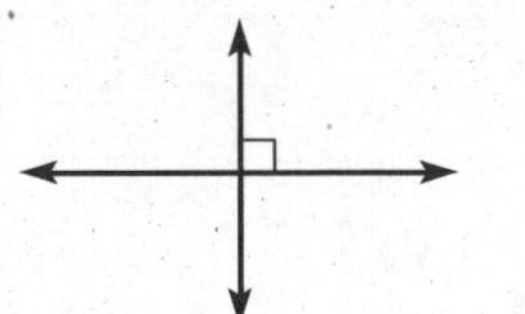

- Lines that appear never to cross or meet and are always the same distance apart are **parallel lines**. They never form angles.

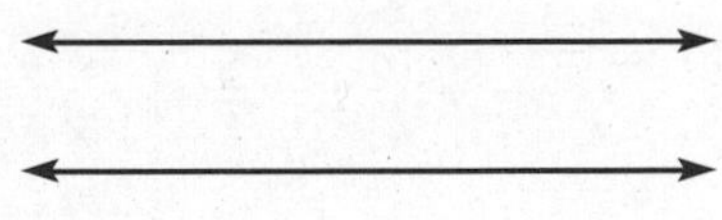

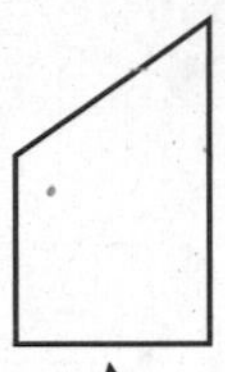

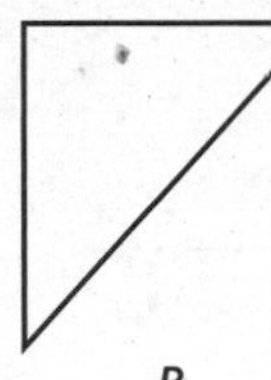

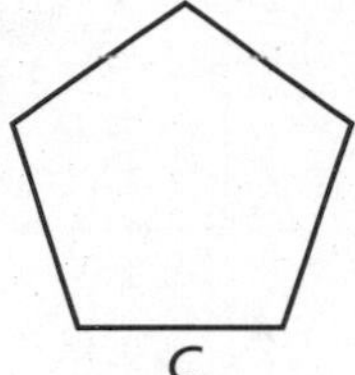

Which shape or shapes appear to have parallel sides? *A*

Which shape or shapes appear to have perpendicular sides? *A, B*

Which shape or shapes appear to have intersecting sides? *A, B, C*

Look at the dashed sides of the polygon. Tell if they appear to be *intersecting*, *perpendicular*, or *parallel*. Write all the words that describe the sides.

1.

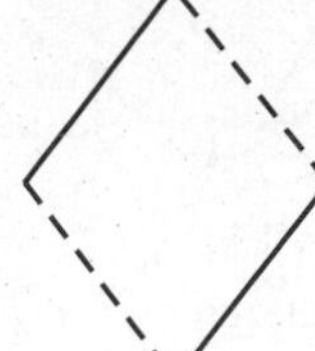

____

2.

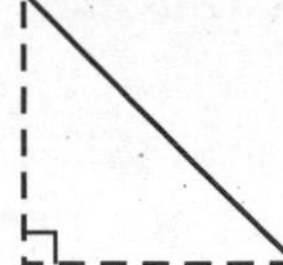

____

3.

____

Name ____________________

Describe Sides of Polygons

Look at the dashed sides of the polygon. Tell if they appear to be *intersecting, perpendicular,* or *parallel.* Write all the words that describe the sides.

1. 

parallel

2. 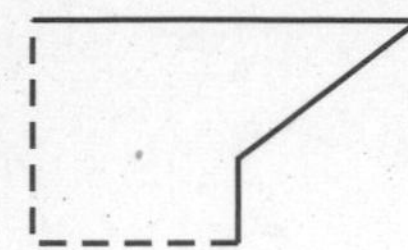

____

3. 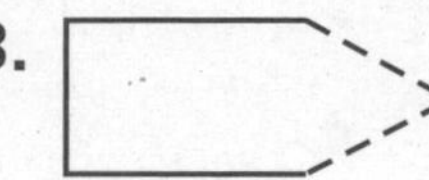

____

4. 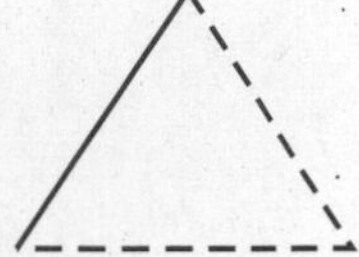

____

5. 

____

6. 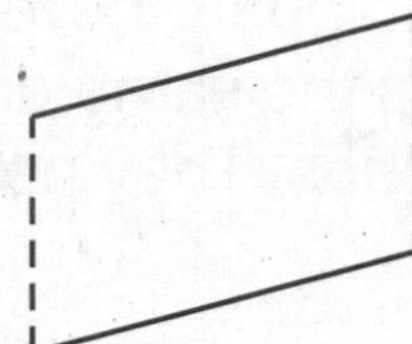

____

7. 

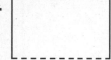

____

8. 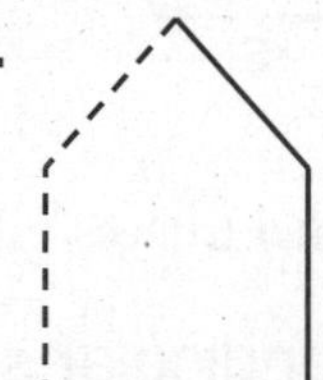

____

9. 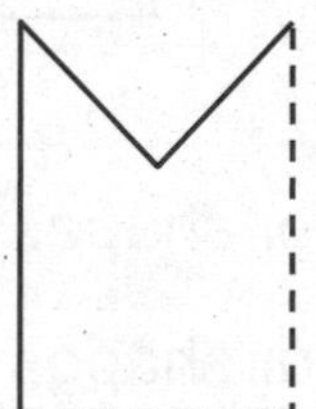

____

Problem Solving REAL WORLD

Use shapes *A–D* for 10–11.

10. Which shapes appear to have parallel sides?

____

11. Which shapes appear to have perpendicular sides?

____

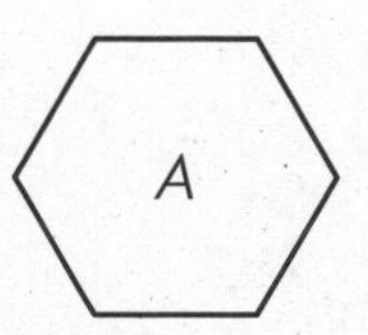

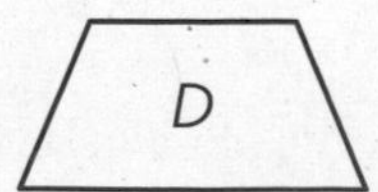

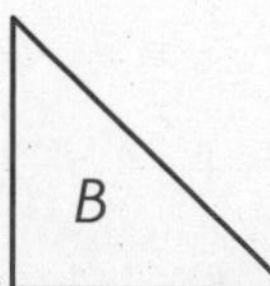

D

Name ______________________________

Lesson 101

COMMON CORE STANDARD CC.3.G.1

Lesson Objective: Describe, classify, and compare quadrilaterals based on their sides and angles.

Classify Quadrilaterals

You can classify quadrilaterals by their sides and by their angles.

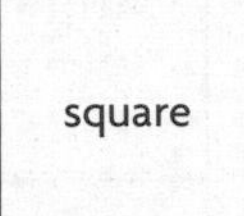

2 pairs of opposite sides that are parallel

4 sides that are of equal length

4 right angles

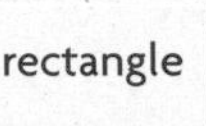

2 pairs of opposite sides that are parallel

2 pairs of sides that are of equal length

4 right angles

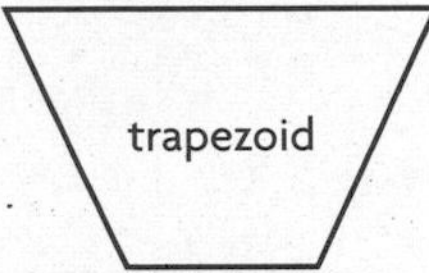

1 pair of opposite sides that are parallel

lengths of sides could be the same.

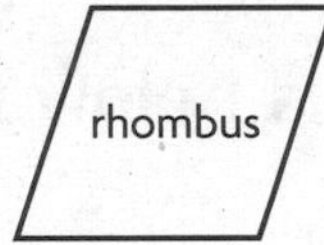

2 pairs of opposite sides that are parallel

4 sides that are of equal length

How can you classify the quadrilateral?

It has only 1 pair of opposite sides that are **parallel**.

The lengths of all 4 sides are **not equal**.

So, the quadrilateral is a **trapezoid**.

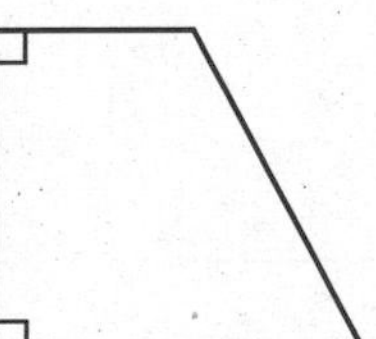

Circle all the words that describe the quadrilateral.

1.

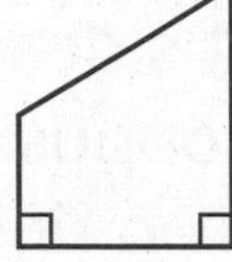

square

rhombus

trapezoid

2.

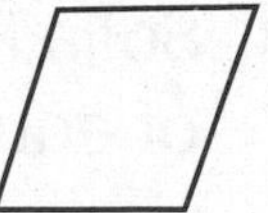

square

rectangle

quadrilateral

3.

square

rectangle

rhombus

Name ______________________________

Lesson 101
CC.3.G.1

Classify Quadrilaterals

Circle all the words that describe the quadrilateral.

1. 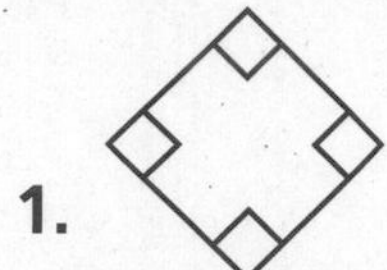

square
rectangle
rhombus
trapezoid

2.

square
rectangle
rhombus
trapezoid

3. 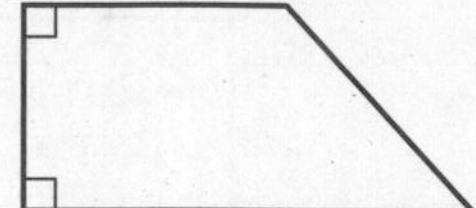

square
rectangle
rhombus
trapezoid

Use the quadrilaterals below for 4–6.

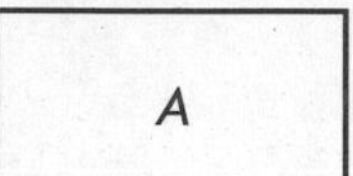

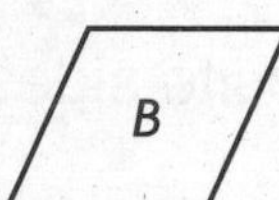

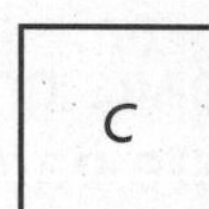

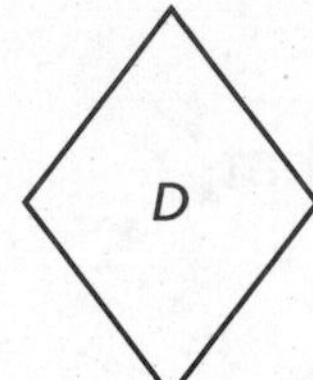

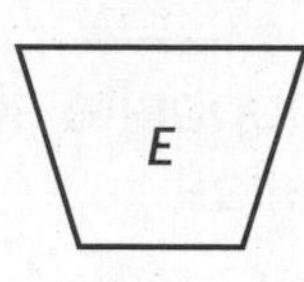

4. Which quadrilaterals appear to have no right angles?

____

5. Which quadrilaterals appear to have 4 right angles?

____

6. Which quadrilaterals appear to have 4 sides of equal length?

____

Problem Solving REAL WORLD

7. A picture on the wall in Jeremy's classroom has 4 right angles, 4 sides of equal length, and 2 pairs of opposite sides that are parallel. What quadrilateral best describes the picture?

____

8. Sofia has a plate that has 4 sides of equal length, 2 pairs of opposite sides that are parallel, and no right angles. What quadrilateral best describes the plate?

____

Name ____________________

Lesson Objective: Draw quadrilaterals.

Draw Quadrilaterals

Use grid paper to draw a quadrilateral.

Step 1 Use a ruler to draw line segments. Connect *A* to *B*.

Step 2 Connect *B* to *C*.

Step 3 Connect *C* to *D*.

Step 4 Connect *D* to *A*.

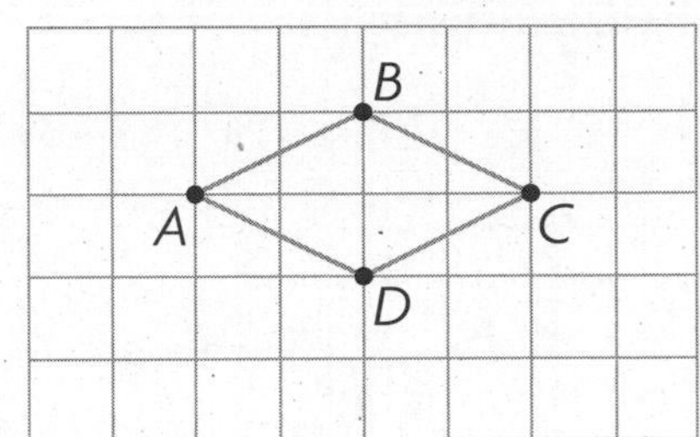

Write the name of your quadrilateral.

rhombus

1. Choose four endpoints that connect to make a square.

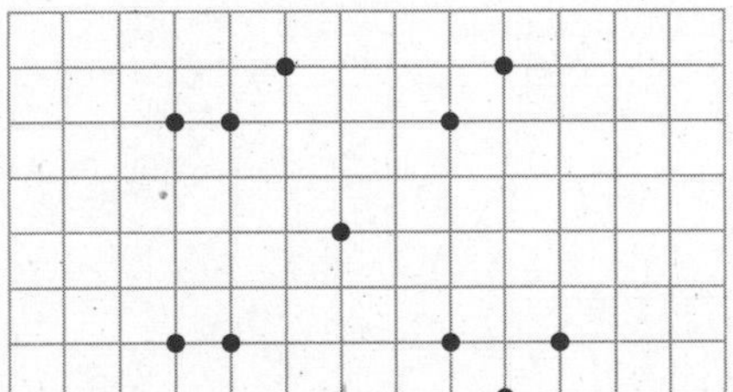

2. Choose four endpoints that connect to make a trapezoid.

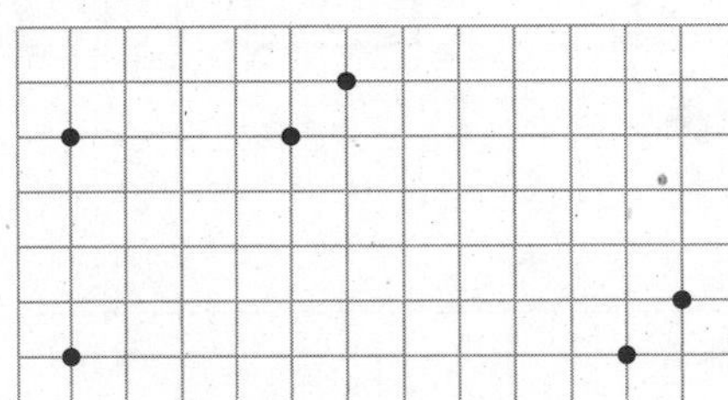

Use grid paper to draw a quadrilateral that is described. Name the quadrilateral you drew.

3. 4 right angles

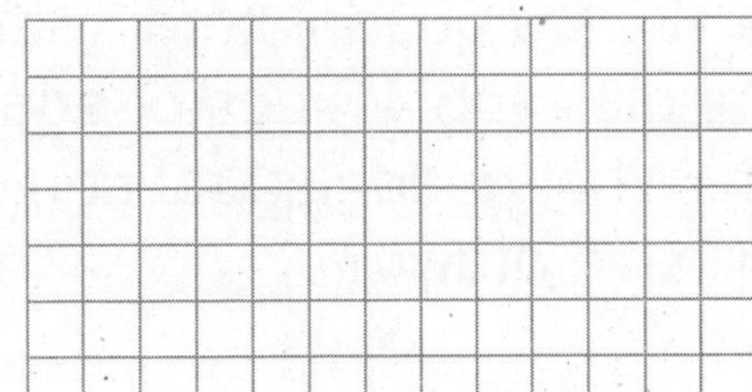

____

4. 2 pairs of opposite sides that are parallel

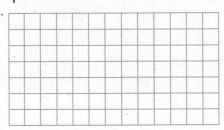

____

Name ______________________

Draw Quadrilaterals

Draw a quadrilateral that is described. Name the quadrilateral you drew.

1. 4 sides of equal length

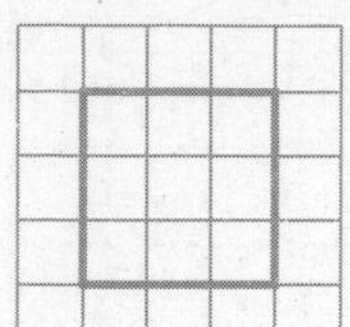

square

2. 1 pair of opposite sides that are parallel

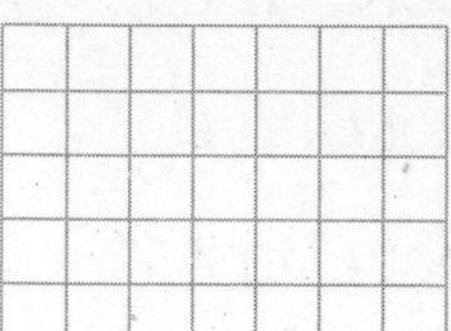

____

Draw a quadrilateral that does not belong. Then explain why.

3.

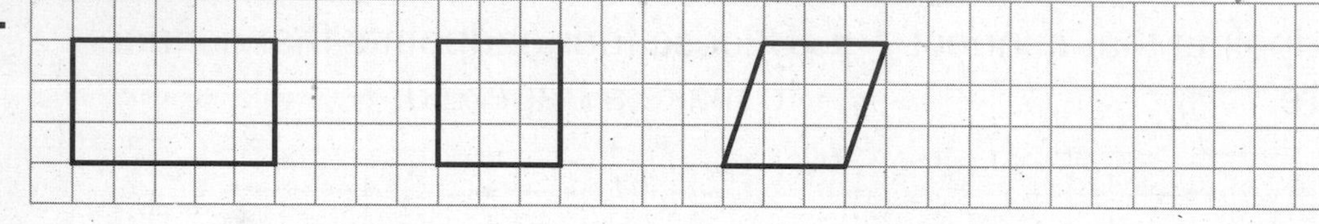

____

____

____

Problem Solving REAL WORLD

4. Layla drew a quadrilateral with 4 right angles and 2 pairs of opposite sides that are parallel. Name the quadrilateral she could have drawn.

____

5. Victor drew a quadrilateral with no right angles and 4 sides of equal length. What quadrilateral could Victor have drawn?

____

Name ___________________________

Describe Triangles

Lesson 103

COMMON CORE STANDARD CC.3.G.1

Lesson Objective: Describe and compare triangles based on the number of sides that have equal length and by their angles.

You can describe a triangle by its types of angles.

This triangle has 1 right angle.

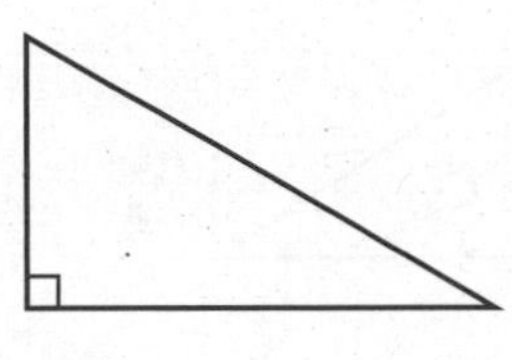

This triangle has 1 angle greater than a right angle.

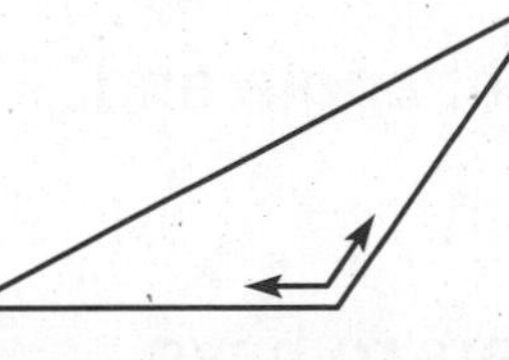

This triangle has 3 angles less than a right angle.

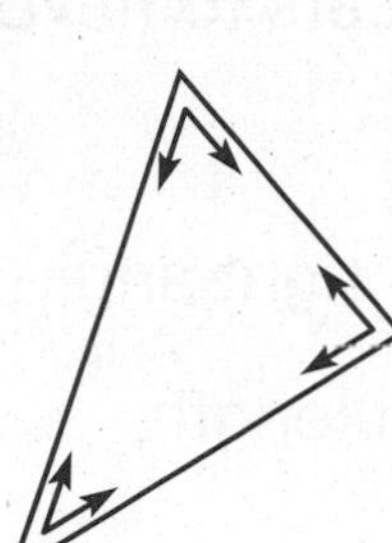

You can describe a triangle by the number of sides of equal length.

This triangle has 0 sides of the same length.

This triangle has 2 sides of the same length.

This triangle has 3 sides of the same length.

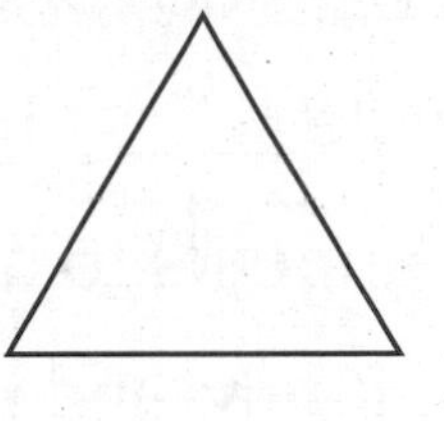

Draw a line to match the description of the triangle(s).

1. One angle is a right angle.

2. One angle is greater than a right angle.

3. Three angles are less than a right angle.

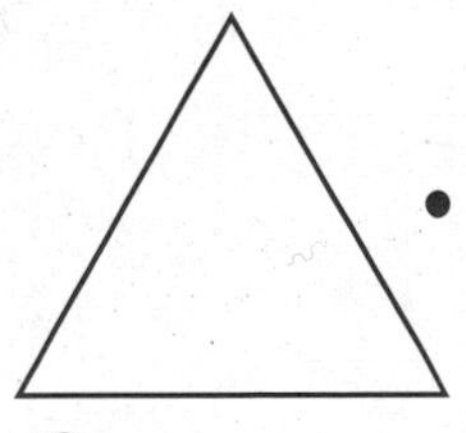

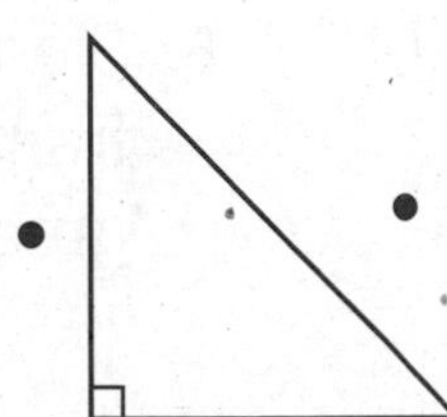

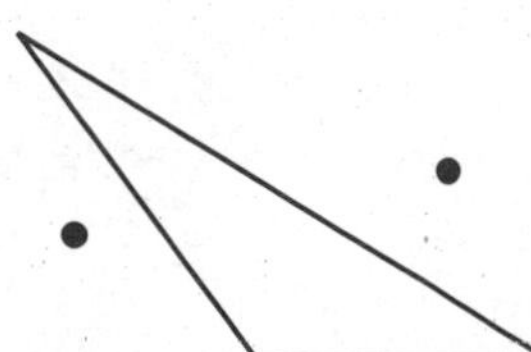

4. No sides are equal in length.

5. Two sides are equal in length.

6. Three sides are equal in length.

Name ___________________________

Lesson 103
CC.3.G.1

Describe Triangles

Use the triangles for 1–3. Write *A*, *B*, or *C*. Then complete the sentences.

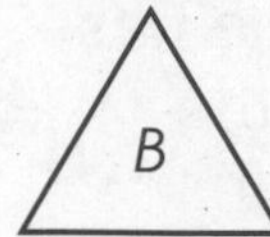

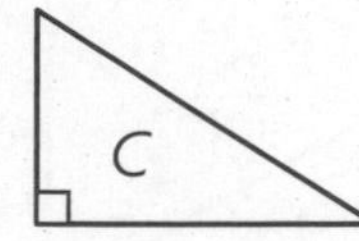

1. Triangle __B__ has 3 angles less than a right angle and appears to have __3__ sides of equal length.
2. Triangle ______ has 1 right angle and appears to have ______ sides of equal length.
3. Triangle ______ has 1 angle greater than a right angle and appears to have ______ sides of equal length.
4. Kyle, Kathy, and Kelly each drew a triangle. Who drew the triangle that has 1 angle greater than a right angle and appears to have no sides of equal length?

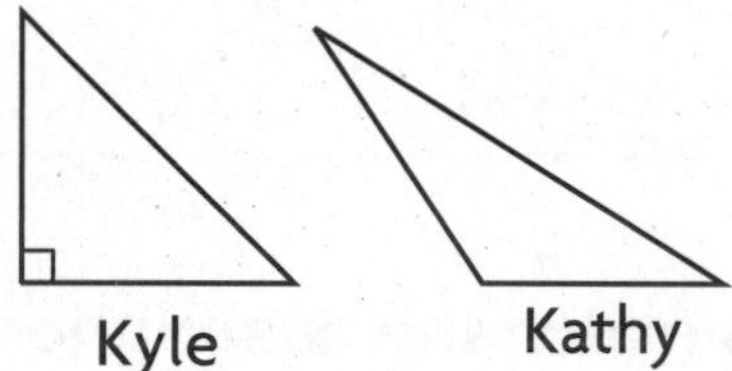

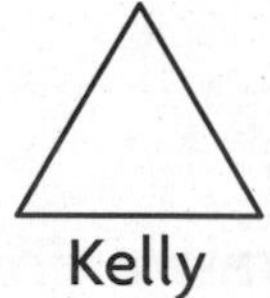

____

Problem Solving

5. Matthew drew the back of his tent. How many sides appear to be of equal length?

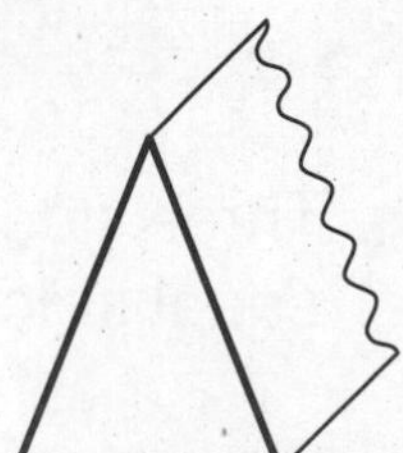

____

6. Sierra made the triangular picture frame shown. How many angles are greater than a right angle?

____

Name ______________________________

Lesson 104

COMMON CORE STANDARD CC.3.G.1

Lesson Objective: Solve problems by using the strategy *draw a diagram* to classify plane shapes.

Problem Solving • Classify Plane Shapes

A **Venn diagram** shows how sets of things are related. This Venn diagram shows how quadrilaterals and polygons with all sides of equal length are related. The shapes in the section where the circles overlap show shapes that belong to both groups.

What types of polygons are in both circles?

Read the Problem	Solve the Problem
What do I need to find? what types of polygons are in both circles	What is true about all polygons in the circle labeled Quadrilaterals? They all have 4 sides.
What information do I need to use? The circles are labeled Quadrilaterals and Polygons with All Sides of Equal Length.	What is true about all polygons in the other circle? They all have sides of equal length.
How will I use the information? I will describe the shapes in the section where the circles overlap.	Which polygons are in the section where the circles overlap? shapes that are quadrilaterals and that have 4 sides that are of equal length So, a square and a rhombus are in the section where the circles overlap.

1. Brad drew the Venn diagram at the right. What type of shapes are in the section where the circles overlap?

____

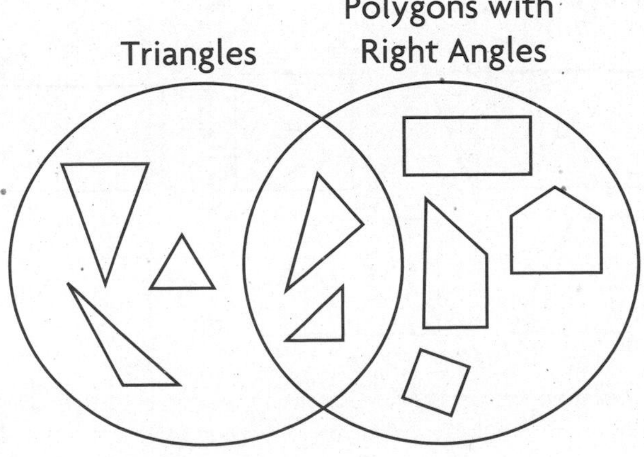

Name ______________________________

Problem Solving • Classify Plane Shapes

Solve each problem.

1. Steve drew the shapes below. Write the letter of each shape where it belongs in the Venn diagram.

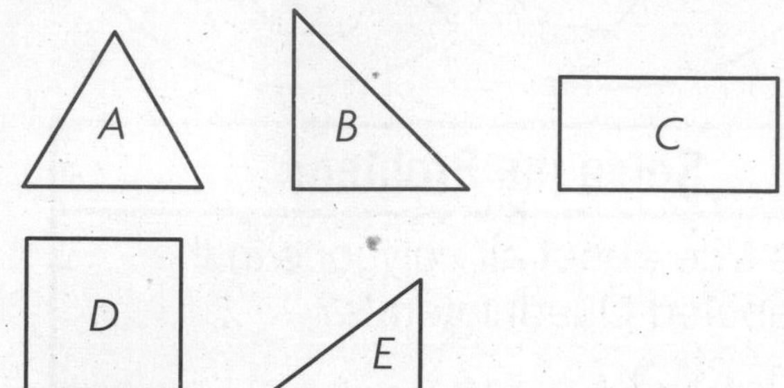

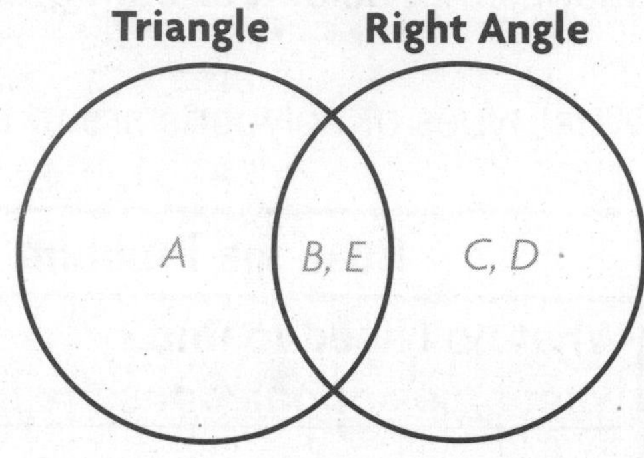

2. Janice drew the shapes below. Write the letter of each shape where it belongs in the Venn diagram.

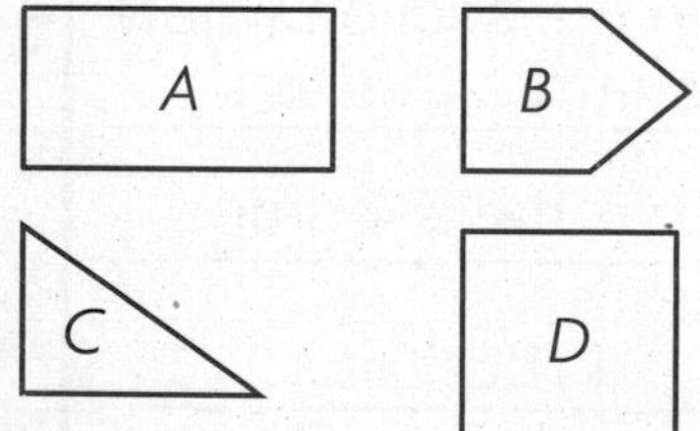

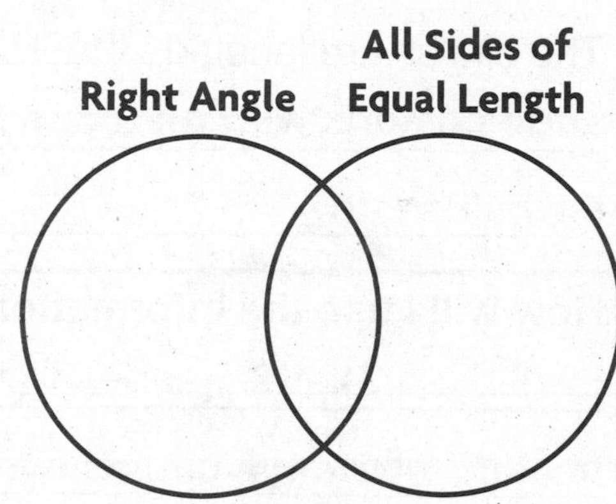

3. Beth drew the shapes below. Write the letter of each shape where it belongs in the Venn diagram.

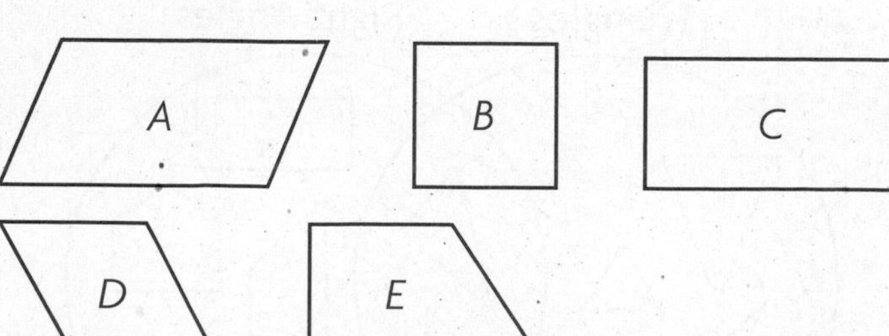

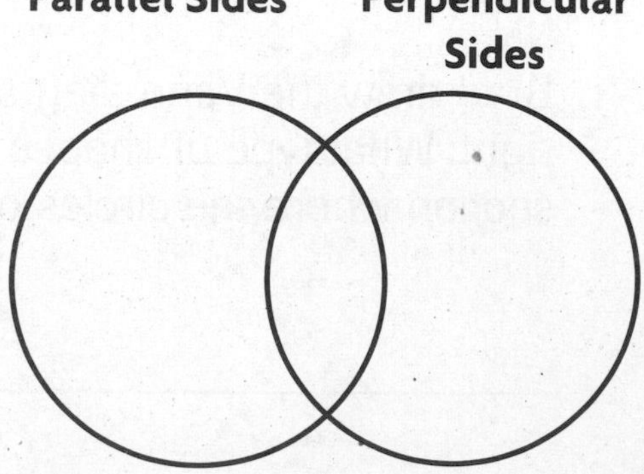

Name ______________________________

COMMON CORE STANDARD CC.3.G.2

Lesson Objective: Partition shapes into parts with equal areas and express the area as a unit fraction of the whole.

Relate Shapes, Fractions, and Area

You can separate a plane shape into equal parts to explore the relationship between fractions and area.

Divide the rectangle into 6 parts with equal area. Write the fraction that names the area of each part of the whole.

Step 1 Draw lines to divide the rectangle into 6 parts with equal area. Use the grid to help you.

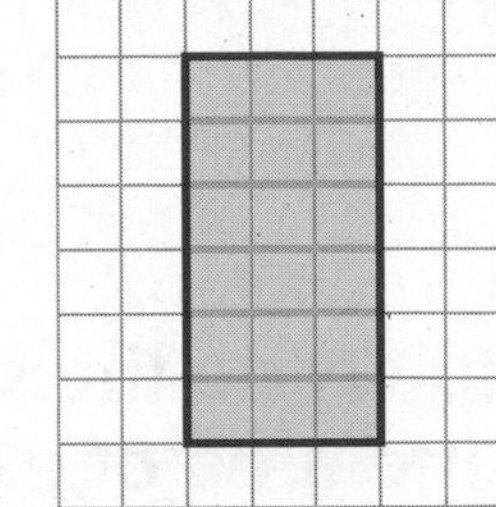

Step 2 Write the fraction that names each part of the divided whole.

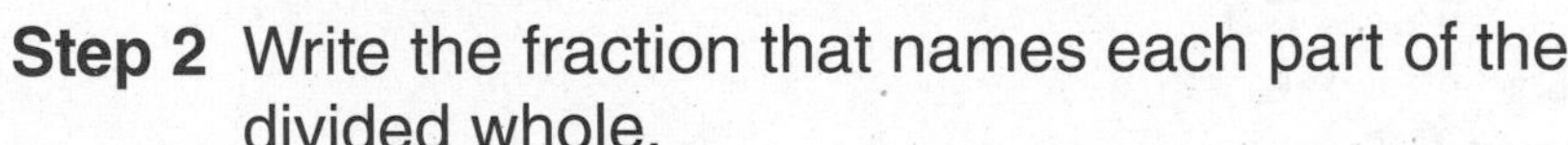

Think: Each part is 1 part out of 6 equal parts.

Each part is $\frac{1}{6}$ of the whole shape's area.

Step 3 Write the fraction that names the whole area.

Think: There are 6 equal parts.

The fraction that names the whole area is $\frac{6}{6}$.

Draw lines to divide the shape into parts with equal area. Write the area of each part as a unit fraction.

1. 4 equal parts

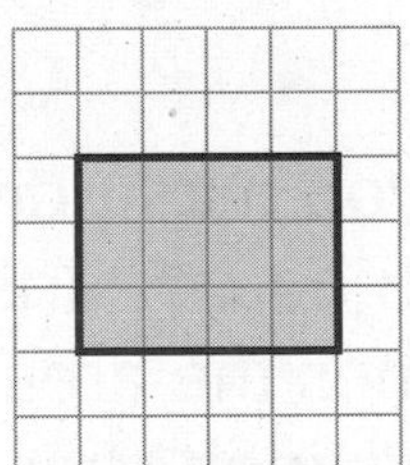

Each part is ______ of the whole shape's area.

2. 8 equal parts

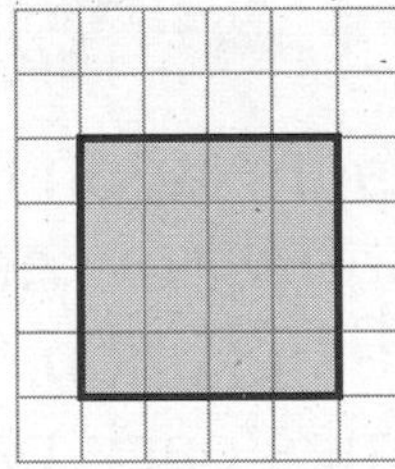

Each part is ______ of the whole shape's area.

Name ____________________

Relate Shapes, Fractions, and Area

Draw lines to divide the shape into equal parts that show the fraction given.

1.
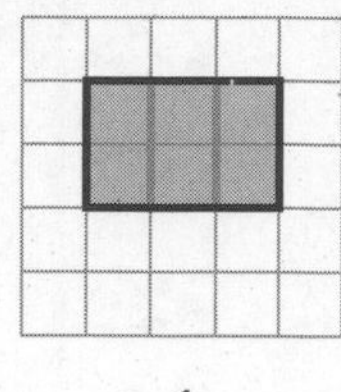

$\frac{1}{3}$

2.
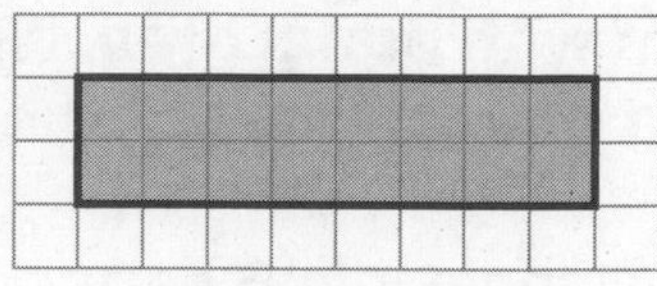

$\frac{1}{8}$

3.
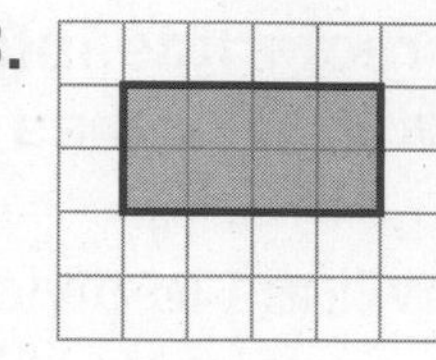

$\frac{1}{2}$

Draw lines to divide the shape into parts with equal area. Write the area of each part as a unit fraction.

4.
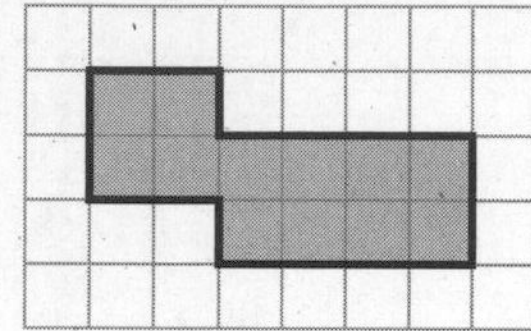

4 equal parts

______

5.
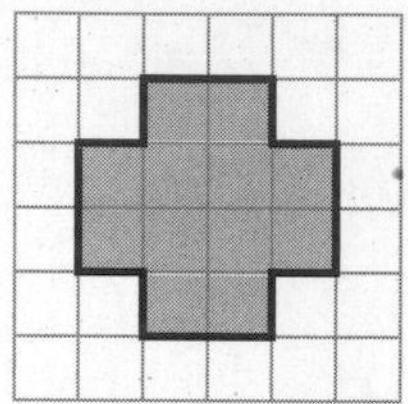

6 equal parts

______

6.
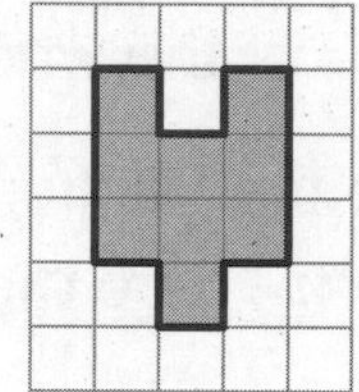

3 equal parts

______

Problem Solving REAL WORLD

7. Robert divided a hexagon into 3 equal parts. Show how he might have divided the hexagon. Write the fraction that names each part of the whole you divided.

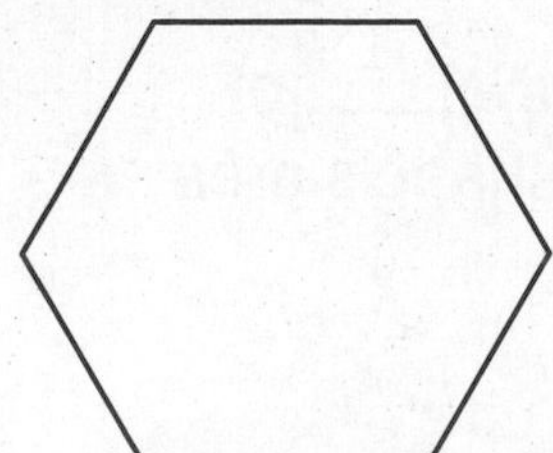

____

8. Show how you might divide the shape into 8 equal parts. What fraction names the area of each part of the divided shape?

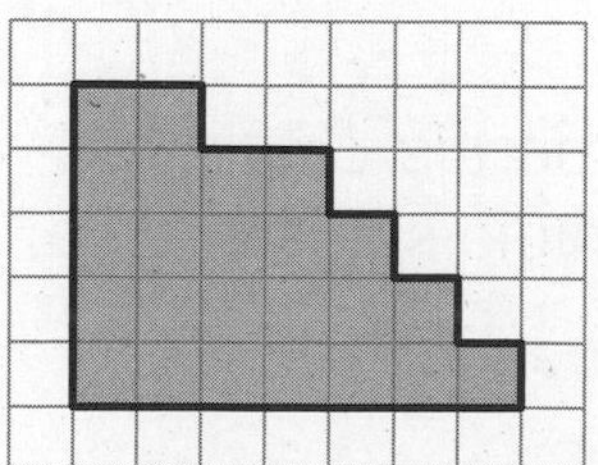

____